HIDDEN HISTORY *of* HERNDON

HIDDEN HISTORY *of* HERNDON

Barbara A. Glakas

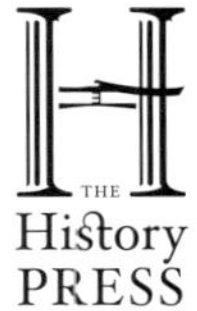

Published by The History Press
Charleston, SC
www.historypress.com

Front Cover: Farm machinery in front of the Hutchison and Mitchell Building on Station Street, circa 1916. *J. Berkley Green Collection of the Herndon Historical Society*.

Back Cover: *Above*: Inside Wilkins Store. *J. Berkley Green Collection of the Herndon Historical Society*; *Below*: The Herndon baseball team, circa 1900. *Herndon Historical Society*.

First published 2019

Manufactured in the United States

ISBN 9781467140966

Library of Congress Control Number: 2018963526

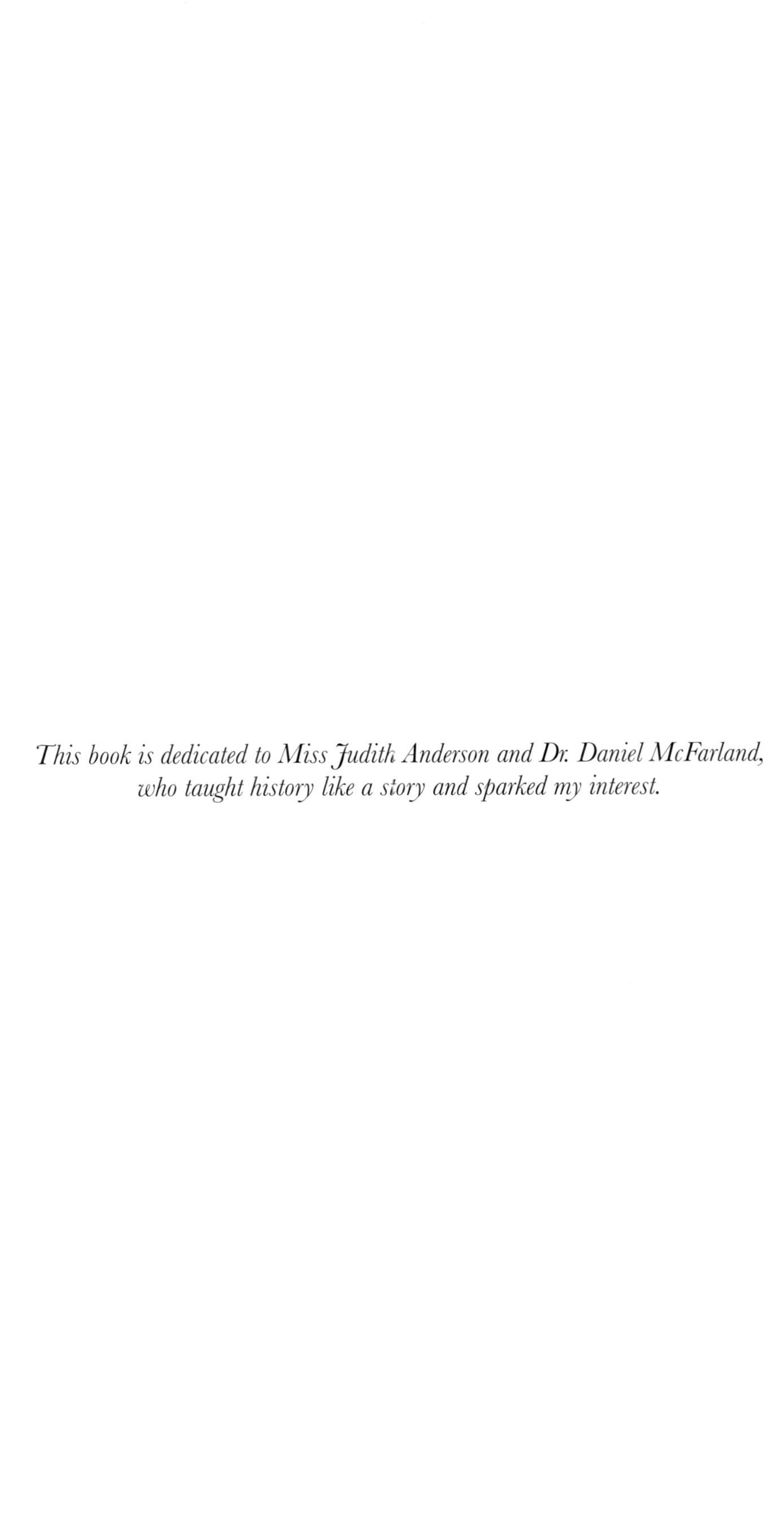

This book is dedicated to Miss Judith Anderson and Dr. Daniel McFarland, who taught history like a story and sparked my interest.

G.M. Hopkins Map, 1878.

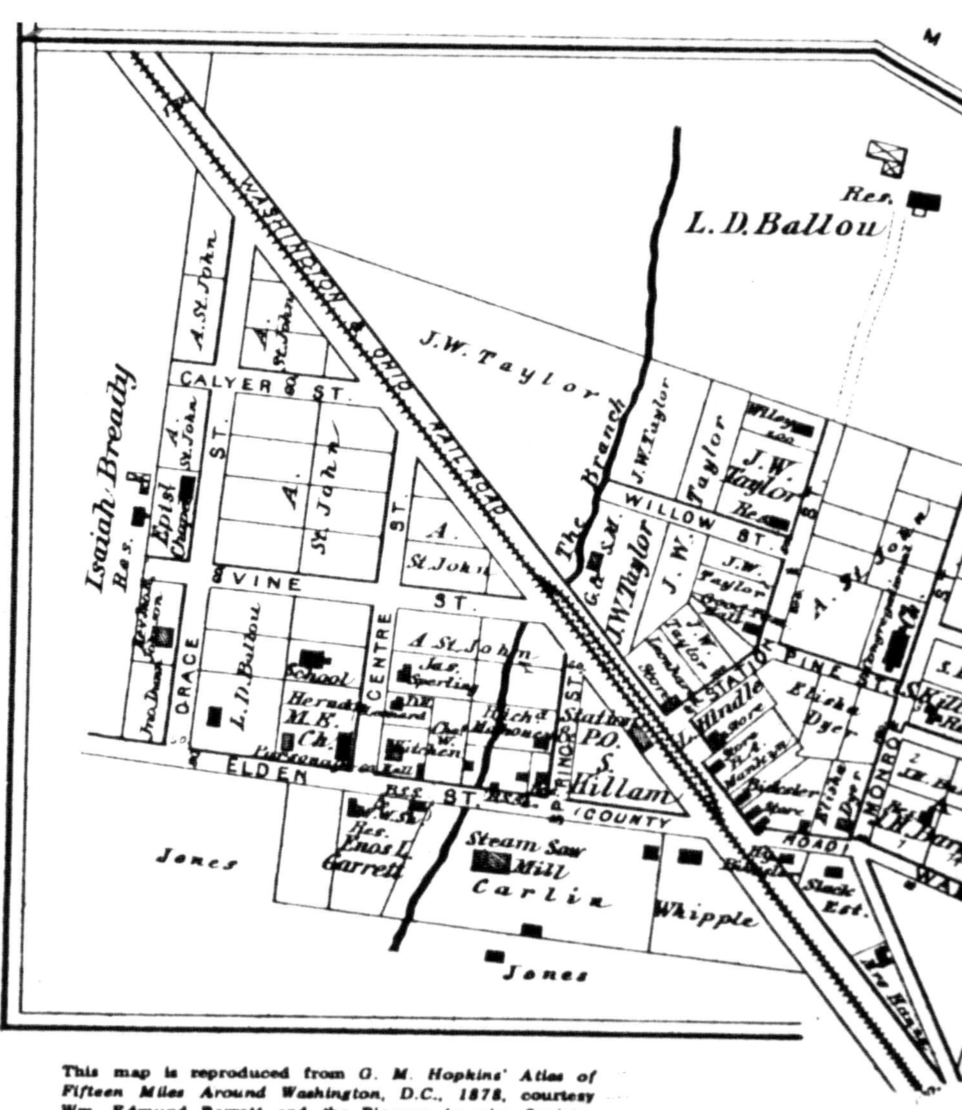

The earliest known map of Herndon, 1878, created by G.M. Hopkins. *Fairfax County Public Library Photographic Archive.*

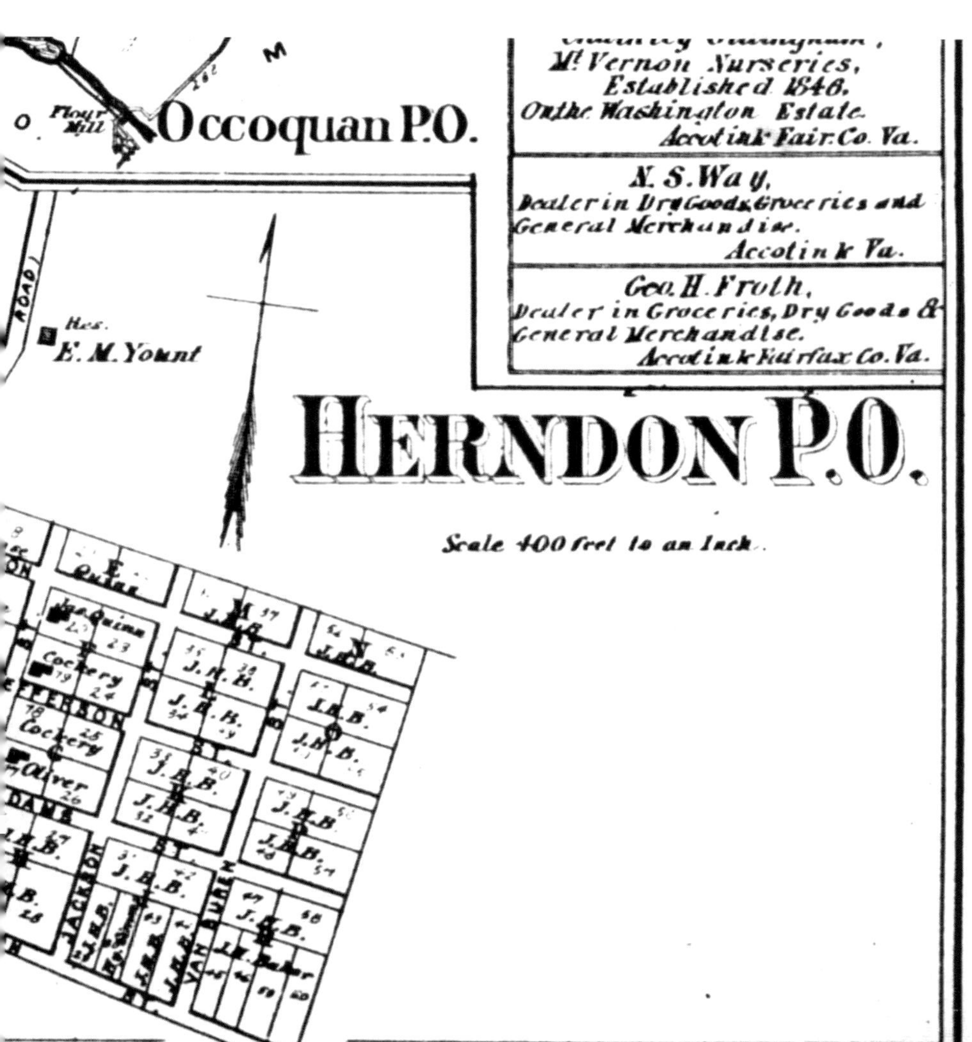
Mt. Vernon Nurseries,
Established 1846.
On the Washington Estate.
Accotink Fair. Co. Va.
N. S. Way,
Dealer in Dry Goods, Groceries and
General Merchandise.
Accotink Va.
Geo. H. Froth,
Dealer in Groceries, Dry Goods &
General Merchandise.
Accotink Fairfax Co. Va.
Occoquan P.O.
Flour Mill
Res.
E. M. Yount
ROAD
HERNDON P.O.
Scale 400 feet to an Inch.
JACKSON
VAN BUREN
Entered according to Act of Congress in the year 1878 by G.M. Hopkins,
in the Office of the Librarian of Congress at Washington D.C.

Contents

Acknowledgements

I would like to extend my heartfelt thanks to the many Town of Herndon and Fairfax County employees and to the many Herndon residents, past and present, who so willingly allowed me to interview them and have access to historic records and family documents. Without their cooperation, I would not have been able to tell the stories of Herndon's hidden past. At the risk of inadvertently omitting someone's name, those individuals are listed below.

Chris Adams
Janet Allder
Lisa Anderson
Art Anselene
Brad Anzengruber
Pat Beckner
Katie Blair
Bob Boxer
Jean Brooks
Carol Bruce
Mary Burger
Jimmy Cirrito and staff
Virginia Clarity
Ron Colan
Eddie Colon
Jeff Colon
Lea Coyell
Anne W. Crocker
Richard Crouch
Ann Csonka
Margaret Cyrus
Diane D'Amico
Tony DeBenedittis
Maggie DeBoard
John DeNoyer
Mrs. and Mrs. Arthur de Butts
Richard Downer
John Dudzinksy
Kevin East
Tom Evans

Wesley Fox
Benjamin C. Garrett II
Lisa Gilleran
Paul Glass
Lucinda Brooks Gormes
Carrol Groff
Sue Groff
Francis Guber
Don Hakenson
Walter Harrison
Anne Harvey
The Herndon Historical Society
Maryana James
Kate Jenkins
Katrina Krempasky
Dave Kochendarfer
Donald M. LeVine
Mary Lipsey
Sonny Lynch
Elma Mankin
Chuck Mauro
Paul McCray
Tim McGrath
Elaine McRey
Steve Mitchell
Mike Moore
Nancy Myers
Sharon and Arthur Nachman
Howard Nachman
Virgie Needab
Theodore Needab
Mike O'Connor
Margaret Peck
Arno Randall
Joy Reed
Doris Rosenberg
Patsy Rust
Paul Sangster
Robert J. Schneider
Dana Singer
Darryl Smith
Ronald Thompson
Town of Herndon Clerk's Office
Gwen Trent
Viki Wellershaus
Mr. and Mrs. Jimmy White
Laura Wickstead
Frieda Wolfe
Carol and Bill Wright

•

Introduction

The town of Herndon is located on the northwestern side of Fairfax County, Virginia. Arrowhead points were once uncovered on the property of the Herndon Centennial Golf Course and in Herndon's Runnymede Park, indicating the long-ago presence of prehistoric Indians, possibly attracted by the abundant wildlife and plant life, as well as the nearby Sugarland Run. Aside from those Stone Age inhabitants, the earliest residents who settled in the Herndon area did so in the late 1700s.

Up until the 1840s, there were only a handful of homes in Herndon. A mill was built in the 1850s. The growth of the yet-to-be-named village of Herndon soon flourished in earnest, marked by the coming of the railroad in 1857. At that time, the Herndon area was predominantly a dairy farming community, and the rail helped the farmers bring their products more efficiently to market to places such as Washington, D.C. Much like what occurs today—where residential and business growth start popping up around transportation hubs (such as today's Metrorail stations)—that same development phenomenon occurred in the village of Herndon when the train depot station was first built. Within twenty years—especially in Herndon's downtown core area along Elden, Station, Lynn, Center, Spring, Grace, Monroe and Pine Streets—buildings started dotting the village landscape. In addition to residences, these buildings included churches, schools, gristmills, sawmills, a blacksmith shop and general stores. Soon after would come other businesses, including a butcher shop, a jewelry store, a pharmacy, a doctor's office, a harness shop and a livery.

Once the train depot was constructed in the center of the village, a post office was established inside the building in 1858. By happenstance (the story is within this book), the post office was named Herndon in honor of the brave Commander William Lewis Herndon, a Virginian who was the captain of the SS *Central America* and died at sea after the ship encountered a disastrous hurricane.

There was a limited amount of war-related activity in Herndon during the Civil War. Units and individual troops sometimes passed around and through the village. One Confederate raid occurred at a downtown lumber mill. Individual Herndon residents were known to support opposite sides of the war.

After the war, the population of the village continued to grow, partially attributed to Northerners investing in Virginia's affordable land. In 1879, the village was formally incorporated as the Town of Herndon, with its boundaries measuring a little over four square miles. By 1880, the town's population was 422. In the early 1900s, Fairfax County led the state in dairy production, and most of the leading dairy producers were located around Herndon.

Through the world wars, Herndon continued to thrive as a close-knit farming community. Gaslights were eventually installed downtown, the rail went electric, the town established its own water system, the first telephone lines were erected, a volunteer fire department was established and residents slowly started replacing their horses and wagons with automobiles.

In the 1960s, rail service stopped, and the construction of the Washington Dulles International Airport—located about one and a half miles outside of Herndon's corporate limits—caused significant growth in the town. The once small farming community eventually developed into a vibrant suburban community.

Today, the population of the town of Herndon is about twenty-four thousand people. Nevertheless, it is still known for its small-town feel with its accessible town government, its many community activities, its many volunteer opportunities and its historic preservation district, which protects historic structures, such as the train depot.

This book will attempt to tell some of the little-known stories of Herndon's history, showcasing some of the noteworthy people, places and events that shaped the town of Herndon's past and led to its future.

I

THE SS *CENTRAL AMERICA*

The Life and Death of Commander Herndon's Ship

The SS *George Law*, a steamship that was later renamed the SS *Central America*, sunk off the North Carolina coast in 1857 at the hand of an overwhelming hurricane. Commanded by William Lewis Herndon, it was the sinking of this ship, and the brave actions of its captain, that gave rise to the name of the town of Herndon.

Commander William Lewis Herndon was born in 1813 in Fredericksburg, Virginia. An accomplished navy officer, he was an outstanding explorer and seaman who served with distinction in the Mexican-American War as the commander of the brig known as the USS *Iris*. He also led an important expedition that explored a vast uncharted area: the Valley of the Amazon. But what really sealed his reputation as a naval hero were his actions on the SS *Central America*.

After the Mexican-American War ended, the U.S. government subsidized private companies to build and operate two fleets of side-wheel steamships to connect the newly acquired California Territory to the rest of the country. One fleet would travel from Oregon to Panama while the other fleet would travel from Panama to New York.

The U.S. Mail Steamship Company was formed in 1848 by George Law, Marshall Roberts and Bowes McIlvaine. They retained a contract to carry U.S. mail from New York to the Isthmus of Panama, where it would then be delivered to California. The company also carried passengers. When the California Gold Rush began in the late 1840s, the company became very profitable. In 1852, it ordered two large ships to be built, one of which was ultimately named the SS *George Law*, after the New York financier and co-owner of the company.

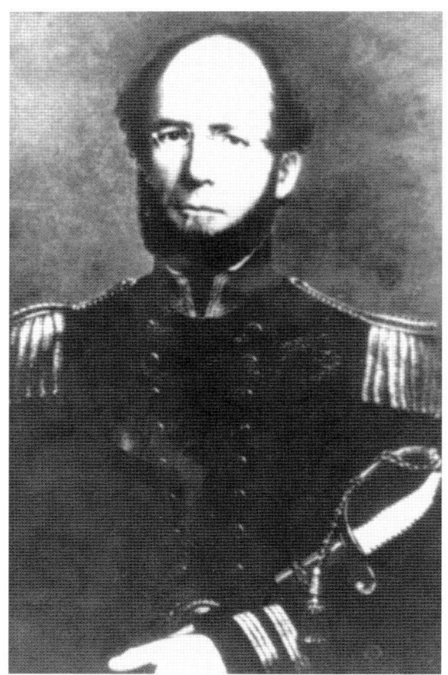

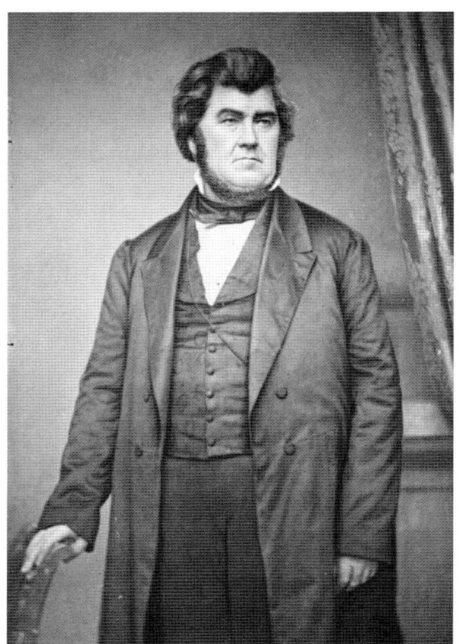

Left: Commander William Lewis Herndon. *Herndon Historical Society*.

Right: George Law, 1855. *Library of Congress*.

Cedric Ridgely-Nevitt, author and a 1939 graduate of the Webb Institute—a naval architecture and marine engineering college—described the life of the SS *George Law* in a 1944 article he wrote in the *American Neptune*, a journal of maritime history.

The SS *George Law* was constructed in the shipyard of the prolific shipbuilder William H. Webb and was located on the East River in New York. The ship was launched in October 1852. The ship measured approximately 278 feet by 40 feet. It had a pair of engines, one funnel and three masts. It had two large red side paddle wheels that propelled the vessel through the water. The hull was wooden with a copper sheath. The upper deck had a large expanse of planking, broken up by a series of hatches, surrounded by wooden benches and open rails, which had rope netting attached to them.

The *George Law* made her maiden voyage to Aspinwall, Panama (now Colon), on October 20, 1853, under the command of John N. McGowan. Passenger ticket prices ranged from $150 to $300. On her way, the ship stopped in Jamaica to pick up additional coal. She then arrived at the isthmus

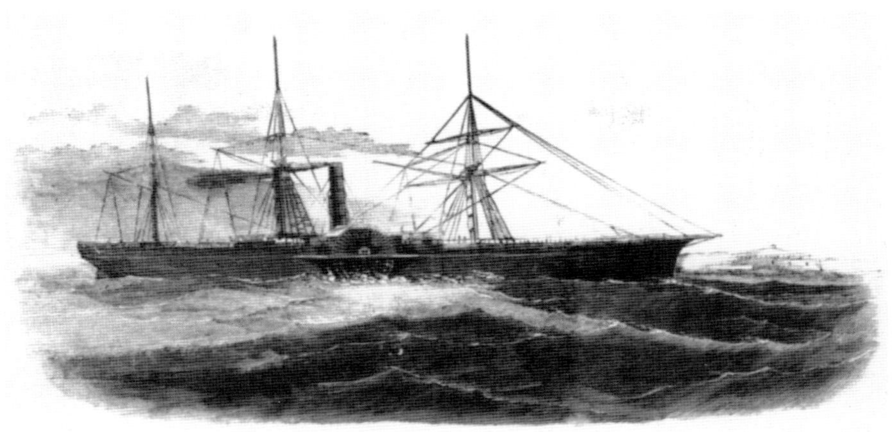

SS *Central America*. *Frank Leslie's Illustrated Newspaper*, 1857. *Herndon Historical Society*.

in Panama. When the ship returned to New York on November 10, she was carrying 465 passengers and $872,831 of California gold.

That began the bimonthly service from New York to Aspinwall that the *George Law* and the *Illinois* conducted, sailing on the fifth and the twentieth of each month. The *George Law* was recorded to have carried between 217 and 817 passengers and between $800,000 and $1,951,721 in gold on each trip. Sometimes on her trips she would go directly to Aspinwall, while other times she would stop at Havana, Kingston or Key West. In 1855, the Panama Railroad was completed, which made it much easier to transfer people across the isthmus.

It was estimated that the voyage from New York to Aspinwall typically took about eight or nine days to complete. It is also estimated that the travel speed was typically around eleven knots. Faster speeds were achievable, although often not used, as coal capacities were limited and speed was not a necessity, so the risk of running out of fuel before returning to port was not chanced.

There were two known groundings of the ship, the last one in 1857 at the southern end of her route. After a dry-dock period back at the Webb Shipyard, the engines were overhauled and some of the hull's copper sheathing was replaced. Some initially speculated that earlier hull damage may have contributed to the ship's sinking, but that assumption was not found to be true. It was during this dry-dock period that the ship's name was changed to the SS *Central America*. It is unknown why the name change occurred, possibly to reflect its most common destination and because George Law had sold his interest to his company back in 1853.

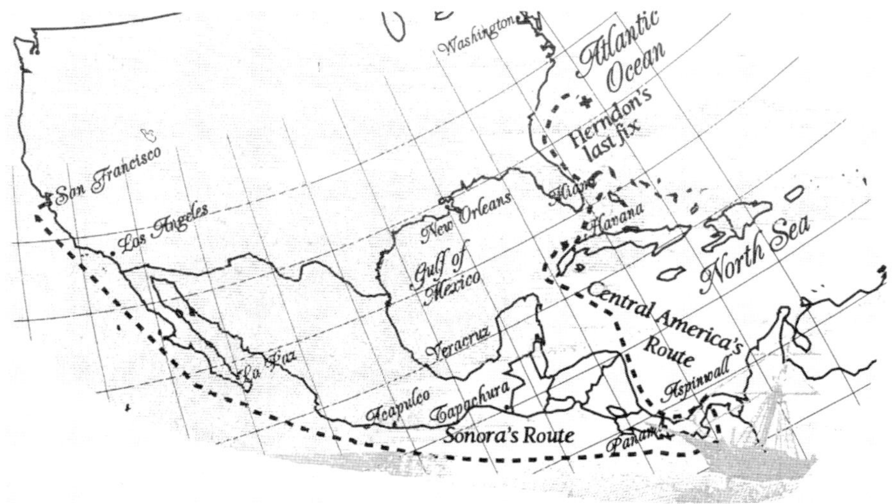

Route of the SS *Central America*. Mariner's weather log, National Oceanic and Atmospheric Administration, 1991. *Herndon Historical Society.*

During her career, the ship was commanded by six different officers. William Lewis Herndon, USN, commanded the ship during her twenty-fifth through thirty-eighth voyages. Herndon later took command of the ship again on her fortieth voyage and remained her commander until she was lost at sea on her forty-fourth voyage. George Ashby held the position of ship's chief engineer throughout the life of the vessel.

The fateful voyage started on August 20 with passengers boarding the steamship *Sonoro* at the Vallejo Street wharf in San Francisco, with many carrying gold. Jack Finney described in his book *Forgotten News* that "some passengers were of large or moderate means…while the greater portion of the passengers [are] returned miners." After about two weeks, the *Sonoro* reached Panama, where passengers took the railway to get to the other side of the coast and to the SS *Central America*. The *Central America* stopped at Havana on her northward route.

The account of the *Central America*'s sinking was well documented by interviews of surviving passengers and crew members and printed in the *New York Times* of that year. The *Central America* left Havana on September 8, 1857, carrying over thirty-eight thousand pieces of mail, about $1 million in gold and well over five hundred passengers. The weather and seas were favorable. In the first two days, she had covered about five hundred miles. By September 11, the seas had grown, and northeasterly gusts of wind and rain were blowing. The ship was about 125 miles south of Cape Fear off the

North Carolina coast. That morning, those in the engine room found that they were taking on considerable amounts of water and were starting to list to the starboard (right) side, making it difficult to use barrows to pass coal.

The ship's waiters were sent to pass coal using buckets and baskets. The bilge pump was fired up, but the ship took on water at a faster pace than the bilge could pump it back out. The storm shutters were closed, but the source of the leak could not be found, since suspected areas were already covered by rising water. The winds increased and the ship could not be kept headed into the wind and sea. Water was overflowing the coal bunker. Wooden berth slats were ripped out and thrown into the furnace, but the pressure in the main boiler finally failed by 5:00 p.m. Without the ability to create steam, the paddle wheels would not work and the ship could not be controlled. Commander Herndon made attempts to have the sails raised, but the canvass of each one was tattered to shreds by the high winds. The listing of the ship to the starboard side increased, making it difficult to walk along the deck.

An attempt was made to create a drag, or sea anchor, in order to bring the ship around. The heaviest anchor hung from the bow out of reach of the crew. A smaller anchor was let out and lowered forty fathoms deep.

The ship continued to be at the mercy of the huge waves, lowering the ship into troughs and then lifting her back up onto swells. Waves crashed down and pounded the leaning ship, with water now flowing in through porthole covers. The ship was ravaged furiously by the wind. The ship then began listing so far to the side that no one could walk along the deck. The three heavy masts leaned over the water. With sails no longer of use, Herndon ordered the front mast to be cut down. They first cut the rigging and then used axes to hack at the base of the mast. They heard a crack, and the mast snapped and tumbled over the rail; as it fell, it got caught in some rigging and summersaulted into the water. Ensnared in the rigging, the mast flung underneath the ship and began pounding against her hull. Later that night, the chafing of the thick rope that held the anchor caused a leak around the right wheel shaft, which they attempted to plug with blankets.

Now with ten feet of water in the hold, Herndon asked the male passengers to go to work bailing. If he could keep the ship afloat long enough, it might allow enough time for another ship to arrive to help them. Despite the seasickness that plagued many of the passengers, hundreds of volunteers started bailing. The exhausted men continued to bail for hours, and the women provided bread, fresh water and liquor. One passenger later reported: "This work of bailing continued all through the night…the captain and his officers making every arrangement necessary, and contributing by their conduct and bearing to increase the hopes and keep the spirits of the passengers."

The following day, the brig *Marine*, of Boston, was spotted. She, however, could not maintain a close position to the *Central America* to offload passengers due to the damage she had sustained in the storm. Another person on board stated:

> *Immediately after the firing of the guns and the hoisting of the signals, Captain Herndon called me into his stateroom. He said he was afraid there might be a rush of passengers for the small boats. He wanted the ladies and children saved first. He desired, he said, some of the passengers to assist in preventing a rush for the boats. He only had five boats…it was his intention to transfer all the passengers to the* [approaching] *brig.*

Another passenger said: "When they were getting into the boat there was the utmost coolness and self-control among the passengers; not a man attempted to get into the boats. Capt. Herndon gave orders that none but the ladies and children should get into the boats, and he was obeyed to the letter."

Herndon attempted to offload women and children on to the three remaining undamaged lifeboats. By the time the third boat got clear, the *Marine* had drifted at least two miles away. After reaching the *Marine*, only one of the three lifeboats returned. The *Marine's* lifeboats were too damaged to be used.

By around 6:30 p.m., the schooner *El Dorado*, of New York, came into view and moved toward the crippled *Central America*. The *El Dorado* captain called for Herndon to start offloading passengers, but there were no lifeboats available. Herndon asked that the *El Dorado* stay by the *Central American* until daylight, hoping the storm would subside and the bailing would keep them afloat. But the *El Dorado* could not hold her position and drifted off.

Bailing continued. Parts of the deck were cut away to form rafts. The *Marine* had now drifted about five miles away.

From a distance, some people in the last lifeboat could see that the water line was now even with the upper deck of the *Central America*. Herndon and his second officer could be seen on the wheelhouse. A final rocket had been shot off from the wheelhouse at an odd angle, straight across the water, signaling the ship's imminent sinking. On the evening of September 12, the *Central America* was lost. Commander Herndon was lost with his ship.

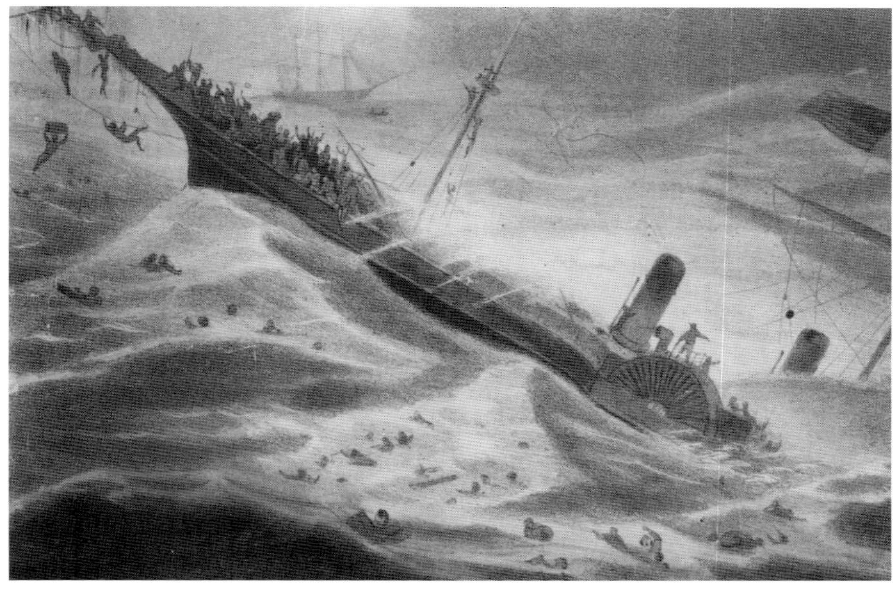

Wreck of the steamship *Central America*. Lithograph by J. Childs. *Peabody Museum of Salem.*

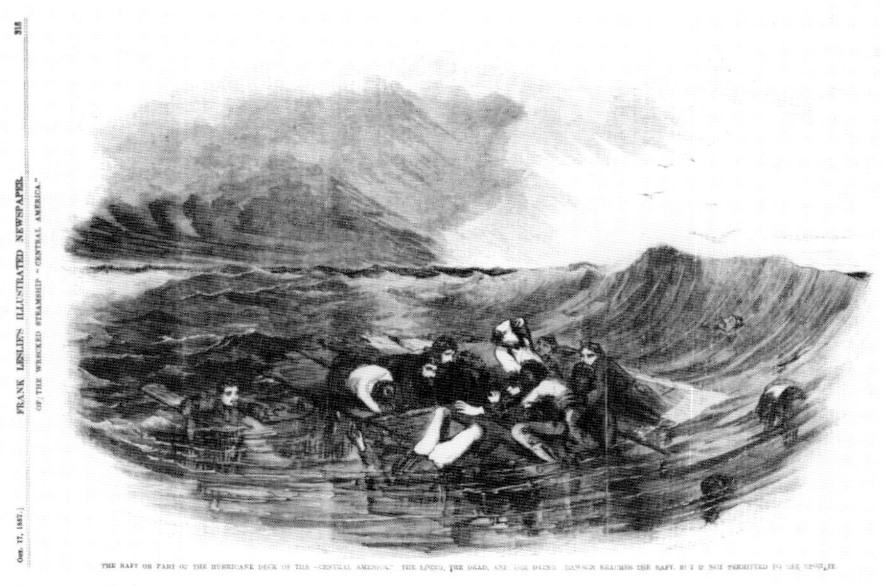

SS *Central America* passengers float on rafts or part of hurricane deck. *Frank Leslie's Illustrated Newspaper*, 1857. *Herndon Historical Society.*

Cedric Ridgely-Nevitt speculated that the wooden ship was so twisted and pounded by the forceful winds and seas of the hurricane that some parts of the watertight hull eventually gave way.

That evening, the Norwegian bark *Ellen* passed by the area where the *Central America* sank and picked up 49 passengers who had been floating on pieces of wreckage. The *Marine* had previously taken 97 others aboard. Nine days later, the brig *Mary* found the final 3 survivors drifting in one of the *Central America*'s lifeboats. All total, 153 people were saved and 425 were lost, along with a shipment of tons of gold, including ingots, coins and nuggets. The *Central America* steamship itself was valued at approximately $140,000 but was, unfortunately, not insured.

New York banks, such as Wells Fargo and the American Bank exchange, expected the much-needed shipment of gold to meet their debts. The enormous loss of gold that resulted from the sinking contributed to the Panic of 1857.

One month after the disaster, the superintendent of the U.S. National Observatory, Lieutenant Matthew Fontaine Maury, USN, wrote a report to the secretary of the navy on the sinking of the SS *Central America*. Recounting what occurred, he added:

> *The law requires every Commander in the Navy to show himself a good example of virtue and patriotism; and never was example more nobly set or beautifully followed. Captain Herndon, by these noble traits which have so endeared his memory to the hearts of his countrymen, and won the respect and admiration of the crew and passengers of that ship in a such a degree as to acquire an influence over them that was marvelous in its effects.*
>
> *After the boat which bore Mr. Payne—to whom Herndon entrusted his watch—had shoved off, the captain went to his state room and put on his uniform. The gold band around his cap was concealed by the oil-silk covering which he usually wore over it. He took the covering off and threw it on the floor; then, walking out, he took his stand on the wheel-house holding on to the railing with his left hand. A rocket was set off, the ship fetched her last lurch and as she went down, he uncovered.*
>
> [Commander William Lewis Herndon] *went down with his ship, leaving a glowing example of devotion to duty, Christian conduct, and true heroism.*

2

How the Town of Herndon Got Its Name

The Happenstance of a Post Office, a Shipwreck and a Mysterious Stranger

It is not believed that William Lewis Herndon ever visited the Herndon area, so the question remains: How exactly did the town of Herndon end up with the name "Herndon"? There many things that are known, but some details still remain a mystery.

In the mid-1800s, and prior to the arrival of the railroad, the town now known as Herndon had no name. Firsthand accounts of people who lived in Herndon during that period referred to Herndon as "the village," or they referred to certain geographic areas by the names of property owners. One of those people was Katherine "Kitty" Kitchen Hanna, who wrote, "How did this town gets its name? It didn't have one before the railroad come through. We used to say, 'goinin' to Cockerilles' or to Purdies' or Colemans'."

In the 1850s, the SS *Central America* sank, the newly constructed railroad arrived and the Herndon train depot was built, becoming a center of the community. The people of the village requested the establishment of a post office at their new railroad station. The first two proposed names for the post office that were submitted by the villagers were rejected by the U.S. Post Office, due to conflicts with names of other post offices that were already used within the state and because the postal department insisted that post offices not be named after local families.

Kitty Hanna went on to explain: "When the first depot was build, jes' after Purdies lef', there was much talk an' choosin' of names, an' many a

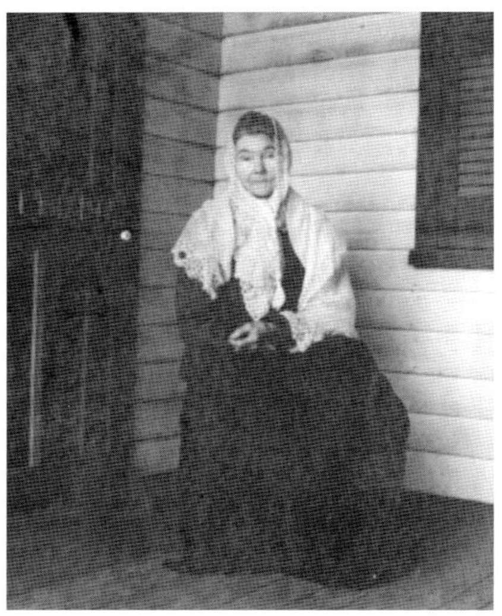

Katherine "Kitty" Kitchen Hanna, circa early 1900s. *Herndon Historical Society.*

name was spoke of by one another; but Mr. Hollin'sworth…chose the name an' it stuck to the place 'midst all the changes, even when the people that named it's dead an' gone."

William W. Hollingsworth was Herndon's first postmaster. However, he did not simply select the name "Herndon" out of the blue and on his own. The name of the new village post office is more closely attributed to a stranger, a passerby who came into the town on a train one evening, on his way to another destination.

At a meeting of village residents, held to select an acceptable name for the post office, the recently arrived passerby was invited to attend the meeting. He was also—supposedly—a survivor of the shipwreck of the SS *Central America*, a shipwreck that coincidentally occurred that same year. This man told of the ship captain's heroism in staying with his ship, leading the effort to keep the ship afloat for as long as possible and ensuring that as many people as possible were safely disembarked. Despite the lack of an adequate number of lifeboats, the captain succeeded in getting the women and children off the ship. The captain no doubt understood the coming fate of his ship. The stranger explained how the captain threw his watch to a sailor in the nearest boat with instructions to deliver it to his wife. Then, bidding the sailors Godspeed, Commander William Lewis Herndon went down with his ship.

The stranger also relayed to the villagers how this same commander, as a lieutenant in 1850–1851, had performed a dangerous and difficult mission of exploring the tributaries in the Valley of the Amazon for the purpose of ascertaining "the benefits might accrue to its [United States] citizens by the establishment of commercial relations with the people who dwell on its banks."

The people at the village meeting were profoundly impressed with the stories about Commander Herndon, and they decided to bestow his name on the village's new post office, a name that Hollingsworth no doubt approved. Kitty Hanna explained: "It was the story of the brave Captain who went down with his ship after savin' so many lives that won all hearts. So 'twas Herndon the town's called."

The name "Herndon" was accepted by the U.S. Post Office. The Herndon Post Office was established on July 13, 1858, with William W. Hollingsworth assigned as its first postmaster, a position he held until 1865. The Town of Herndon would become incorporated twenty years later, in 1879.

The story of this stranger is considered by some as a legend. But upon further research, it has been concluded that this legend is most likely true. The remainder of this chapter explains various pieces of information that may reveal the identity of that passerby.

Recently found in a storage closet in the Herndon Depot Museum was a paper that was written by an unknown author. The paper recounts the story of Herndon's beginnings. The part of the paper that recounts the story about the naming of the town is very similar to stories heard before; however, this particular paper added more detail. Moreover, this paper's provenance is very substantial, due to its association with the family history of William S. Blanchard.

This typed paper is entitled *Herndon—Virginia, Past, Present and Future.* On the cover it also said, "Preliminary Draft, July 24, 1948." There was a handwritten note on the back page, written in 1993 by former Herndon planning commissioner Edward N. Stirewalt. It read, "This document was given to me around 1955–57 by Mr. William S. Blanchard, a Herndon native and former town official, himself elderly at the time. He told me it had been prepared by a man whose name he did not recall who stayed for some time 'in the rest home on Monroe Street.' April 21, 1993."

William S. Blanchard would have been seventy years old in 1955, the time period he handed this paper to Stirewalt. Blanchard had once served as Herndon's town manager, and he also served on the town council in the 1940s. He also happened to be the son of Howard W. Blanchard, who was Herndon's first town clerk when the town was incorporated in 1879.

To add another piece of provenance to this paper, it is also known that Howard W. Blanchard happened to be the nephew and son-in-law to two other former town officials—William Drinkwater Sweetser and Stephen Killam—who also both served on the first town council in 1879. Additionally, William S. Blanchard's middle name was St. John, no doubt a connection to Ancel St. John, another original town councilmember and good friend to Howard Blanchard. All these family and friend associations are not surprising, given that town of Herndon's population in the year 1880 was less than five hundred.

As mentioned earlier, the villagers had twice tried to name their new post office, with no success. That part of the story recounted in the paper that William S. Blanchard passed along to Edward Stirewalt went like this:

> *As more homes were built, and the settlers were thrown more together, they began to talk about a post-office and a name for their hamlet. A railroad had come near their farms, but troublesome days coming on when a brother was arrayed against brother in daily strife, the rails were not carried farther than the outskirts of this yet unnamed community. Finally, the farmer folk gathered and took a vote upon a name, which was submitted to the authorities in Washington, but was rejected because there was another post-office of the same name in the state. Again a name was selected, only to meet the same fate, and the people were almost at a loss what name to choose.*

The author then went on to describe the 1857 sinking of the SS *Central America* and its brave captain, an event that occurred the same year the villagers were attempting to select a name for their new post office. The author continued, providing more details about the arrival of the stranger who came into the village:

> *On a fateful night, in the little village in Fairfax County, the men of the community were gathered to choose for it a name. At that moment a worn-out and bronzed man alighted from the train and announced his intention of remaining until morning in the village, until he could continue his journey. As the men were lingering before the door of the house in which the meeting was held, the stranger sauntered up, and with true Southern hospitality the farmer invited him into the meeting.*
>
> *There is always curiosity aroused when a stranger arrives in a place, and that time those people were no exception to the rule. We surmise that questions were asked the stranger, as to whence he came and whither he was going, and his answers brought out the fragments of a remarkable story of shipwreck, suffering, bravery and such virtues in one who went down with his ship, that as with one voice the farmers said, "We have our name—it shall be Herndon."*

Although the story about the stranger who suggested the name "Herndon" was similar to other stories that have been written and told over the years, this particular paper—with its connection to early Herndon founders—gives

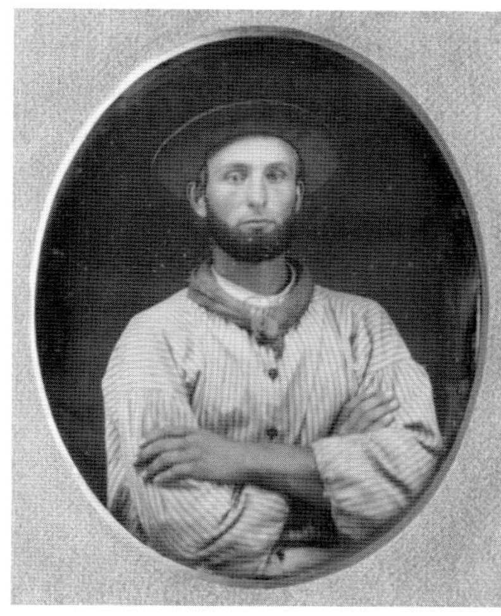

An 1860s miner and author's conception of what the "Bronzed Man" many have looked like. *Fine Daguerreotypes & Photography.*

one pause and reinforces the notion that this "legend" must have a good level of truth to it.

In an attempt to solve the mystery of the identity of this stranger, the following questions were asked: What was his name? Where did he come from? Where was he going? And why was he described as "a worn out and bronzed man" by the local villagers?

In researching this mystery, there are assumptions that must be made and a certain amount of speculation. The first step was to look at old records surrounding the sinking of the *Central America*. In looking at the survivor list, there was gentleman on board the ship by the name of Robert Hutchinson, who had the abbreviation "Va" marked next to his name. He was the only survivor with Virginia listed next to his name. Upon reading this, the first speculation is that Hutchinson's destination was Virginia.

The shipwreck of the *Central America* was a massive news story in 1857. Major newspapers such as the *New York Times*, the *New York Daily Tribune* and the *Sacramento Daily Union* covered the story, sometimes filling whole pages with lists of the dead, lists of the survivors and interviews of some of the survivors.

In an issue of the *Sacramento Daily Union* dated October 24, 1857, Robert Hutchinson was interviewed. The newspaper described him as being "a resident of Nevada City, California, who had been on the *Central America*, bound on a visit to Virginia." This confirmed that Virginia was his destination. In the newspaper article, Hutchinson is quoted as saying:

> *The Captain's conduct, from first to last, was worthy of all praise. He was very active in the beginning and very self-denying in the end. He went around in every part of the ship, urging the men to do their duty, and showing them how to do it to the best advantage. He brought the men fresh water whenever anyone wanted it. Every man felt encouraged continually by the Captain's untiring devotion. He has left a fine example.*

This quote indicates that Hutchinson was highly complimentary—not critical—of Commander Herndon's performance during the course of the disastrous shipwreck, much like how the stranger who later passed through the village was complimentary as he told the residents the story of the brave ship's captain.

Next, research was conducted to figure out more about the identity of this Robert Hutchinson. Census documents reveal there was a man named Robert Hutchinson living in California during this time. The gold and many passengers being transported on the *Central America* originated from California.

Robert Hutchinson was found living in Nevada City, which was part of Nevada County in California. This location matches the information reported in the *Sacramento Daily Union*. Census documents indicate that Hutchinson was born around 1825 or 1826, was from Scotland, came to the United States in 1851 and was naturalized in 1870. His name was found on several California census documents that placed him in various counties located just north of Sacramento. Census documents from various years listed him as a miner and/or farmer.

Robert Hutchinson was also listed on California voter lists from the 1870s to the 1890s. On all those lists, he was shown as being in Nevada County, California. On the 1892 voter list, he was described as being a miner with "light hair and complexion."

A death notice for a man named Robert Hutchinson, born around 1825, shows he died in 1907 at the age of eighty-one in Nevada, California. A grave for him was not found in the United States, but there was one found in Scotland for a man named Robert Hutchinson, who died in 1907.

One slight conflict of information is that the 1900 census said Hutchinson immigrated to the United State in 1851, but he also showed up on an 1850 California census document. Of note, though, is that the 1850 census was taken in the month of October, late in the year, and that slight gap of time was simply an unimportant technicality. Or, by 1900—fifty years later—could it be that Hutchinson simply did not accurately remember the exact year he arrived?

All these California census documents describe Hutchinson as being a single man born around 1825 or 1826 in Scotland, with both of his parents having been born in Scotland as well. It also said he could read, write and speak English.

Looking in Scottish census documents, it was found that a couple named Thomas and Janet Hutcheson, who lived in Angus, Scotland, had a son named Robert Hutcheson who was born on April 7, 1825. Although the spelling of the name is slightly different, that could be a census error, as names on old census documents are often misspelled. The facts on a family tree for the Hutcheson family, however, did seem to align. It showed Robert Hutcheson living in Scotland from 1825 through 1851, and then the Scottish record went blank on his whereabouts from 1851 through 1907, the years it is believed he was present in the United States, until he died in California.

The California counties where Hutchinson lived (Nevada, Yuba and Colusa Counties) are all adjacent to one another, so it seems he never moved too far. Doing some research on the geography of California during the 1850s, it was discovered that those counties were located in key areas where gold was found during the California Gold Rush. Reading about the history of that area, one source said that Nevada City was described as "the County seat of Nevada County, settled in 1849 during the California Gold Rush. In 1850–51 it was the most important mining town in the state." This was during the time that Hutchinson immigrated to the United States.

All this information fits a possible scenario of a young man who may have left his home in Scotland around 1850 to find his riches in the California Gold Rush, who later took a calamitous trip from California to Virginia on the SS *Central America* in 1857, who subsequently stayed in California

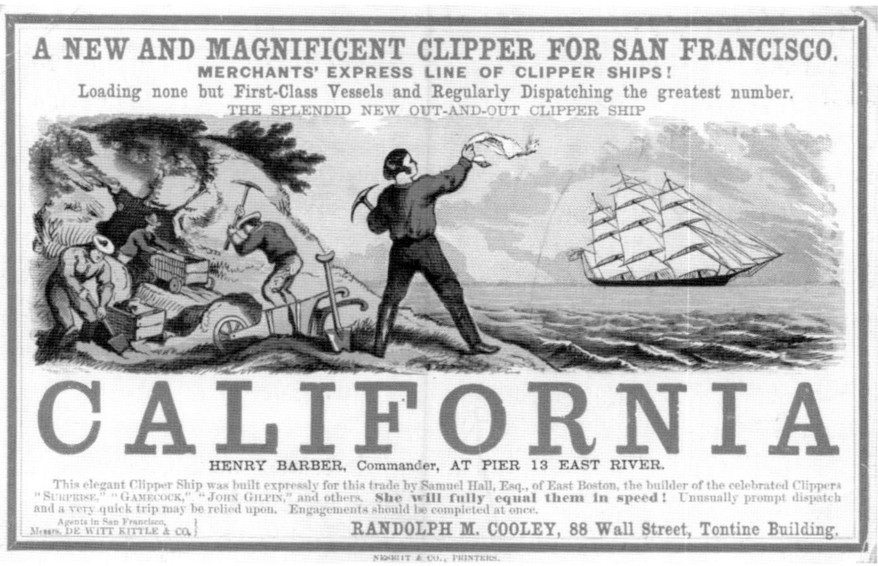

An advertisement about sailing to California during the Gold Rush, circa 1850. G.F. Nesbitt & Company, printer. *Wikimedia Commons.*

throughout the rest of his adult life until he died in 1907 and who was then returned to Scotland to be buried.

In the *Sacramento Daily Union*, Hutchinson was listed as a steerage passenger on the *Central America*, which most likely indicates that he was a passenger of modest means. In his newspaper interview he indicated that during the sinking he had been taken aboard the brig *Marine* in the last, or one of the last, boats that left the *Central America*. The newspaper reported that Hutchinson said the following:

> [He] *leaped into it at a narrow risk of losing his life by drowning. All the ladies had been taken off, and the Chief Engineer had deserted the ship. One of the lifeboats came near the ship—he hardly knew where from—and he succeeded in getting into it. It was manned by a regular boat's crew. Some other persons, in attempting to get into the boat, fell into the sea, though they were got out of the water and saved. The brig was then almost five miles off, and the sea was very high.*

A female passenger who had also been picked up by the brig *Marine* was interviewed by the newspaper as well. She said, "We were all weak and reduced from having nothing to eat of any consequence for two days before the ship went down." She also described how the lifeboat tossed violently in the water and how it took over two and a half hours to get to the brig. Once aboard, she described how there were food shortages and how they spent three more days on a food allowance.

Was Robert Hutchinson the man who showed up in the village (of Herndon) on a train in 1857? Was he the worn-out stranger who, after stepping off the train, "announced his intention of remaining until morning in the village, until he could continue his journey?"

If this man was born in 1825, he would have been about thirty-two years old when he came through the village. Blanchard's manuscript described the stranger as being a "worn out and bronzed man." The term "bronzed man" is an interesting description. One California document described him as having "light hair and complexion." Could it be that the stranger who showed up in the village appeared to be "bronzed" because he was a gold miner or panner by trade, spending long hours out in the sun and making his highly tanned skin appear "bronzed" against his light hair? In one newspaper account, one ship passenger in 1857 described some of the steerage passengers and crew members as "hard sun brown men." Or could it be that he appeared worn out and bronzed because he recently

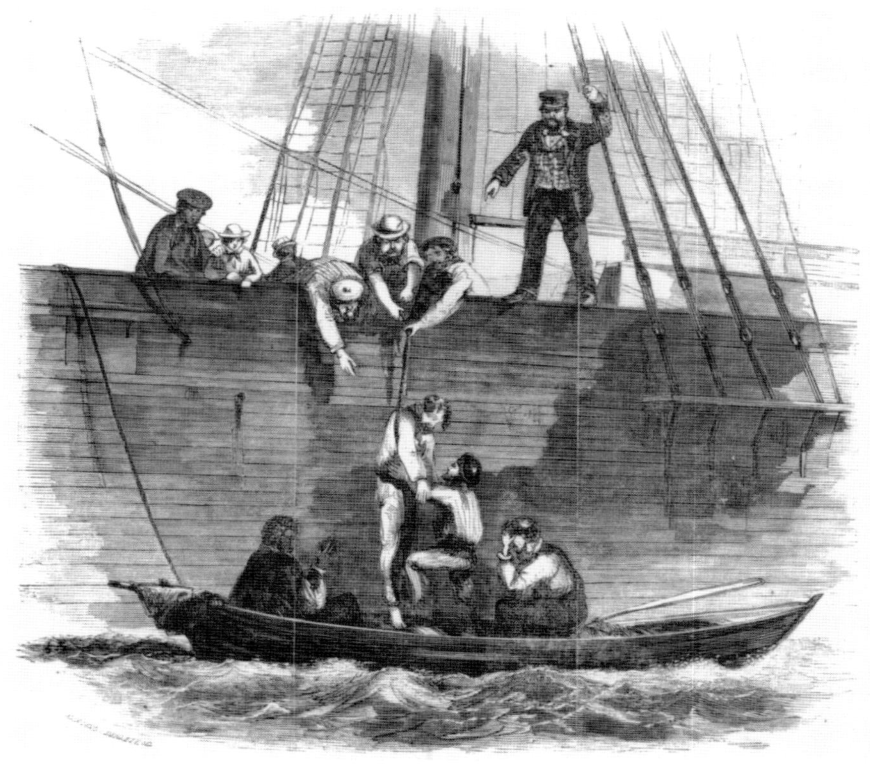

SS *Central America* survivors being rescued. *Frank Leslie's Illustrated Newspaper*, 1857. *Herndon Historical Society.*

survived a shipwreck and spent two days "working like [a] horse" to bail the ship and then floated in the lifeboat until he was rescued? Or maybe it was because he also spent additional days in the sun on the deck of the brig *Marine*, waiting to get back ashore. Could this physically, emotionally and exhausting experience, and the lack of food during the shipwreck, be why he also appeared "worn out" to the villagers?

Was Hutchinson's recent harrowing experience of the shipwreck in the forefront of his mind when he spoke so highly of the brave Commander Herndon at the village meeting, which caused the townspeople to choose to honor the brave captain by selecting Herndon's name for the new village post office?

Additional information about the identity of the stranger came in the form of a 1988 letter found in the Herndon Depot Museum. The letter was written by author Normand Klare to a Herndon Historical Society member. Klare lived in California and wrote the 1992 book *The Final Voyage*

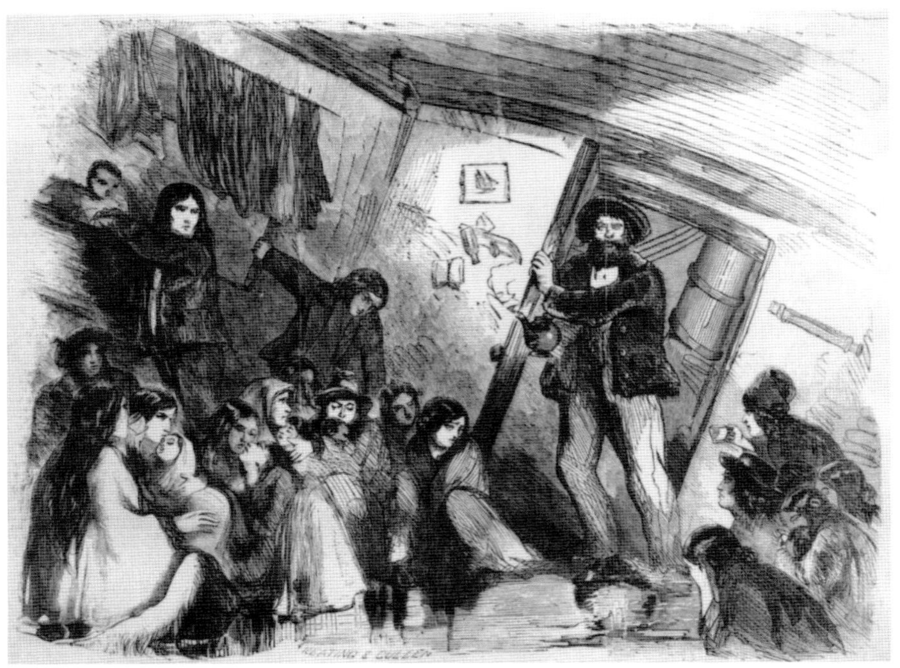

Rescued female passengers from the SS *Central America* in the cabin of the brig *Marine*. *Frank Leslie's Illustrated Newspaper*, 1857. *Herndon Historical Society.*

of the Central America, 1857. Klare looked into the question of the infamous stranger who had passed through Herndon in 1857. He wrote the following to the historical society member:

> *It would be rewarding to learn the identity of the passenger who suggested naming your town after William Lewis Herndon, although I understand that the story is thought by some to simply be folklore.*
>
> *There is a distinct possibility that the suggestion may have come from one of the two known survivors who were Virginians. Robert Hutchinson, a resident of Fairmount, Virginia, may have passed through the area when en route home after his rescue. I could not locate a town by that name in Virginia, and we consider the name Falmouth may have been garbled in the passenger list. I think this is a likely prospect because he spoke admirably of Herndon. Additionally, his passing through the Herndon area to Falmouth would seem quite feasible.*
>
> *The other passenger, Captain Thomas Badger was a native Virginian from Cedar Rapids, near Marionville. This seaman, owner and master*

of sailing vessels, and a California '49er, played a major role in assisting Captain Herndon during the emergency on the steamer. After their rescue, he remained in Virginia until 1861, when he and his wife, Jane, returned to California. Badger died in November 1899 in Oakland, California, about two miles from our Piedmont residence. Of the master of the Central America he said, "Captain Herndon behaved nobly." Captain Badger's route to Cedar Plains, on what is now Delmarva Peninsula, does not seem likely.

Robert Hutchinson seems to be the more likely candidate. Here are the reasons why:

If Captain Badger was on his way to the Delmarva Peninsula, it does not make sense that he would have gone through Herndon on his way home from the shipwreck. Herndon is too far out of the way and would not make sense for a traveler to go to Delmarva from Herndon. Also, the train would have not connected Herndon to Delmarva. Additionally, both Badger and his wife were on the *Central America.* Herndon history stories never indicated anything about a stranger and his wife stopping off in Herndon, only a single stranger.

Klare indicated in his book that Hutchinson was one of the bailers on the ship when it was sinking. Many of the men on the ship did this, and it was hard and constant work for at least two days straight. This helps support the villager's description of the bronzed man as looking "worn out."

A footnote in Klare's book said: "Robert Hutchinson was from Fairmount, VA, had been in California, working in Kidd's Tunnel for eight months; lived in Nevada City, Nevada County; was a business partner of Thomas McNeish, of Grass Valley." Looking at Klare's newspaper citations, it was noted that on page seven of an issue of the *New York Daily Tribune* that Hutchinson was a resident of Nevada City, California, and was bound on a *visit* to Virginia. While on page eight it said that he was *from* Fairmount, Virginia, and had been in California for eight months working in Kidd's Tunnel.

So was Hutchinson from Nevada City, California, or from Fairmount, Virginia? It is conceivable that he could have lived in Virginia for a short while before heading out to California; however, there are no found census documents placing him as living in Virginia. If he ever lived there, it would not have been for too long. It is more likely that he lived in California (as the newspaper said) and went on a *visit* to Virginia, where he may have had family or friends in Fairmount.

Regarding Fairmount, Virginia, Klare said he could not find a place named Fairmount in Virginia and so he surmised that the name got lost in translation and they must have meant Falmouth, Virginia, instead. It is doubtful it was Falmouth, as Falmouth is located near Fredericksburg, Virginia. Again, it would not make sense for Hutchinson to go through Herndon on his way to Falmouth. No trains would have taken him from Herndon to Falmouth.

A Fairmont, *West* Virginia, was found, however. Klare may not have considered that West Virginia was still part of Virginia in the 1850s; it did not break away from Virginia until the early 1860s. Therefore, in 1857, Hutchinson may have been going to Fairmont, Virginia, which today is Fairmont, West Virginia.

After getting off the lifeboat from the *Central America*, Hutchinson was picked up and saved by the brig *Marine*. The brig *Marine* brought survivors into Norfolk, Virginia. Instead of going from Norfolk to an unlikely destination of Falmouth or Delmarva on his way to West Virginia, it makes much more sense that Hutchinson would have sailed from Norfolk up the Chesapeake Bay and Potomac River to Alexandria, Virginia, where he could have caught the train out to Herndon.

Looking at maps, there is a route from Herndon to Fairmont that makes perfect sense. The railroad line that ran through Herndon (now the Washington and Old Dominion Trail) headed in a northwesterly direction, closely aligned with a route toward Fairmont, West Virginia. Using a little imagination, one can envision a route in 1857 in which a person could take the train from Herndon to Leesburg. From there, he may have switched over to a horse and carriage. The route would be continued over land from Leesburg Pike (Route 7) all the way out to Frederick, Maryland. From there, Route 50 could be taken farther west until it took a person to what is now Interstate 79, which is just a stone's throw away from Fairmont, West Virginia. Fairmont is located between Clarksburg and Morgantown on Interstate 79. Some of these roads may have been little more than dirt roads in 1857, but the point remains: the trajectory of the route from Herndon to Fairmont is a logical and direct one. This imagined route that Hutchinson may have taken from Herndon to Fairmount makes more sense than any other routes that Hutchinson would have supposedly taken to Falmouth, or that Badger would have taken to Delmarva.

Another footnote in Klare's book described Thomas McNeish as being "24 years old, born in Canada to Scottish parents. He now lived in Bloomsburg, Columbia Co. PA, and had been a merchant in Grass Valley,

Nevada Co., CA." This was the gentleman who Klare said was Hutchinson's business partner. Could it be that Hutchinson and McNeish had been previously acquainted with each other or had a kindred relationship based on their common Scottish heritage?

Both McNeish and Hutchinson had apparently worked in Kidd's Tunnel (a mining tunnel located in Grass Valley and named after an important mining man named George Washington Kidd). This puts Hutchinson in Grass Valley, which is in Nevada County, one of the locations where Hutchinson had lived. One article indicated that Grass Valley, during this time, had a lot of Northern Europeans working there.

As was stated at the outset, this story must include some assumptions and speculation at an effort to figure out the identity of "the bronzed man." His name was never recorded in any Herndon documents. Nevertheless, this information strongly supports that theory that the California miner of Scottish heritage, who was bound for a visit to Virginia, who survived the sinking of the *Central America* and who shortly thereafter showed up in the yet-to-be-named village of Herndon on a train—"worn out and bronzed"—was Robert Hutchinson. He stayed the night, enthralled the villagers with this impassioned story about the brave Commander Herndon and then went on his way to a town farther west.

3

Facts about the Washington & Old Dominion Railroad You May Not Know

A Short Chronology of the Railroad that Bisected the Town

The small dairy community of Herndon thrived and grew around the railroad and its depot. Here are some lesser-known facts about the railroad and the Herndon Depot:

- The Alexandria port had become overshadowed by port competitors in Washington, D.C., and Baltimore, further exacerbated by the construction of the Baltimore & Ohio Railroad. The beginning of the Washington & Old Dominion (W&OD) Railroad came about as an effort of Northern Virginia investors to connect the Alexandria port to the farmlands and coal mines in West Virginia for the purpose of commerce.
- The rail line starting in Alexandria was charted in 1847 under the name Alexandria & Harper's Ferry Railroad. Over the years, through various acquisitions and reorganizations, the railroad changed names several times. It became the Washington & Old Dominion Railroad in 1936.
- The land of several Herndon landowners was condemned in order to build the railroad through the Herndon area: Jane Farr, Thomas Cox, James Miller, Henry Kipp and Joseph Orrison. Compensation for the land ranged from $150 to $556. They were also compensated for "good and substantial fencing" that would run along the owner's land parallel to the

railroad right-of-way. Their fence compensation ranged from $87 to $415.

- The railroad started being constructed in 1855 under the name the Alexandria, Loudoun & Hampshire (AL&H) Railroad. "Hampshire" referred to Hampshire County, Virginia (which later became part of West Virginia after the Civil War started).
- The Herndon Depot was constructed circa 1857, with a post office officially opening inside the depot in 1858.
- The Herndon Depot was originally very small, a wood board-and-batten structure, measuring about twenty feet by fifty-five feet, with a ticket office and freight room.
- The size of the Herndon Depot has changed over the years, with additions being constructed on each end, including "separate but equal" waiting rooms.

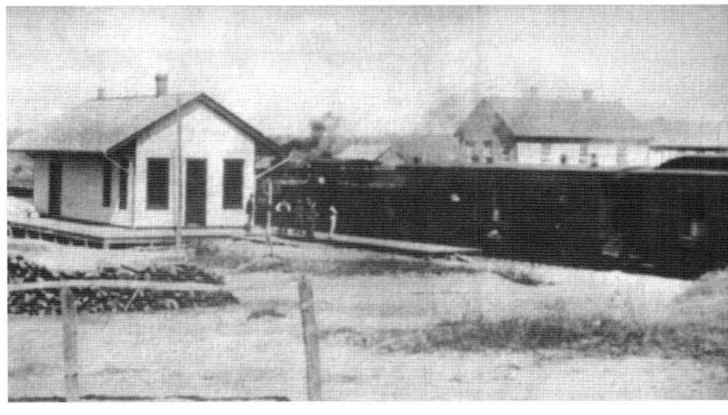

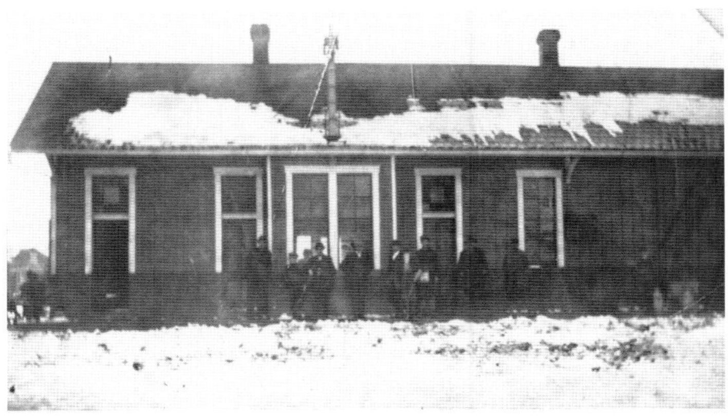

Top: The Herndon Depot, circa 1890. *From* Washington and Old Dominion Railroad: 1847–1968 *by Ames Williams.*

Bottom: The Herndon Depot, pre–1912. *J. Berkley Green Collection of the Herndon Historical Society.*

- By early 1861, trains were running out to Leesburg. Stagecoaches picked up passengers at Leesburg to transport them to points farther west. That same year, the AL&H bought the triangular piece of land on the south side of the depot, which became known as the railroad park and was later the location of many community events.
- Herndon had a siding (a parallel side track) on the north side of the depot. Herndon also had a railroad wye, a triangular configuration of railroad track that allowed trains to pass each other or to turn and change direction. Herndon's wye was located just northwest of Center Street, in the vicinity of the Fortnightly Square neighborhood.
- During the Civil War, the Confederates took two AL&H locomotives to be used on the Orange & Alexandria Railroad. They also destroyed many railroad cars and tore up many of the railroad tracks along the W&OD west of Vienna. Railroad bridges were destroyed as well, including the 110-foot span over Difficult Run.
- After the war, the damaged railroad property was turned back over to its original managers. Service was resumed to Herndon around 1866 or 1867. But the dream to go to West Virginia

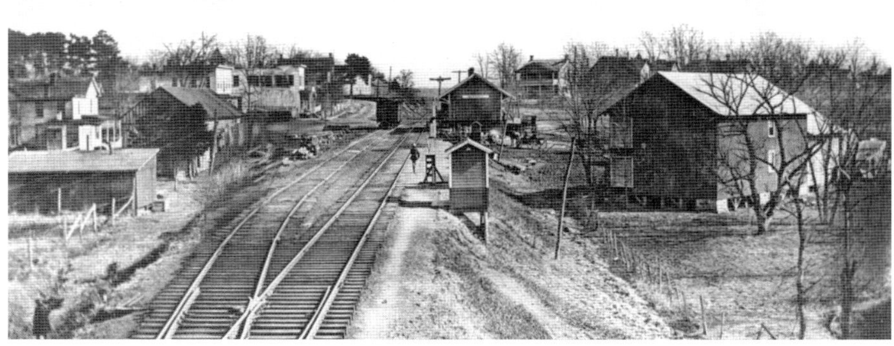

The siding on the railroad track in Herndon, circa 1905. *J. Berkley Green Collection of the Herndon Historical Society.*

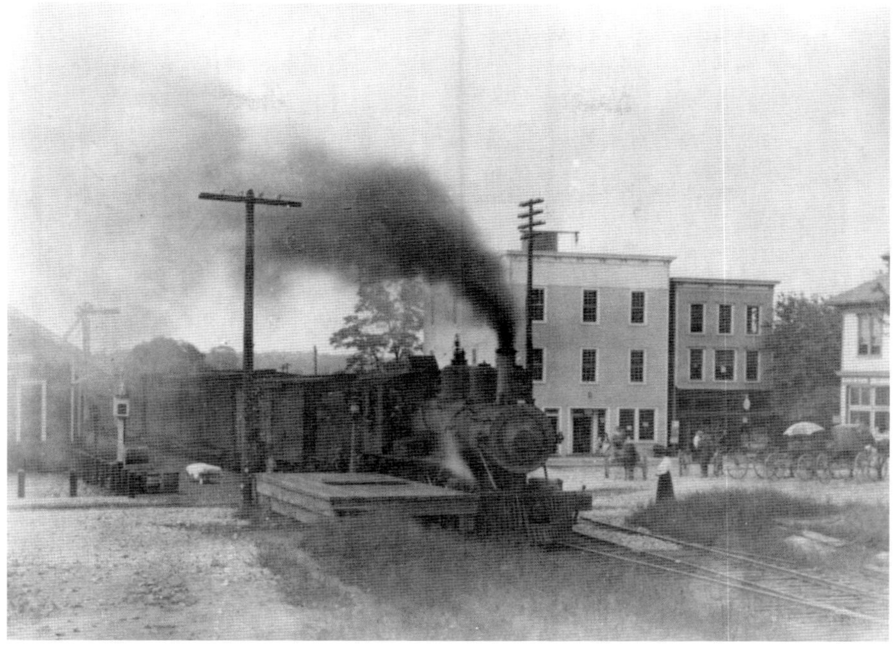

A steam locomotive next to the Herndon Depot, circa 1910. *J. Berkley Green Collection of the Herndon Historical Society.*

never came about. By 1900, the railway extended to its last stop: Bluemont, Virginia.

- The locomotives that originally ran on the railroad were steam locomotives (using wood or coal fuel) and later changed over to electric and diesel. The rail went electric in 1912, creating an interurban electric trolley system. A brick substation was built on the east side of the Herndon Depot. The electric lines were taken down in the 1940s, and the substation was demolished in 1969.
- The popularity of automobiles caused the railway business to wane. Freight outpaced declining passenger service. Mail and passenger service officially stopped on the W&OD in 1951.
- One of the last uses of the railroad was to haul materials for the construction of Washington Dulles International Airport. Once the airport opened in 1962, the railroad's profits dropped and deficits accumulated. The railroad ceased operations in 1968 and went into disuse. The Herndon Depot was abandoned.

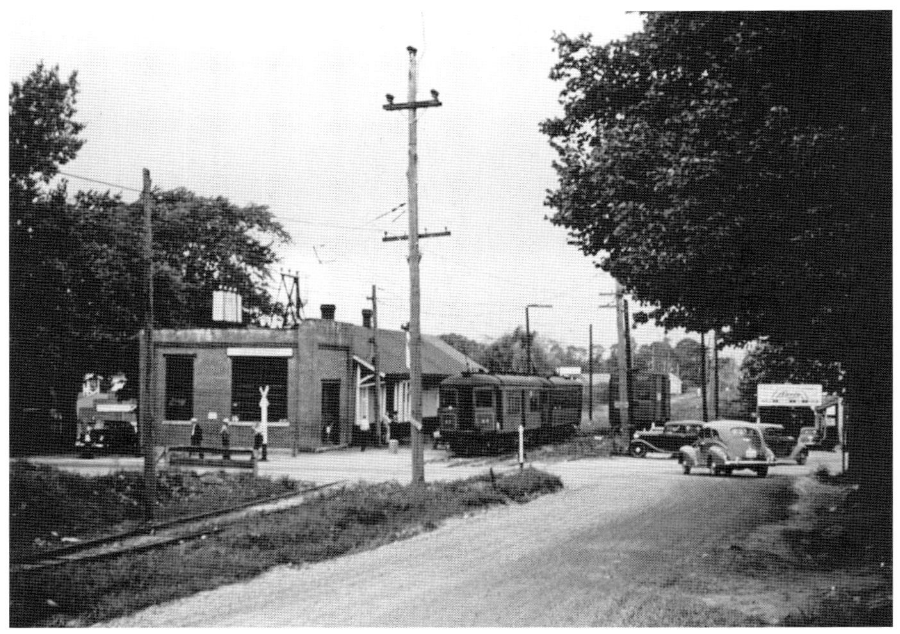

A 3:00 p.m. train enters Herndon around 1940. Note the brick substation next to the depot. *Herndon Historical Society.*

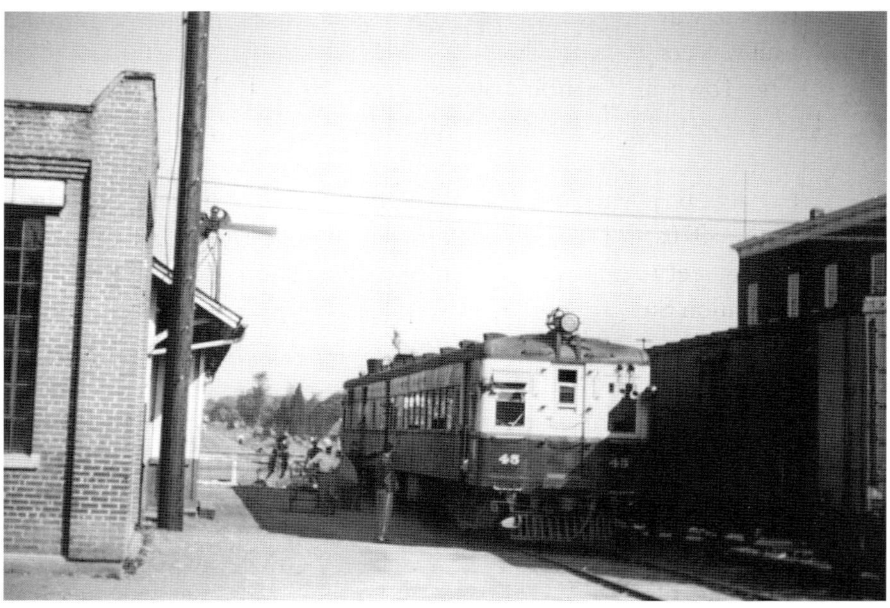

Train stopped at the Herndon Depot, 1951. *Herndon Historical Society.*

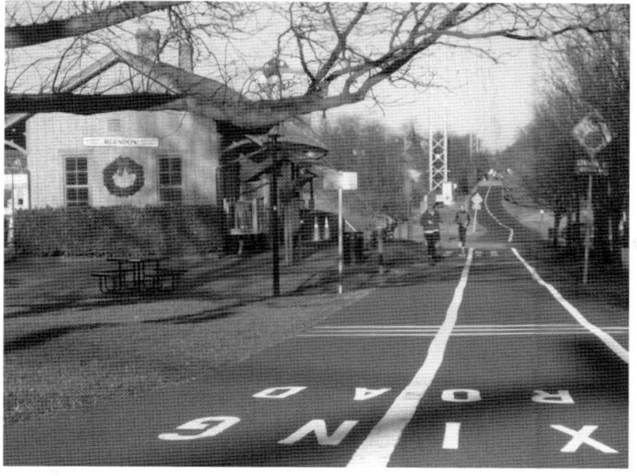

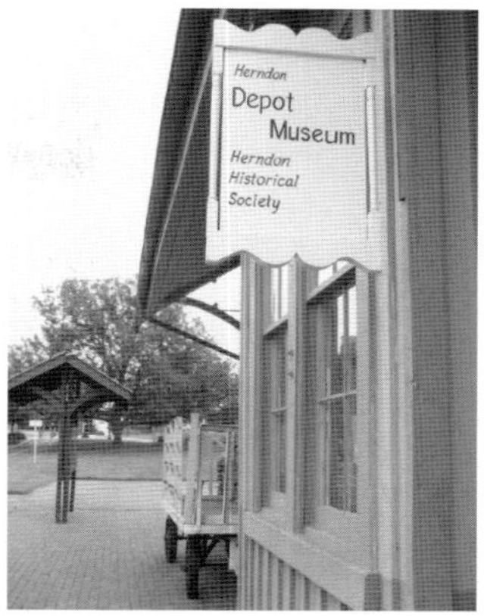

Left: The Washington and Old Dominion Trail by the Herndon Depot. *Right*: The Herndon Depot Museum. *Barbara Glakas.*

- The Virginia Electric and Power Company (VEPCO) bought the railroad right-of-way for its electric power transmission lines. In 1977, the Northern Virginia Regional Park Authority reached an agreement with VEPCO to acquire the railroad right-of-way for use as a hike and bike trail. The paving of the trail was completed to Herndon in 1981.
- The Town of Herndon obtained the Herndon Depot from VEPCO. The Herndon Town Council considered tearing down the old depot building to make way for additional parking, but by a close vote, the council decided to save it.
- In the 1970s, the west end of the depot was shortened by about twenty feet to accommodate the newly constructed extension of Station Street behind the depot.
- After the town renovated the depot, the Department of Public Works temporarily moved into the building. At one point, it was thought that the newly acquired depot might be turned into a teen center, but it was leased to the Herndon Historical Society instead, to be used as a town museum. The museum officially opened in 1981 and still occupies the depot today.

4
The Civil War Experience in Herndon

A New Look at Herndon Participants and Observers

The Impact of the Manassas Battles on Herndon Residents

Given the position of Herndon in Northern Virginia, the residents were not oblivious to the sights and sounds of war and the troop movements that swirled all around them. Some residents, depending on their individual political leanings, occasionally felt compelled to quickly escape the village in order to avoid approaching troops, depending on whether those troops were Union or Confederate.

Two such people were Nathaniel "Nat" Hanna and his wife, Kitty Kitchen Hanna. They were a married couple of different state origins—Kitty was a lifelong Virginian who was a Southern sympathizer, and Nat was a native New Yorker who supported President Lincoln. Kitty and Nat were also loyal to each other.

The Confederates were victorious in the First Battle of Manassas (or Bull Run), the first major land battle of the Union and Confederate armies in Virginia. The battle took place in July 1861. Both sides experienced significant casualties and injuries. The Confederate victory gave the South a surge of confidence.

In Virginia Castleman's book *Reminiscences of an Oldest Inhabitant,* Kitty Hanna told the story of how her husband, Nat, who had signed up for the Home Guards, received orders to join the militia at Manassas with three days of rations. Nat and one of her brothers went to "Vienny" that same night to take the railroad to Union lines. Kitty's other brother John, however, wanted to join the Southerners. Kitty said, "After supper the [Southern] men all went away by the lane leadin' across fields—Cedar Lane, they called it, 'count of that clump of cedars still standin' in Urick's field. I was left with Mother and the boy."

William Uric[h]'s farm was located in the vicinity of the present-day Chandon subdivision. Kitty continued: "The nex' Sunday, we heard firin' at Manassas—little guns an' big guns above the res'. James White, my cousin, come to spen' the day; he was a terrible Secessioner, an' all day long he kept saying to hisself…'Oh Lord, I'm feared the ammunition'll give out!' Jim told me about the big cannon that kep' boomin', how it was the Southerns firing.'" Kitty said she knew "the Southerns has whipped," explaining, "I know 'cause the big gun's comin' nearer this way, an' it must be the Southerns has won." And so it turned out to be.

The Second Battle of Manassas occurred in August 1862. A follow-up battle took place on September 1 near the present-day location of Fair Oaks Mall as the Union army was in retreat to the city of Washington. The battle is commonly referred to as the Battle of Chantilly or Ox Hill. It was the only major battle fought in Fairfax County. Again, the Confederates were victorious, handing the North another blow to its morale.

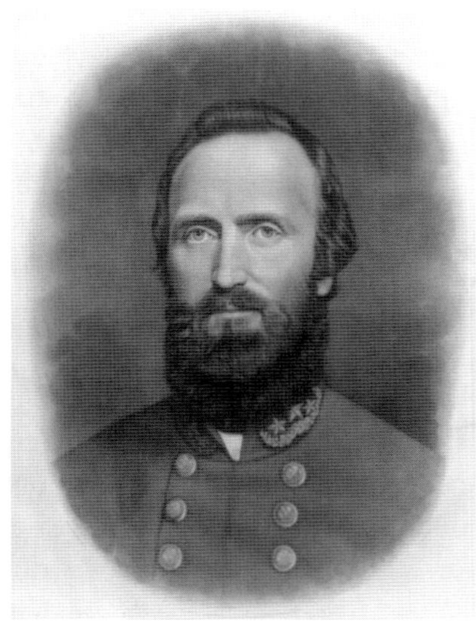

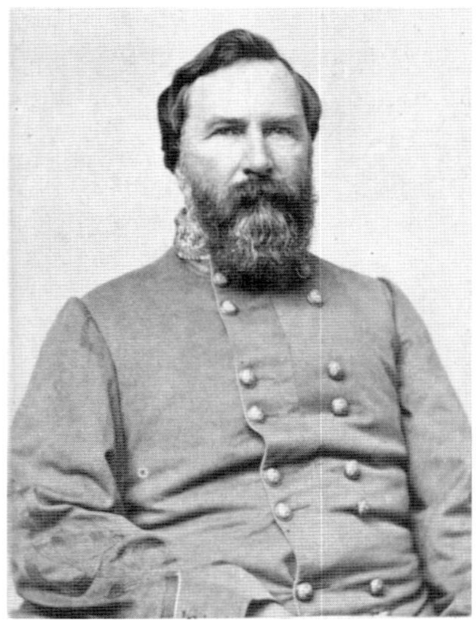

Left: Stonewall Jackson, circa 1871. *Right*: James Longstreet, circa 1861. S.T. Blessing, publisher. *Library of Congress*.

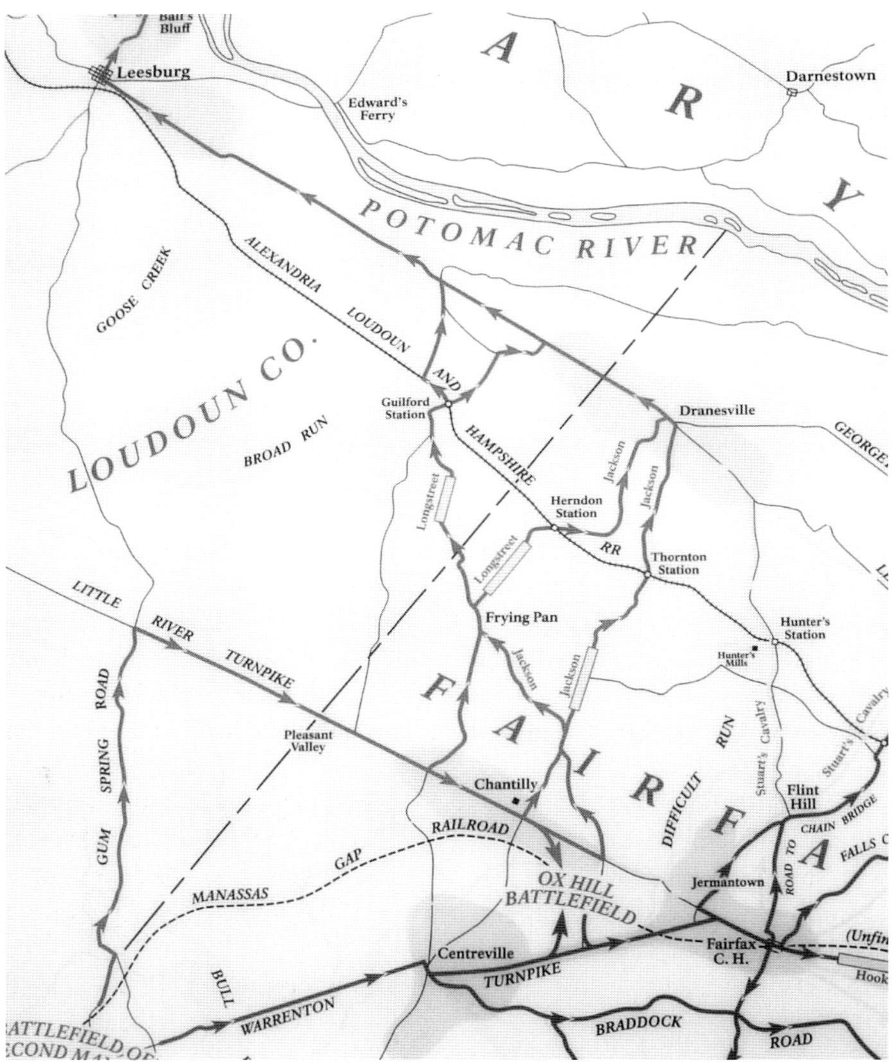

Map showing post-battle movement of Confederates through Herndon after the Battle of Ox Hill. *Fairfax County Park Authority.*

Encouraged by his victory, General Robert E. Lee decided to continue his offensive and quickly moved his Confederate army northward toward Leesburg, where he would cross the Potomac River and move into Maryland and on to Sharpsburg. On September 3, Lee and his generals—Stonewall Jackson and James Longstreet—exited Chantilly and moved the Army of Northern Virginia through present-day Reston, Herndon and Sterling to reach Dranesville. They then headed northwest to Leesburg.

Those who lived in the village of Herndon could hear the sounds from the second battle at Manassas. Kitty, Nat and their young son had been living in the Herndon Depot, operating a supply store and making a prosperous living. Kitty recalled that the months of April through July were quiet, but all that changed later in the summer.

One day when Nat was away from the store, business picked up considerably. Kitty said:

> *I was sellin' all day long, standin' on my feet till I was ready to drop, 'cause customers would come crowdin' an' crowdin' till I began to suspect somethin' was up...I'd listen to guns firin' over yonder, an' I said to mother, who'd come by to visit me—"I've been hearing guns boomin' near two days, Mother. The Southerns must be comin' back this way."*
>
> *Lookin' up the railway, I saw about a dozen bluecoats comin'. They rode without a word...an' lef' us wonderin' what's nex'. We found out later they was deserters from the Union Army, headin' for the river toward Seneca.*

A friend named McDaniel stopped by the store and whispered to Kitty, "Kitty, Southerners has come back to Manassas, their old battleground." Kitty knew that was true, based on the gunfire she could hear and the sudden buying of supplies.

Nat heard about the nearby action and came riding home fast. Kitty said, "Long 'bout dark, I heard such a clatter of hoofs comin' downhill, I knew it was Nat drivin' at breakneck speed." Kitty did not want to leave her home again, but Nat insisted that they "skedaddle" and join his folks, who were also leaving the area again.

McDaniel bought out the Hannas, who then left the store. They started off in the dark, working their way through the pines out toward the Bickslers' property (now near Dranesville Road and Park Avenue). They made their way to Sugarland Run and then joined Nat's parents at a house near Dranesville Tavern. They ate and then pushed on until they came to a fort where pickets were out and troops were mustering. The troops would not let them pass that evening so they camped outside the city.

The next day they reached Georgetown. While there, Kitty recalled: "'Twas the night of Manassas, an' we could hear the cannon boomin' an' boomin', an' nex' day the ambulances kep' comin' with the wounded."

Kitty sat quietly in the wagon, listening intently to the sounds of the guns. Her father-in-law asked her which way the battle was going, to which she replied, "The Southerns has whipped again—we won't go home very soon."

Nat left after Kitty found her brother's home, where she stayed for some time. One night while in Georgetown Kitty recalled seeing a passing army: "I heard trampin' an' runnin' an' saw an army passin'. It was the Northerners goin' to Antietam where that awful battle raged. They'd gathered forces an' took a week for them to pass—wagons, ammunition, soldiers an' all. There wasn't room on the sidewalk for common people!"

Nat later returned safe and sound. After the roads were clear, the Hannas were free to return home to Herndon. Soon after, the marching armies clashed again on September 17 in Sharpsburg, Maryland, in the Battle of Antietam, the bloodiest one-day battle in the Civil War.

THE LIVES AND ACCOUNTS OF THOSE WHO WERE PRESENT AT MOSBY'S RAID

The village of Herndon experienced one military raid that took place near the railroad depot in 1863. At that time the village had not yet been incorporated and did not have a name. However, the post office located inside the railroad depot had been named the Herndon Post Office.

During the Civil War, the Union army set up pickets around the nation's capital in order to protect the city of Washington from Confederate advances. One of those pickets was positioned at a sawmill located close to the Herndon Depot station.

On March 17, 1863, the Herndon picket was manned by a detachment of twenty-five soldiers from the First Vermont Cavalry, commanded by Lieutenant Alexander G. Watson. The First Vermont Cavalry was headquartered in Dranesville, located about three miles north of the Herndon Depot. Major William Wells and a couple of other Vermont officer colleagues had just arrived in the village that day to investigate complaints from local residents that soldiers had been stealing from nearby farmers. In the meanwhile, Confederate captain John Mosby was conducting guerrilla operations around the Northern Virginia area.

John Singleton Mosby was born in Powhatan County, Virginia, in 1833. After graduating from the University of Virginia, he opened a law office in Bristol, Virginia. Although he objected to succession, once Virginia voted to secede Mosby enlisted in the Confederate army in the First Virginia Cavalry. Later, General J.E.B. Stuart gave Mosby permission to lead an independent cavalry unit, which came to be known as Mosby's Rangers. Mosby did not

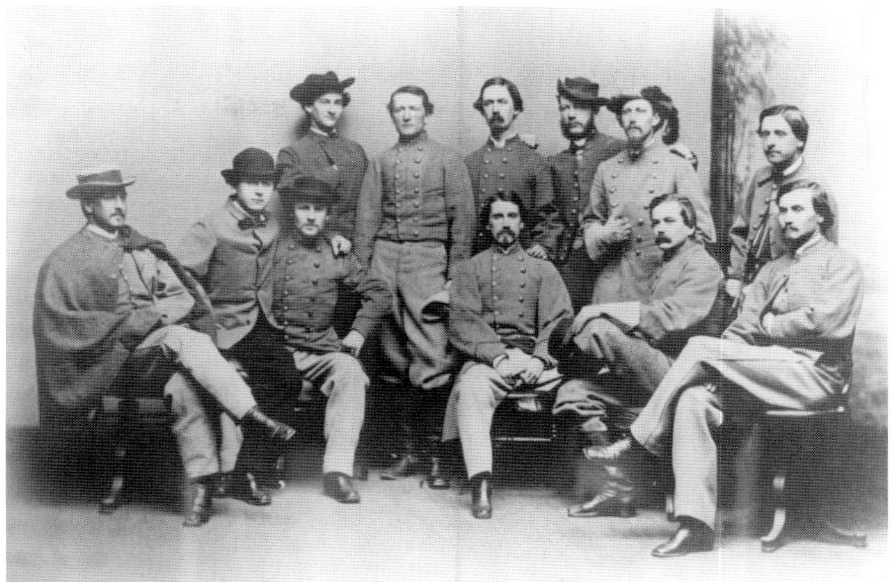

Colonel John S. Mosby and some members of Mosby's Rangers, 43rd Virginia Cavalry Battalion, 1861–1865. Bendann Bros., photographer. *Library of Congress.*

look the part of a warrior. He stood five feet, seven inches tall; had a slight build at 128 pounds; with blue eyes, fair hair and skin and was most often clean shaven. But he was also energetic, confident, quick and elusive, earning him the nickname "The Gray Ghost."

On March 8, 1863, Mosby conducted a very successful raid in Fairfax City. Soon afterward, Mosby headed to the village of Herndon, where an exposed outpost had been reported.

In *The Memoirs of Colonel John S. Mosby*, published in 1917, Mosby wrote about an addition to his command, a man named John Underwood. Son of a stonemason who had died before the war, by the 1860s Underwood was a young farmer in his mid-twenties, who lived with some of his siblings in the Herndon area. Mosby said he found Underwood in the Fairfax forests, explaining: "Why he had stayed at home and let me discover him is a mystery to me…I was largely indebted to his skill and intelligence for whatever success I had in the beginning of my partisan life, for he was equally at home threading his way through the pines or leading a charge." Mosby said Underwood "knew every rabbit path in the county." Another of Mosby's men said that Underwood's knowledge of Fairfax was "better than the wild animals that roamed over it by night or by day."

In his book *Partisan Life with Col. John S. Mosby,* author John Scott describes the meeting between Mosby and Underwood in more detail:

> *On the 10th of January we started from the neighborhood of Middleburg for Fairfax County, and proceeded to the house of a farmer who lives near Herndon Station, on the Loudoun and Hampshire Railroad* [later the Washington and Old Dominion Railroad]. *As we approached the dwelling, Mosby observed a man pass rapidly out of the back door into the pines which cover the rear of their house with their dense growth. We found no little difficulty in convincing the farmer of our Confederate character, for in Fairfax a grey uniform often conceals a Yankee. Soon however, his doubts were removed, he became more cordial, and, by a particular whistle, called from the pines the man to whom I have just referred. He seemed about 30 years of age. His person was short and thick-set, and he had a shock of white hair, which stood erect in unrestrained independence. His whole appearance was that of a wild man, but his eyes, ever in motion, indicated watchfulness and an intelligent mind. His name was John Underwood, whose value as a guide to Mosby's eye soon discovered, for he is distinguished, above all other men whom I have known, by a wonderful faculty which enables him to thread with unerring certainty, in the darkest night the intricate forests and tangled brushwood of the country in which he lives. Without much difficulty Mosby prevailed upon Underwood to join him, and, being thus furnished with a guide, prepared at once to strike the enemy near Herndon Station, where they had a cavalry picket.*

It was Underwood who had reported the exposed Herndon outpost to Mosby. Referring to the outpost, Mosby said, "I could hardly believe it; the Yankees seemed to have learned nothing by experience. It looked much as though they had been put there just to be caught, or as a snare to catch me, so I resolved to give them another lesson in the art of war."

Mosby's men gathered on March 16 in Atoka, Virginia (near Route 50, west of Middleburg), and then rode north toward Dranesville. At noon the next day, they crossed the railroad bed of the Alexandria, Loudoun & Hampshire Railroad, a couple miles west of Herndon. Once they reached the road toward Dranesville, they turned south and headed to the Herndon Station.

Concerned that the Vermonters may have set a trap for him, Mosby decided to attack during the daytime, when the Yankees would least expect it. Underwood led them through the woods until they arrived at a road leading to the Herndon picket. A sentry was there, but he was caught before he could fire and alert the others.

Just a few hundred yards away, Mosby observed that the Union troops were lounging around the sawmill, with their horses tied to a fence. Mosby described: "It was past twelve o'clock, there was bright sunlight, and there was snow on the ground. They were Vermont cavalry, and they had no suspicion that an enemy was near. It was just the hour for their relief to come, and as we came from the direction of their camp, they thought, when they saw us, that we were friends."

As Mosby's Rangers got within a hundred yards of the Yankees, the order was given to charge.

> *They were panic stricken—they had no time to untie their horses and mount—and took refuge in the loft of the mill. I was afraid that if they had time to recover from their shock, they would try to hold the mill against us with their carbines until reinforcements came. There was a pile of dry timber and shavings on the floor, and the men were ordered, in a loud voice, to set the mill on fire. When we reached the head of the stairs, the Yankees surrendered. They were defenseless against the fire, and it was not their ambition to be cremated alive. Not a shot was fired.*

Soon after the event at the sawmill, Mosby saw four finely equipped horses tied in front of a nearby house on Elden Street. The house—then known as the Purdy house—was formerly located on the property of what is now a bank located at 727 Elden Street. Nat and Kitty Hanna, who married in 1855, sometimes stayed there. Although they had built a small home on Monroe Street shortly before the war, at the time of the raid, Kitty, pregnant with her second child, and her son Charlie were staying at the Purdy house.

Nat, born in New York, was a cooper (barrel maker) in his youth and later a lumberman who worked at local Herndon mills. For a time, he also ran a store out of the Herndon Depot. His wife's lifelong ties to Virginia occasionally caused problems for Nat, as he was sometimes suspected of being a Southern sympathizer himself. But he could not bring himself to fight against the Union. As a result, he joined the Home Guard and was often away from home on patrol.

Nat was not home the day Mosby arrived in in the village of Herndon. But earlier that day, Nat's brother told Kitty that Lieutenant Watson—a friend of Nat's—would be coming over for dinner along with some other

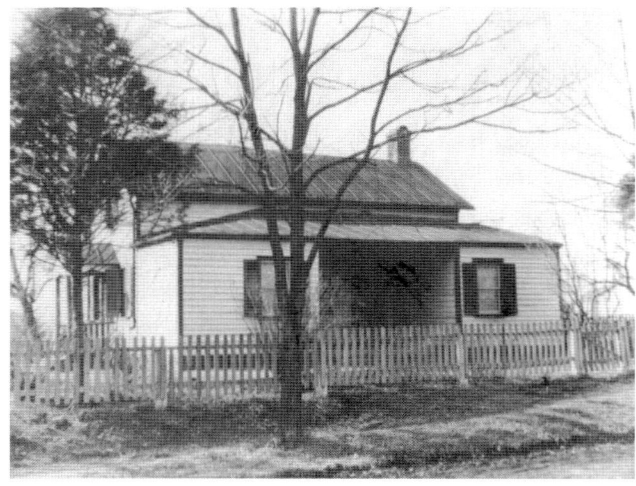

Kitty and Nat Hanna's home on Monroe Street. *Herndon Historical Society.*

visiting Vermont officers. Watson was joined by Major William Wells, Captain Robert Schofield and Lieutenant Perley Cheney.

Immediately following the raid on the sawmill, a squad of Mosby's men rushed the Purdy house to find the riders who belonged to the horses that were hitched there. As Kitty looked out a window, she saw a squad of grays coming her way, hollering their rebel yell as they charged toward the house. As the bullets started flying, Kitty ran to a neighbor's house, hiding her son Charlie under her hoop skirt.

Upon entering the house the rangers found a table spread with food. Mosby explained:

> *One of the men ran up-stairs where it was pitch dark; he called but got no answer. As a pistol shot could do no harm, he fired into the darkness. The flash of the pistol in his face caused one of the Yankees to move, and he descended through the ceiling. He had stepped on the lathing and caved it in. After he was brushed off, we saw that he was a major. The three other officers who were with him came out of their holes and surrendered. My men appropriated the lunch by right of war.*

Mosby had captured Lieutenant Watson and the other officers on the investigating commission who had come to Herndon with Major Wells. Underwood was sent off with the prisoners to Culpeper, where they were eventually taken by train to a Confederate prison in Richmond.

The following day, Mosby sent a communication to his commander, General J.E.B. Stuart, explaining that he had completely routed the enemy

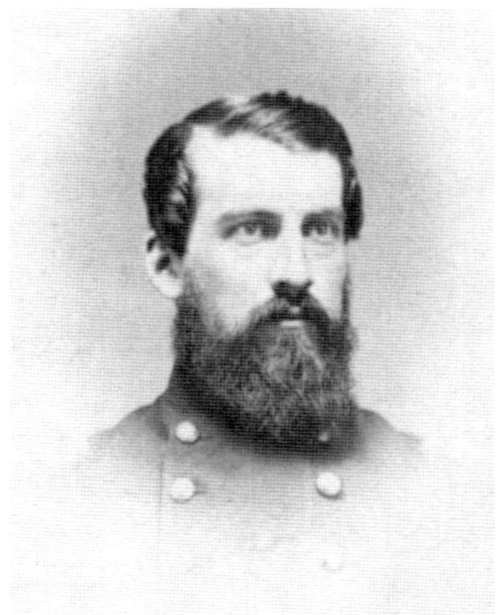

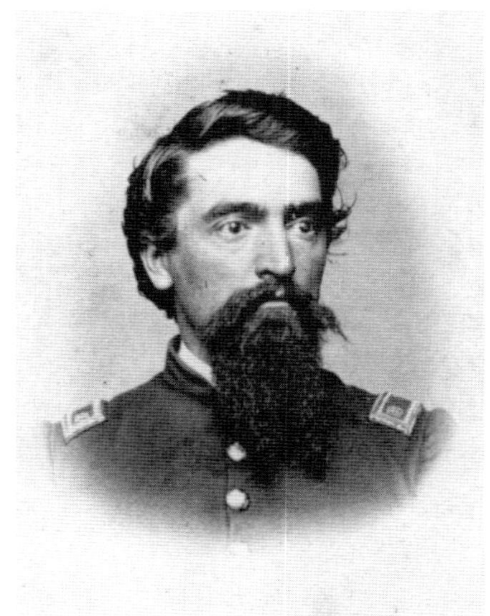

Above, left: Major William Wells. *Above, right*: Captain Robert Schofield. *Right*: Lieutenant Perley Cheney. *Francis Guber, collector of Vermont Civil War Photographs.*

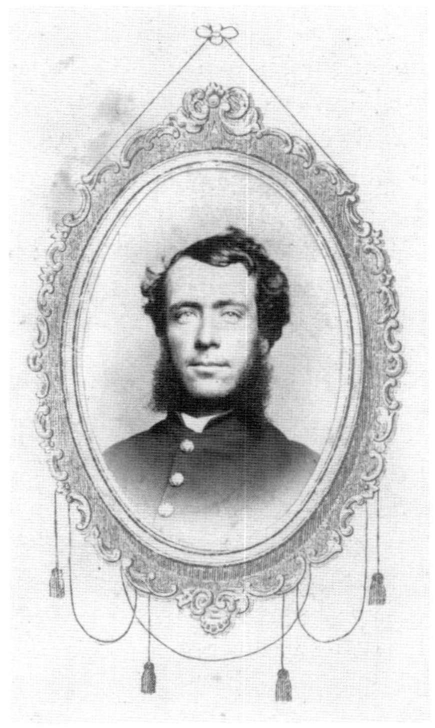

cavalry at the Herndon Station and had sustained no losses. He wrote, "In this affair my officers and men behaved splendidly."

During the raid, the commotion caused the proprietor of the store at the Herndon Depot, Mayo Janney, to be caught off guard, startled and frightened. According to the book *The First Vermont Calvary in the Civil War: A History*, Janney had been draining a jug of molasses for a customer when the raid commenced. "Forgetting about the flowing sweetener, he wasted no time in distancing himself from the scene of action."

In his memoir, Mosby also confirmed this "ludicrous affair" involving Janney:

> [He] *had just brought a barrel of molasses from Washington to retail to his neighbors, and he was in the act of filling a jug for a customer when he heard the yell of my men as they rushed at the picket post. As the place was occupied by the Unionists, he could not have been more surprised if a comet had struck it. Janney did not aspire to be a hero, so he ran away as fast as his heels could carry him, and, if possible, the molasses ran even faster. When he ventured to return to the store, he found the molasses spread all over the floor, and not a drop in the barrel.*

In various tax and census documents, a man named Mayo C.W. Janney was sometimes listed as living in Guilford (now called Sterling) and at other times listed at a house one mile south of Frying Pan Church, a house he bought in 1856 and sold in 1870. This may have been the same Mayo Janney who once worked in the depot. At various times, he was listed as being a farmer, a liquor dealer and a butter dealer. He died in 1894.

As a result of the raid, Major Wells spent several weeks in Richmond's Libby Prison. He was later exchanged from prison, returned to his Vermont regiment and distinguished himself in several military engagements, including in Gettysburg, where his gallantry earned him a Medal of Honor. He was promoted to the rank of general in 1865 and mustered out of the army in 1866. He led a distinguished civilian life, becoming a partner in a druggist firm, a state adjutant general and a state senator. He died in 1892 and is buried in Vermont.

Captain Schofield later participated in the Battle of Gettysburg. He lost his left eye and was seriously wounded in Hagerstown, Maryland, where he was captured and sent to Libby Prison for nine months. He was later transferred to other Confederate prisons. He was discharged from the army in 1865 at the rank of major and later promoted from brevet to colonel by the president. He married in 1867 and had five children. For many years, he was the manager/owner of Schofield Cottage, a popular resort hotel in Wisconsin. He died in 1918.

Lieutenant Watson later went on to fight at Gettysburg as well. Census documents show that after the war he returned to Vermont where he attended law school and then became an attorney.

Lieutenant Cheney, who also fought at Gettysburg, was shot in the back by a sharpshooter in a battle near Little Round Top. The bullet exited the front of his body where it stopped when it hit a pocket watch in his front pocket. After months of recuperating, Cheney returned to participate in several more battles. After the war, Cheney moved to Boston, where he became a salesman and later got married.

In 1910, Cheney wrote a letter to Colonel Mosby, which began, "Dear Colonel and Friend." He went on to acknowledge, "You will be surprised to receive a letter from me." He reminded Mosby of the Herndon raid and wrote, "Your treatment and [that of] your men to us on that occasion has always been gladly remembered by us all—in every respect courteous. And you kindly gave us our horses to ride from Upperville to Culpeper Court House, which was an act of the highest type of man, and should bury deep forever the name of 'guerilla.' " Perley Cheney died in Minnesota in 1916.

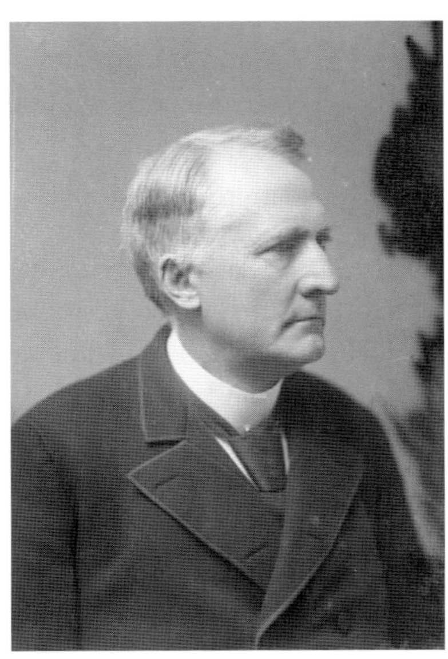

Colonel Mosby, circa 1873. Bell, photographer. *Library of Congress.*

Suspected as a Southern sympathizer, Nat Hanna was arrested in 1864 and spent some time in the Old Capitol Prison in Washington, D.C. Nat later deserted his wife, Kitty, and left her with their two boys. Nothing is known of Nat's whereabouts after he left Kitty.

Kitty had her second child, John, shortly after the Herndon raid. She lived out her days in Herndon at the house that she and Nat had built at 681 Monroe Street. The house still remains today. Kitty died in 1907 and is buried at Herndon's Chestnut Grove Cemetery.

John Underwood was killed a few months after the raid in Herndon by a Confederate deserter near Oatlands, Virginia, south of Leesburg. When speaking of Underwood's skills, Mosby recalled in his memoirs, "I never found his like again." Underwood is buried in Middleburg.

Mosby disbanded his rangers after the war. He reestablished his law practice and became Ulysses S. Grant's campaign manager in Virginia. However, the Southerners were not ready to follow his lead and turned bitterly against their former hero. Mosby served in various appointed positions under several presidents. Some of the jobs he held included a lawyer for the Southern Pacific Railroad, a U.S. consul to Hong Kong, a special agent for the Department of the Interior and an assistant attorney in the U.S. Department of Justice.

After a series of physical debilitations, Mosby died in a Washington hospital in 1916 at the age of eighty-two. Southerners' view of Mosby eventually softened over the years. After his death, the president at the University of Virginia issued a statement saying, "The University lost one of her bravest and noblest sons."

One eulogy that was printed in the *Fauquier Democrat* and the *Richmond Virginian* said:

> *With the bitterness of war all gone, there remains to Americans, North and South, a precious heritage of valor, of self-sacrifice, of sturdy, unflagging never-give-up spirit, a heritage which, in future days of possible stress, will prove inspiration unto us. Mosby is dead—peace to his ashes.*

Mosby is buried in Warrenton, Virginia.

TWO LOCAL CONFEDERATE FIREBRANDS: DOCTORS WILLIAM AND JOHN DAY

Two well-known and well-respected local horse-and-buggy doctors from mid-nineteenth-century Herndon were Dr. William B. Day and his brother Dr. John T. Day.

Both men were born in Calvert County, Maryland. William was about twelve years older than John. It is unclear when they first moved to Fairfax County, but census documents found them both in Fairfax County in 1850. At that time, William, thirty-three, was already a physician while John, twenty-one, was in school. By 1860, John was also listed as a physician. They both settled in Dranesville, living on

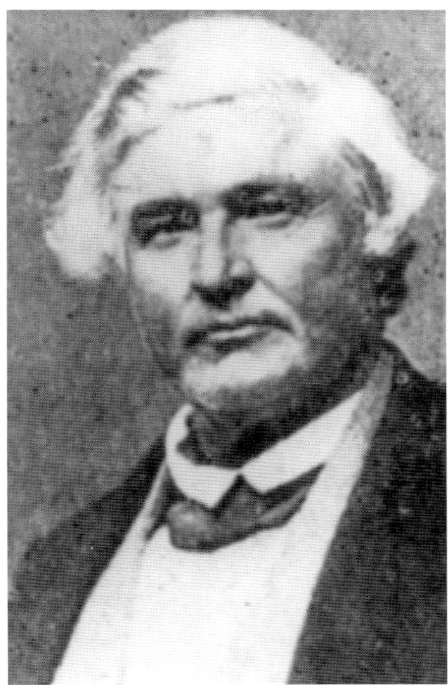
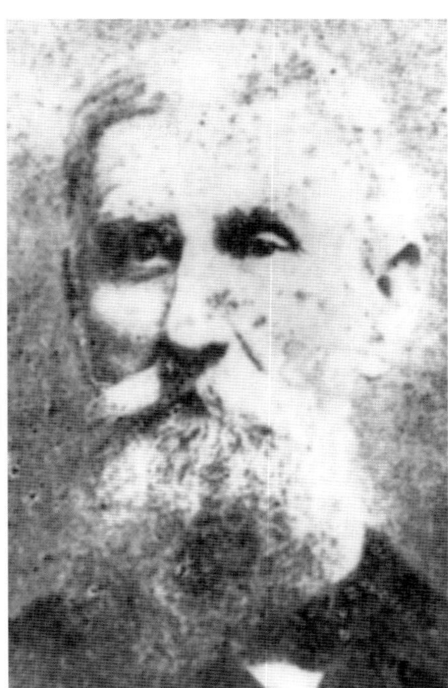

Left: Dr. William B. Day. *Right*: Dr. John T. Day. *Fairfax County Public Library Photographic Archive.*

Leesburg Pike with their respective families. Both of their adjacent homes, at 11700 and 11706 Leesburg Pike, still stand today and are historical landmarks in the Dranesville District.

William and John split their medical practices. The blue-eyed William, who was known to be corpulent, weighing approximately 275 pounds, primarily served patients who lived east of Dranesville, as far as Langley. The thin and bearded younger brother, John, primarily served the patients south and west of Dranesville, including Herndon and Leesburg. The residents' dependence on these two doctors, who served such a large geographical area, earned them popularity and influence.

Lottie Dyer Schneider, who was born in Herndon in 1879 and lived there until 1920, remembered how it was sometimes necessary for one of the doctors to come to Herndon. Mothers would handle minor ills and injuries, using concoctions of sulphur and molasses, slathers of mutton tallow on their chests or asafoetida bags worn around their necks. Nevertheless, she recalled that the doctors had to be called in cases of emergencies. Lottie's younger sister, Ruth Dyer, also remembered being treated by John Day for scarlet fever and subsequent days of a severe earache.

William had retired in Lottie's youth, but she had old receipts in her family records that showed that his house call cost one dollar. Lottie primarily remembered John, sometimes referred to by locals as "Dr. Jack": "I see him so plainly—tall and straight with iron-gray hair and beard. He drove a span of horses with several dogs barking at their heels."

Kitty Kitchen Hanna also remembered the two doctors. She recalled when her father was sick: "When he was took with consumption, which went hard with him, Dr. Bill Day—the 'old doctor' they called him after Doc Coleman was gone—tended him faithful; an' his brother, Doctor Jack, who was the 'young doctor' then, he used to come sometimes too, an' sometimes they'd stay to dinner."

Kitty Hanna also recalled a skirmish during the Civil War when one of John Mosby's Confederate soldiers, French Dulaney, was shot and wounded in the area. "They sent for Doctor Jack, who came at once; an' the doctor sent to me for some brandy, knowing I had little on hand. I gave all I had, but poor French died."

John Day was known to sometimes allow patients to pay bills in installments or through bartering. In December 1867, John treated Herndon resident William Robey for two days in a row. The total bill, including the visit, treatment and medicine, was $4.75. Dr. Day's records showed that he received $2 in 1869 and $1 in 1871. The bill was finally settled in 1875 when Dr. Day obtained two slop jars from Robey's general store in Herndon.

Despite these appreciative memories of the two doctors, many of their local activities during the war were sometimes controversial, depending on one's perspective about "Yankees" and "Rebels."

William Day, a slaveholder himself, was described as being a conservative man of great wealth and influence who hated the idea of the abolition of slavery and wanted to preserve the South. One informant reported that William had once said that "he would do all that lay in his power against Lincoln" and would try to persuade others to join the rebel army.

One of his most famous affairs was when he and several other Dranesville residents, including his brother John, were accused of seeking out and attacking four Union pickets in the vicinity of Lowes Island, about six miles north of Herndon. Two of the Union pickets ended up being killed. Recounted from statements on the General Records of the Department of State, one woman reported that William had stripped the clothes off the dead bodies, boasted about having taken them from the "damn Yankees" and gave the clothes to his own slaves. John was reported to have sent a man named Jimmy back to bury the two stripped dead men. Jimmy later reported that he buried one man but the other had already been "eaten up" by hogs. Yet another man stated that William was "the most bitter secessionist in the neighborhood, that he has been particularly active and influential in the persecution of Union men." Another resident said William attempted to gather men to form a company to go to Bull Run. When one man expressed reluctance about going, Dr. Day responded that if he did not go "he would have me, dead or alive." Still another resident reported that William had used his influence in favor of the rebellion and said, "In my opinion, William B. Day had done more against the Union than any other man in town."

At one point a notice was placed on the Herndon Station calling up all citizens to come forth a take an oath of allegiance to support the Confederate States government or leave the country. William Day also tried to pressure residents to vote for secessionist candidates, threatening them with being "marked" if they did not do so. Needless to say, William Day was well known to be a rabid secessionist.

In 1862, William was appointed as assistant surgeon at Winchester Hospital as well as other Confederate hospitals, serving as a contract surgeon for the Confederacy. He was also known to have enlisted in Cobb's Georgia Legion as a physician. John was not known to have ever enlisted in the military but worked in support of the Confederacy.

Both doctors ended up in the Union's Capitol Prison in Washington, D.C., in 1861. Colonel George D. Bayard, who commanded the 1st Pennsylvania Cavalry, reported that he "arrested six of the citizens of Dranesville who are known to be secessionists of the bitterest stamp." Those six citizens included both William and John Day. They were charged with murdering and robbing the Federal soldiers at Lowes Island.

William Day later said that while in prison they could hear carpenters hammering, and they feared gallows were being constructed to hang them. He said his brother John prayed on his knees, loud and often, to be spared from the gallows.

Kitty Hanna recalled:

> [Dr. Jack] *an' his brother, Doctor Bill, was put in old Capitol Prison.... The folks got up a petition an' everybody signed it, to get 'em out, for they was good an' useful men, an' badly needed in our country. It was summer time when they got out'n prison. Doctor Bill went to Richmond for a time, but Doctor Jack stayed at his house in Dranesville as long as he could, tho' at las' he too went to Richmond, bein' a hot Secessioner.*

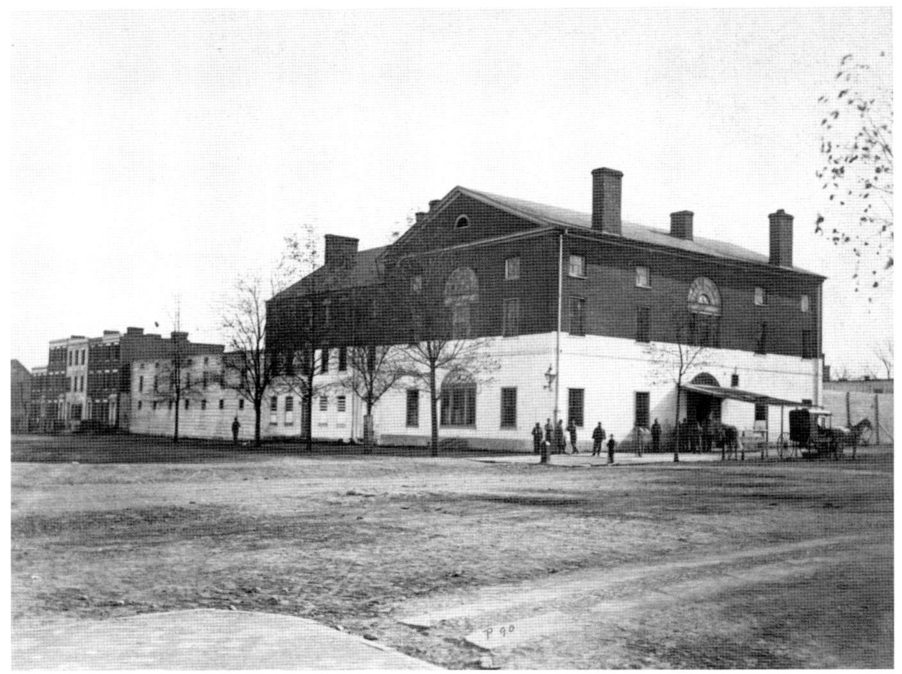

The Old Capitol Prison, Washington, D.C., circa 1861–1865. *Library of Congress.*

John was released conditionally upon taking an oath of allegiance to the United States. William's murder charges were never indisputably proved, and he was released in 1862 as a result of a prisoner exchange.

Both doctors were listed as still living in Dranesville in the 1870 and 1880 census documents. John continued to practice as a local physician after William retired. John also became a devoted Episcopalian. He was one of the earliest members of St. Timothy's Episcopal Church in Herndon, formerly located at the corner of Elden and Grace Streets. His name appeared as a trustee on the deed in 1876. According to the 1877 church mission records, he was elected to the vestry and agreed to be the treasurer. He was a senior warden for fifteen years. The Herndon Masonic Lodge occupies the old church building today at 820 Elden Street.

Kitty again recalled:

> *Doctor Jack was the mos' enthusiastic of all, 'cause Mis' Jack, she'd won him over to be 'Piscopal, an' he never done things by half; so in all sorts of weather he'd drive miles to church, given' so many of his hard earned dollar to support The Mission, he died poor, they say....I know he had treasures*

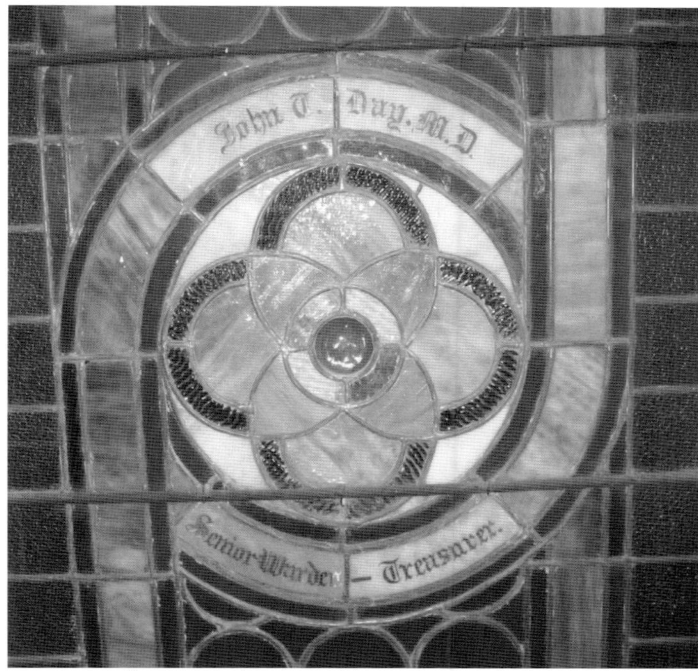

Detail of the John T. Day, MD, memorial window. *Barbara Glakas.*

> *laid up, as you say, an' the picture on his memorial window is topped by crown above the cross….Anyhow, we love to think of Doctor Jack, so tall an' redfaced, with long gray beard an' flowin' locks, drivin' so fas 'round the county, in a two horse buggy, his dogs followin' him a-barkin' an' racin'.*

Dr. William Day died in 1886 and is buried at the Day family cemetery off Brown's Mill Road in Vienna, Virginia. Dr. John Day died in 1893 and is buried at Herndon's Chestnut Grove Cemetery. John's funeral consisted of both an Episcopalian service and a Masonic Ritual. A *Fairfax Journal* obituary said of the funeral, "There was the largest attendance…that was ever seen at this place."

Around 1900, devoted church members, friends and patients of John Day purchased and installed a stained-glass window in the old St. Timothy's Church on Elden Street, dedicated in his memory. The beautiful memorial stained-glass window—measuring approximately fourteen feet high by five feet wide—is still in Herndon's Masonic Lodge today.

5

The Inside Story of Herndon's Incorporated Beginnings

Herndon Becomes an Official Town

Incorporation Day and the First Town Council

Herndon officially became an incorporated town on January 14, 1879—Incorporation Day!

Prior to becoming an incorporated town, Herndon was a small, unnamed village within the Dranesville District of Fairfax County. Sources indicate that between 1790 and 1840 there were only a handful of homes within what is now Herndon's corporate limits.

The coming of the railroad and its depot in the late 1850s stimulated greater growth. The depot became the center of the village, with homes and businesses popping up all around it. The village also got a new post office in 1858.

By 1878, schools, churches, general stores, a blacksmith shop, a wheelwright shop and a Good Templar Hall dotted the downtown area. The businesses around the depot supported the local farmers and their families. Milk was shipped into Washington via the rail. Village commuters also used the rail to travel to Washington for work and for cultural opportunities. Conversely, Washingtonians used the rail to travel out to the village for a summer respite away from the city heat.

By 1879, the village had about four hundred inhabitants. At some unknown point in time prior to that year, the village people decided to increase their self-determination by becoming incorporated. As an incorporated town, the village—which adopted the name of its post office—was allowed to become a municipality within defined geographic limits and was authorized to govern itself. The grant of these powers, and the authorization for a town charter, was provided by an act of the Virginia General Assembly on January 14, 1879.

Specifically, the Town of Herndon's original charter explained:

> *Be it enacted by the General Assembly of Virginia, that the following described territory in the County of Fairfax shall be and the same is hereby declared a town corporate, under the name and style of the Town of Herndon and by that name and style shall have and exercise the powers hereinafter granted.*

The original boundaries of the town were described in a very lengthy way, using the names of resident's properties to describe its boundaries. For example, an excerpt of the boundary description is as follows: "Beginning at the southwest corner of William Urich's farm, on the county road, and running thence southeasterly on the line between Urich and Coleman; also, on the line between Williams and Webster farm, and across the land of C.H. Bliss to the Thornton tract."

As a result of incorporation, a town council was formed—a group of elected men who would govern the town by a system of ordinances. The council had the authority to levy road and corporation taxes, mark the boundaries of the streets and sidewalks, regulate large animals, provide trees, adopt health regulations, provide for order and quiet and punish those who violated ordinances.

The original town charter provided that the town council would be made up of seven people, elected annually, with the mayor to be elected from and by the council for a term of one year. (Later, the town charter was amended to provide for the popular election of the mayor and council every two years.) The mayor was to be the presiding officer of town council meetings but was to have no vote except in the case of a tie. The mayor would also have the jurisdiction and authority as a justice of the peace within the town limits.

On February 8, 1879, about one month after incorporation, a group of men met in the railroad depot for the purpose of organizing a board of councilmen for the newly incorporated Town of Herndon.

It is not clear how these seven men—along with the town clerk and the town sergeant—came to be selected as the first official officers of Herndon.

Presumably an election may have been held among the townspeople sometime either prior to or right after the January 14 Incorporation Day, but such an election was never mentioned in the town minutes. The first town council minutes were taken on February 8—not on January 14—when these men gathered to be sworn in. They took an oath of office that is similar in part to the one that is used today:

> *Declaring ourselves citizens of the Commonwealth of Virginia and do solemnly swear that we will support and maintain the Constitution and laws of the United States and the Constitution and the laws of the state of Virginia; that we recognize and accept the civil and political equality of all men before the law; and that we will faithfully perform the duties of councilmen, Clerk , and Sergeant according to the act passed and approved January 14, 1879 to incorporated the Town of Herndon to the best of my ability, so help me God.*

Richard Coleman was the Fairfax County justice of the peace who swore in the councilmen. The seven councilmen were Isaiah Bready, Ancel St. John, William Urich, Stephen Killam, William D. Sweetser, Lawrence Hindle and C.H. Hathaway. The first town clerk was H.W. Blanchard, and the first town sergeant was C.M. Burton.

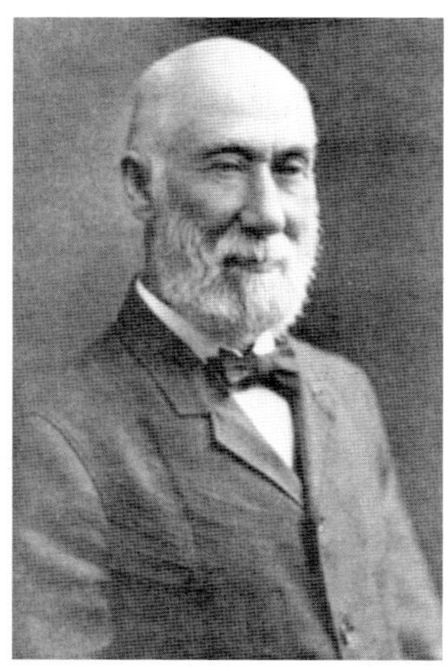

Mayor Isaiah Bready. *J. Berkley Green Collection of the Herndon Historical Society.*

Once the men were sworn in, Stephen Killam was selected as president of the meeting. The men then proceeded to the business of electing the town's first mayor. William Sweetser was appointed as the teller. The ballots were counted, and Ancel St. John was duly elected mayor. However, St. John immediately "respectfully declined" the job. The meeting minutes only stated that he "gave his reasons," but unfortunately, the minutes did not specify what those reasons were. As a result, Isaiah Bready was then elected, and he became the Town of Herndon's first mayor.

The meeting was then adjourned, and the council planned to meet the next time in the schoolhouse on Center Street on February 22. The first and only order of business at that meeting was to "borrow five dollars on six months' time" to pay expenses of "Stationery & C."

By the March meeting, conducted in Councilman Hindle's home, the council had prepared a bond in the sum of $200 to pay the town sergeant. The town sergeant was the first paid employee of the town. They next voted on a committee of two, appointed to recommend ordinances to the council.

The council had no official location to meet, so meetings were held in various places, such as in homes, in the Herndon School and in the depot. (A permanent location would not come until 1938, when the Town Hall was constructed in the railroad park behind depot as a Works Progress Administration project, part of President Franklin Roosevelt's New Deal reforms.) By late March, the first ordinance had been drafted. This ordinance directed the opening of certain streets for public use by May 15. The streets mentioned in that ordinance were parts of Adams, Madison and Jackson Streets.

The men serving on the first town council were all prominent men and/or landowners. They were all Northerners who moved to the Herndon area sometime between the 1850s and 1870. Following is a short description of the seven men who served on Herndon's first town council.

Born in Pennsylvania in 1830, Isaiah Bready's family had already come to the village of Herndon sometime in the 1850s, investing in land. Bready was a dairy farmer. After his father died in 1859, he was left with the land that is now Herndon's Centennial Golf Course, as well as additional land that lay east of the town's golf course over to Grace Street. His home was the grand stone house at the northwest corner of Vine Street and Main Drive, which was built in 1876 and still stands today. He had several children, and he continued serving as mayor until 1882. He died in 1913.

William Urich was born in Pennsylvania around 1832. The townspeople of Herndon often referred to him as "Colonel" or "General." It is believed he served in the Pennsylvania militia, in a Lebanon County unit. He lived in the stately square white house at the northeast corner of Elden and Grace Streets. He was a farmer, and his farm was located in the vicinity of the current Chandon subdivision. He and Mayor Bready served on the subcommittee that started forming the town's first ordinances. Urich was later elected as the town's second mayor. He served in that position until 1886.

Stephen Killam was born in Nova Scotia, Canada, in 1811. He was known to have lived on Monroe Street. He was a retired merchant and later a railroad agent. He served as the town's postmaster from 1868 to 1882,

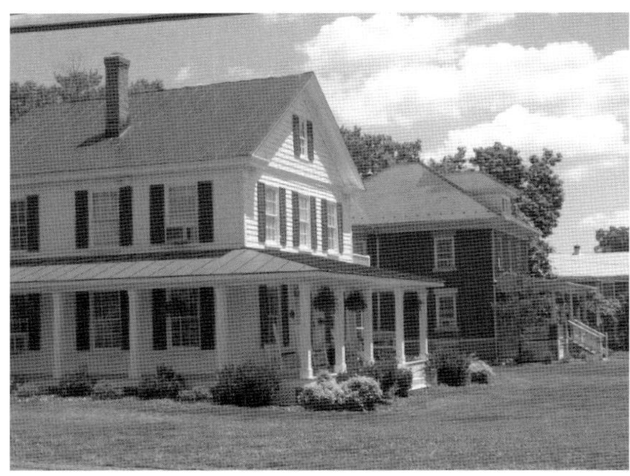

William Urich formerly lived in the white house at 814 Elden Street. *Barbara Glakas.*

and for a while, he operated a store in the railroad station. He served on the council until 1880. He became the first president of the Cemetery Association, a group of citizens that established and cared for the local cemetery, now known as Chestnut Grove Cemetery. Lottie Dyer Schneider once commented that she revered his memory because "he had done so much in planning the town, in planting trees and helping to beautify the community." He died in 1888.

William D. Sweetser was born in Maine around 1824. Sweetser lived in a house that formerly stood on Station Street, at the west end of Pine Street, now the parking lot between the Great Harvest Bread Company and the Dominion Animal Hospital. Looking out his front window, he could see directly up Pine Street. Lottie Dyer Schneider described him as being "straight and tall." Before moving to Herndon, he was a house carpenter and joiner. He was known to be one of the town's early teachers, teaching at a little school on Monroe Street, which burned down around the 1860s. He served on the council until 1880. He served, off and on, as the town's postmaster between the years 1882 and 1901, and he also kept a store in the railroad station house. He died in 1902.

Lawrence Hindle was born in Lancaster, England, in 1809. He was a farmer. He lived in New York before the Civil War. He started buying land in Herndon in the 1860s. He was a member of St. Timothy's Episcopal Church, which was, at that time, located at the corner of Elden and Grace Streets. He was also a trustee for the Herndon School Association in 1871–1872. He owned land in various spots around town, including on Lynn Street. An 1878 map of the town showed his store on Lynn Street, which is now known as the Nachman Building. At one point, he transferred a piece of his land to the town for public use, which

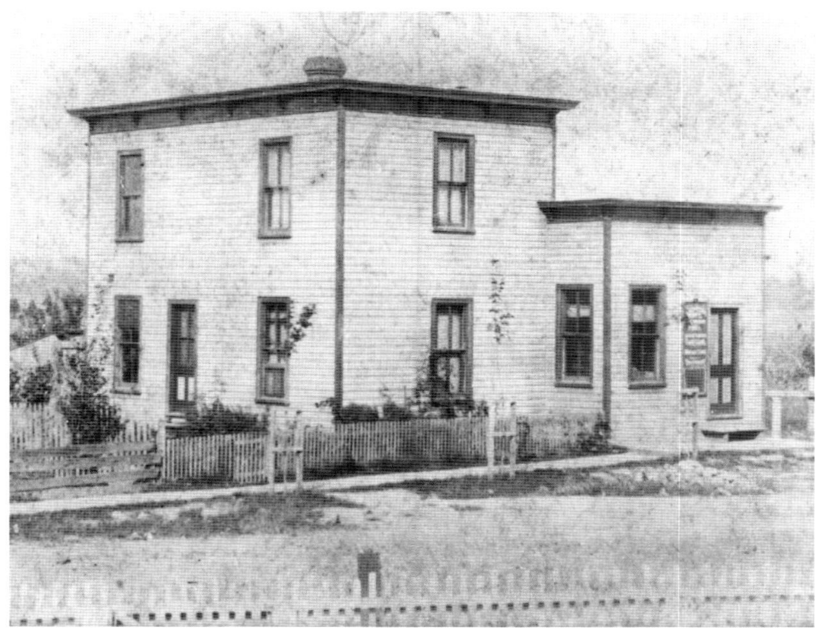

William Sweetser's home and the post office, formerly located at the corner of Station and Pine Streets. *J. Berkley Green Collection of the Herndon Historical Society.*

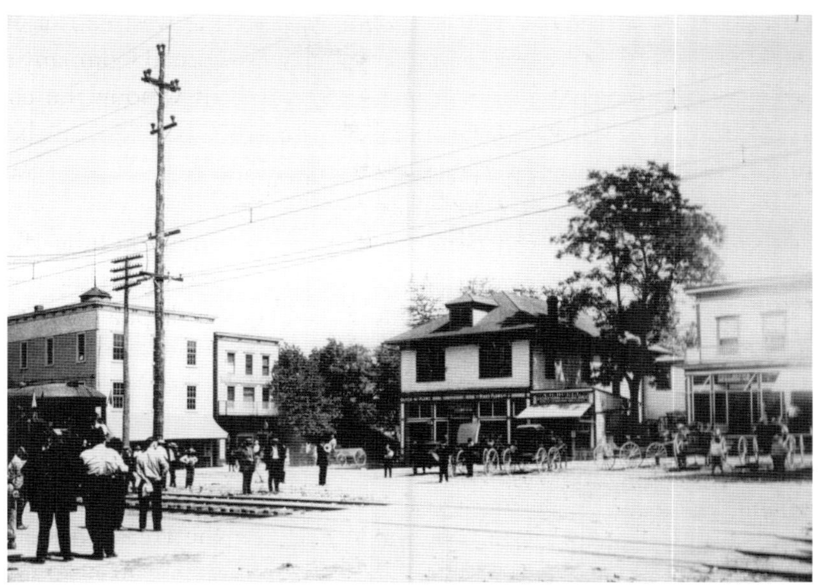

Ancel St. John and Lawrence Hindle ensured that land adjacent to the depot was given to the town for public use. *Courtesy Buell family collection.*

ultimately became the town plaza, now the parking area in front of a small strip of stores on Lynn Street. He served on the council up to 1882. He died in 1886.

C.H. Hathaway was the least known of all the first councilmen, with no census documents placing him in this area. However, some Fairfax County birth and death records show that a Charles H. and Hellen C. Hathaway had one baby who died in 1875 and two others who were born in 1877 and 1879. This is the time frame that the town was being incorporated. Charles was born in 1843 in Massachusetts and owned a farm. He spent most of his life in New England, and a census document dated 1880 placed him back in Massachusetts. Town council minutes also show that he served on the town council up until March 1880. Clearly, Hathaway did not spend much time in Herndon. He died in 1903.

Ancel St. John—the oldest of the councilman—was born in 1799. St. John ended up being a very consequential figure to Herndon's early history; therefore, more is written about him in the next section.

Many of these first councilmen presumably came to the village of Herndon out of opportunity. Some of them ultimately returned to their Northern homes, but many stayed in the town of Herndon, remaining there for the rest of their lives, putting down family roots and helping the town grow, prosper and thrive.

THE IMPORTANCE OF ANCEL ST. JOHN

Although Ancel St. John's contributions were many, he arrived in Herndon later in his life and never set down long-term roots, which may have contributed to his name being lost to history. However, the more that is learned about him, the more it becomes increasingly clear how important a figure Ancel St. John was to Herndon's early history.

The first known official map of Herndon, dated 1878, was drawn by cartographer G.M. Hopkins (see map on pages 6–7). It is commonly referred to as "the Hopkins map." It shows that many parcels of land in the downtown Herndon area were owned by someone named St. John. It was later discovered that the Hopkins map represented only a fraction of St. John's original landholdings.

St. John, along with another man named John Harry Thompson, bought a little over four hundred acres of land in the central part of Herndon in

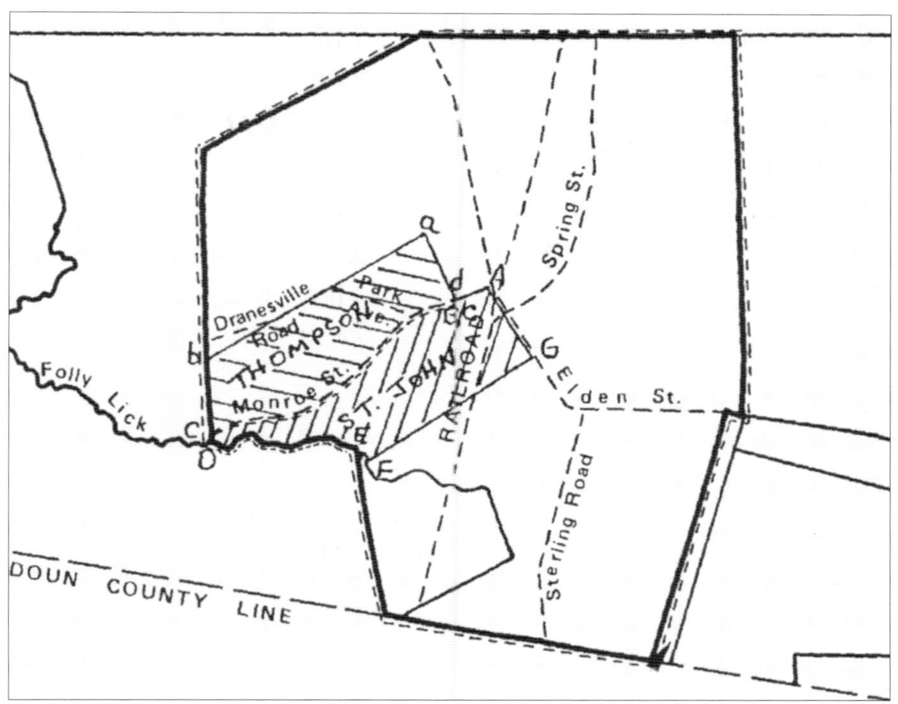

Map showing the St. John and Thompson land tracts in Herndon, 1865. *From* Herndon, The Land: 1649–1900 *by Donald LeVine.*

1865. They eventually divided the land into two large tracts, and by 1867, each owned about two hundred acres.

In 1869, St. John sold a significant portion of his land to Lyman Ballou. But he kept other lots, which he subdivided into reasonably small parcels, many of which were in Herndon's central downtown area. Many of the current lots in the area of Station, Lynn, Pine, Grace and Center Streets are those that St. John had subdivided. Many of those boundary lines still hold true today. By the time the 1878 Hopkins map was drawn, St. John had already sold off a good portion of his land.

The year after the Hopkins map was drawn, the town was incorporated and St. John was elected to the first town council. He was subsequently chosen by his fellow councilmen to serve as the town's first mayor. However, as stated earlier, he declined the job.

Before going any further with this story, we must first go back and look at where St. John came from and how he ended up playing such a major role in Herndon's beginnings.

Ancel St. John was born in Moreau, New York, in 1799. He married his wife, Isabelle, in 1823. They went on to have nine children, although several of them did not survive childhood.

St. John was very active in Ithaca, New York, in the 1820s and 1830s. He was the first cashier of the Bank of Ithaca, he served on Ithaca's first Board of Health and he served as treasurer of Ithaca's First Presbyterian Church.

Notably, St. John—along with three other men—laid out a plan for the village of Ithaca, the section referred to as University Hill, now part of Cornell University. St. John and his colleagues planned the community with the intention of creating growth in the area. St. John appears to have done a similar thing in Herndon, laying out an informal town map of land parcels with cross streets that would develop into a community. This was later the basis of what was reflected in the Hopkins map.

In the 1840s, St. John spent time in New Jersey, where one of his sons lived. He was one of the founders of the Masonic Lodge in Lambertville, New Jersey, and became the first Worshipful Master of the Lodge there.

An 1850 census indicated that St. John and his family were boarders in New York City. Although his whereabouts in 1860 are not clear, it is known that he bought land in Herndon in 1865. An 1866 IRS tax record showed that St. John was living in Washington, D.C. But in 1870, now seventy-one years old, he and his wife were boarding back in Lambertville. Various documents from the 1840s through 1870 listed his occupation as either "broker" or "retired banker."

Across the years, it is clear that St. John moved frequently between New York and New Jersey and—toward the latter part of his life—to Washington, D.C., and Herndon.

The book *Fairfax County, Virginia, 1870–1900* by Patrick Reed described St. John, of New Jersey, as "a leader of the new arrivals after the war, a group which also included families from New York and Pennsylvania." To explain the possible reasoning for St. John's movement south, Reed explains:

> *If Edward Curtis Gibbs's "success in raising Wheat" contradicted the Department of Agriculture's report for Fairfax County that "wheat has been an uncertain crop for several years," his accomplishment was to be typical of the experience of other former Northerners who were finding their way to Fairfax. While many long-time residents were saddled with debts and deprived of their accustomed labor, newcomers were able to take advantage of deflated land prices and the local demand for cash. These conditions must at least partially explain the decision of seven Union veterans from*

> *New York, who had seen the area during the war, to settle with their families near Merrifield on land made available to them at $25 per acre. This may explain as well the arrival of Harrison G. Otis whose family "was among several that migrated to Clifton from the North just after the Civil War," and the actions of Ancel St. John*[s] *of New Jersey, who "with a number of friends," bought up much of the land surrounding Herndon.*

As a broker, St. John invested in Herndon land, but he also lived in Herndon for an undetermined amount of time. Kitty Kitchen Hanna described St. John this way:

> *He lived here many a year after war times, off'n an' on, comin' an' goin', did St. John; an' he wore a red wig to distinguish him; a large han'some man he; an' he bought all the lan' either side of the railroad that he could lay holt of, but mostly to south an' west side....Mister St. John was a smart man for trade. He made a map of the town-to-be with streets an' cross streets laid out on it, an' he sol' many a lot for far more he paid; yet was he fair in dealin' mostly, an' his was the trouble o' layin' off an surveryin' an gettin' titles right, an' he got many people to come in to settle, too, after firs' owners lef'. Owin' to him, where 'twas all buckwheat field...there's a many housetop showin' now.*

According to Donald LeVine's book *Herndon: the Land, 1649–1900,* Ancel St. John donated some land "for a public tract along the railroad." As he must have intended—in collaboration with fellow Town Councilman Lawrence Hindle—the area would later become the town's public plaza and is now the wide parking area on Lynn Street adjacent to the Herndon Depot.

It is unclear if St. John ever owned a house in Herndon. He could have possibly boarded. St. John drew up his last will and testament in 1878, the year before the town was incorporated. It was written in his hand, and he described himself as being "now of Herndon, Virginia." He bequeathed to his wife the remaining land he owned in Herndon, which was about seventeen acres by then. The witnesses to St John's will were Stephen Killam and H.W. Blanchard, who, in 1879, would become St. John's fellow town councilman and the town clerk, respectively.

St. John had a hand in helping to establish some of Herndon's early churches and schools. Kitty Hanna said, "An' churches were built on the St. John tract, lots being bought—or given—for the Northern Methodis' an' the 'Piscopal churches."

In 1868, he assisted Herndon families who wanted to establish a Congregational Church in Herndon by writing a letter to the council of delegates in Washington/Baltimore in support of the proposed church. The Herndon Congregational Church was constituted, and in 1871, St. John sold a half-acre lot, at a low price, at the corner of Monroe and Pine Streets for the Herndon Congregational Church, which was built in 1873.

St. John also had a hand in the first public school in Herndon, located at 725 Center Street. St. John donated half an acre to the Town of Herndon for the Herndon School Association to use for the school, which was built in 1868. He was also the Herndon School Association's first president. The deed for the school land, signed by St. John and the school trustees, was rather explicit in its purpose. The land was for the "maintenance, support and perpetuity of a Public School for the diffusion of knowledge among the children of men…regardless of any particular religious faith."

In 1881, Mary Lee Castleman bought some land from St. John along Grace Street, where she built a home and established a private school called the Herndon Seminary. St. John also sold one acre of land to St. Timothy's Church for the use of its rectory.

It is evident that when it came to land uses that benefited the public good—such as, schools, churches, a public plaza and even a Good Templar Hall—St. John either donated the land or sold the land at below average prices.

Earlier it was stated that Ancel St. John's election as the Town of Herndon's first mayor in 1879 would not come to pass. After respectfully declining the honor of the position, Isaiah Bready was subsequently elected Herndon's first mayor instead.

It is suspected that St. John's age may have been one reason why he may have declined the position of mayor, but that is not known for sure. He would have been eighty years old that year, well over the average life expectancy for that time.

St. John went on to serve on the first town council, which first convened in February 1879. During that term, the town's first ordinances were passed, taxes were imposed and roads and bridges were improved.

By April 1880, St. John resigned from the town council. St. John, then eighty-one years old, returned to Lambertville. St. John died in 1882 and is buried at the Mount Hope Cemetery in Lambertville, a cemetery that he and five others incorporated in 1848.

An obituary in the *Belvidere Apollo*, a weekly newspaper from Belvidere, New Jersey, simply stated: "Ancel St. John Esq., many years ago a prominent

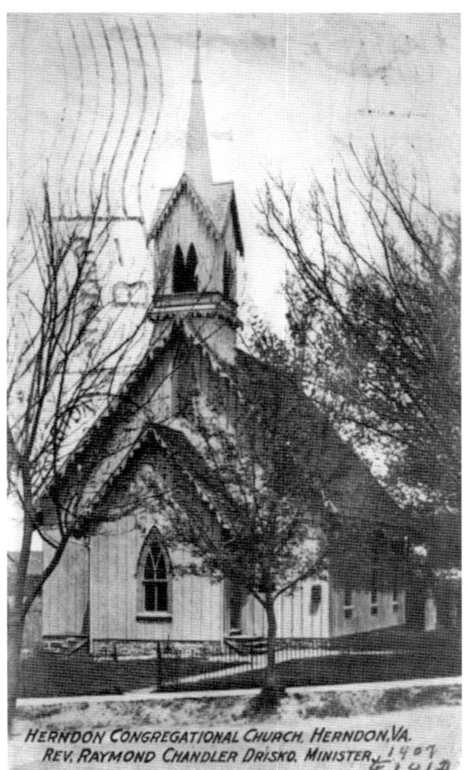

Right: The Herndon Congregational Church, 1907–1912. *J. Berkley Green Collection of the Herndon Historical Society.*

Below: The Herndon School, circa 1888. *Herndon Historical Society.*

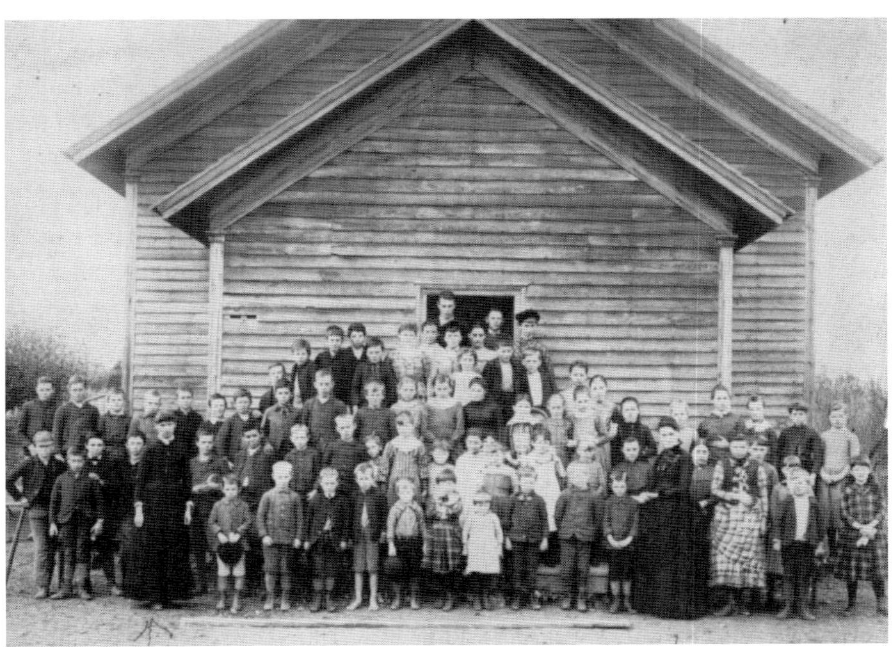

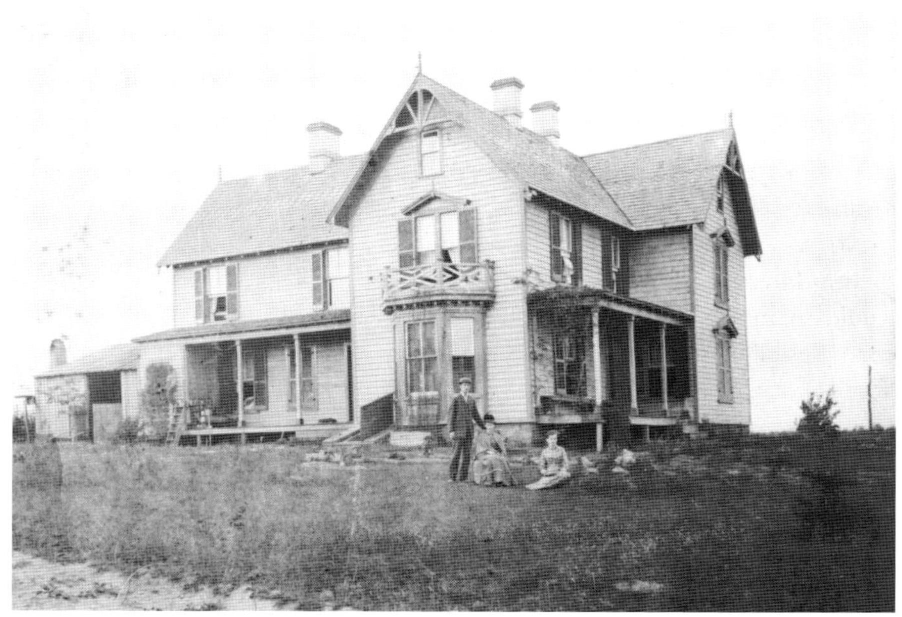

The Herndon Seminary, circa 1895. *Herndon Historical Society.*

citizen of Lambertville, died at Plainfield, on the 1st of April, in the 83rd year of this age, and his remains were interred in Lambertville."

Although St. John was only associated with Herndon for approximately fifteen years, he was well respected and was instrumental in helping to settle and grow the town after the Civil War. He was selected as the town's first mayor and served on the first town council. He thoughtfully mapped, parceled, sold and donated key pieces of land for both private and public purposes. And he helped to establish some of Herndon's first churches and schools. It is curious that for all the important roles that Ancel St. John played in the formative years of the town of Herndon that more is not widely known about him.

There are no Herndon streets, parks or subdivisions named after St. John. His life in Herndon appears to have been born out of land speculation. Nevertheless, his contributions and importance to Herndon's beginnings cannot be denied. Ancel St. John—the man who would have been Herndon's first mayor—seems to have been lost to history.

EARLY LAW AND ORDER ORDINANCES IN NINETEETH-CENTURY HERNDON

One of the early actions the first town council took after the Town of Herndon was incorporated in 1879 was to start drafting a set of town ordinances.

Not surprising, some of these ordinances addressed taxes, but many of them addressed behavior, clearly stating expectations that the council felt would maintain good law and order in town. Outlined below are a few examples of these ordinances:

- Fast Driving: "It shall be unlawful for any person to ride or drive any horse or mule on any street or highway within the corporation at a rate of speed exceeding six miles per hour."
- Trees: "It shall be unlawful for any person or person to girdle, break, bend, wound, or in any manner damage the trees… within this corporation."

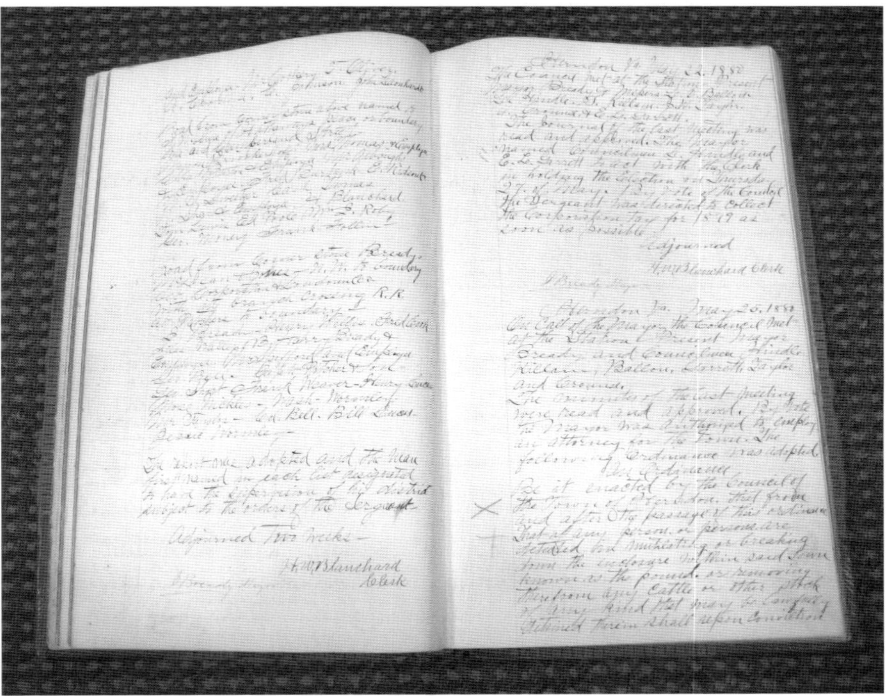

The 1879 Herndon Town Council minute book in the Town Clerk's Office. *Barbara Glakas.*

- Parking and Sidewalk Control: "It shall not be lawful for any person to tie in any manner or fasten any horse, mule, or any other animal to any lamp-post or tree, or to drive or lead any horse, mule or other animal, or cart, wagon or other vehicle on any sidewalk with the corporation."
- Disorder: "It shall be unlawful for any person or persons to congregate at the corners of streets, or in any street, avenue or highway, or on the steps or porticoes of any building, public or private, and be engaged in loud and boisterous talking, or to insult or to make rude or obscene comments or remarks on passersby, or to crowd, or obstruct, or to incommode the footway or entrance to any building or to prevent the free and uninterrupted passage thereof."
- Disturbing Religious Services: "It shall be unlawful for any person to molest or disturb any religious exercise or other proceedings in any church or place of worship or in any public building used for said purposes."
- Vandalism: "It shall be unlawful for any person to cut, break or deface in any way, or cover or rub with filth or excrement of any kind any public or private [property] or to deface any public notices within the Corporation."
- Missiles and Guns: "It shall be unlawful for any person to throw any missile in any street or public place…nor to fire any gun, pistol, cannon or other firearm in any street or within one hundred yards of any building within this Corporation, except to protect himself or property."
- Concealed Weapons: "If any person carry about his person any pistol, dirk, razor, bowie knife, or other dangerous or deadly weapon, he shall be fined from five to twenty dollars, and in default of payment thereof, he shall be confined in jail, not more than three months."
- Trespassing: "It shall not be lawful for any person to walk, ride or drive across the land owned or leased by another without his consent."
- Profanity and Indecency: "If any person shall be guilt of any profanity or the use of any obscene language or any public lewdness or indecency, whether by words or actions in any public place, or expose himself or herself in public view in any indecent manner, or shall exhibit publically any indecent

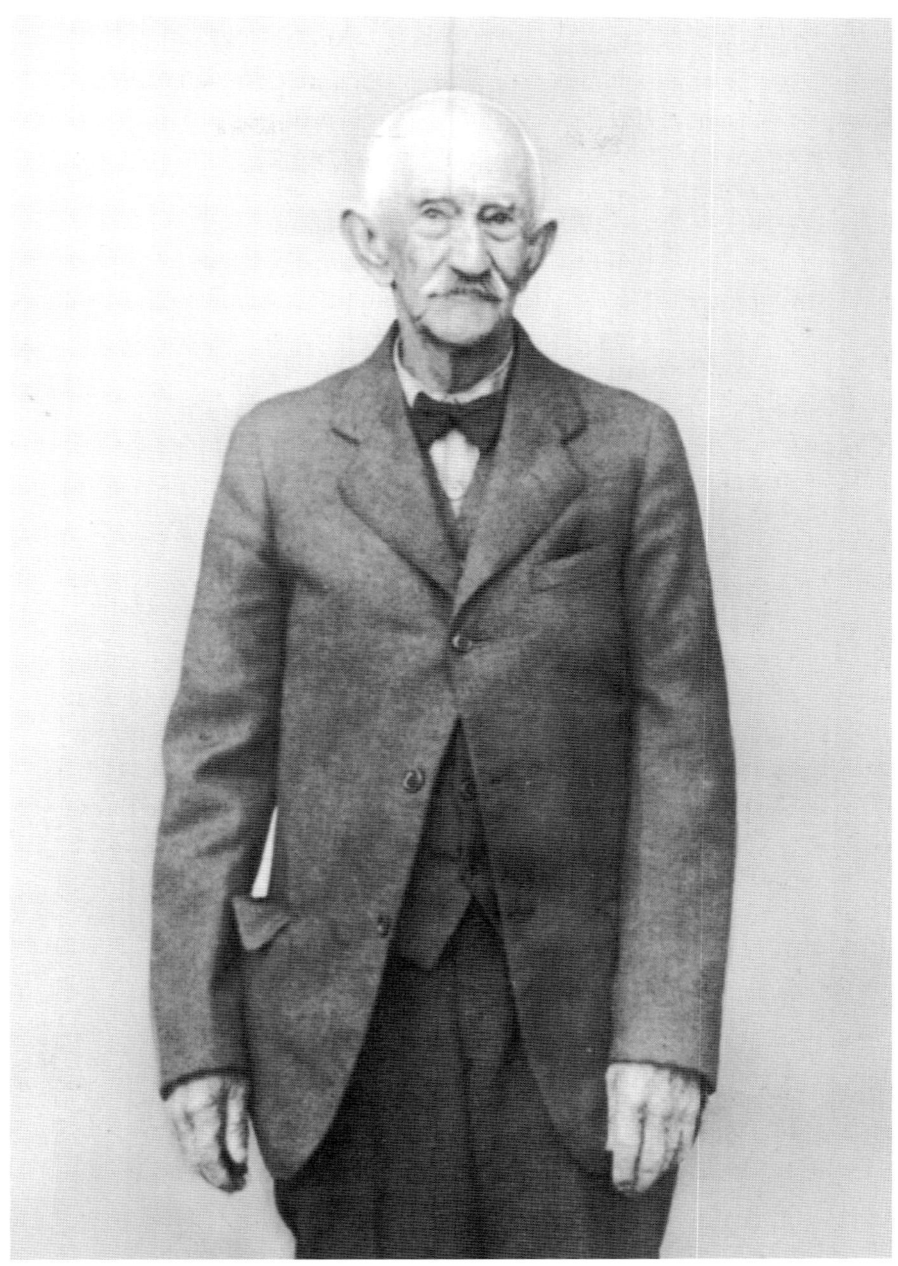

Charles M. Burton, Herndon's first town sergeant. *Herndon Historical Society.*

painting, engraving, print, sculpture or other representation… he shall be liable to a fine of not less than one and not more than ten dollars for each and every offence."

- Stealing from Gardens: "It shall be unlawful for any person to take fruit or garden or farm produce from any farm or garden within the limits of this Corporation except by permission."
- Games: "It shall not be lawful for any person to use a bean shooter or to throw any missile in any street or public place.… The playing of marbles on any sidewalk is prohibited.…It shall be non-lawful for any person or persons to play the game of football or to play bandy, or shindy, or any other game by which a ball, stone, or other substance is thrown, or propelled by any stick can or bat in any street or highway within the corporation."
- False Alarms: "If any person shall willfully make or cause to be made any false alarm, or shall cry fire, or ring any bell, or make any bonfire with a view of creating or causing any false alarm, or shall in any way aid or abet in so doing, he shall be liable to a fine of not less than one nor more than five dollars."
- Hedges: "It shall not be lawful for any person to set a thorn hedge within two feet of the line of any sidewalk within the corporation."
- Grazing Animals: "It shall be unlawful for any person to permit any horse, mule, colt or hog to graze on any of the sidewalks or highways of the Town…or for any ox, bull, or young cattle to graze or run at large on any portion of the improved limits of this Corporation."
- Swine and Dangerous Animals: "The keeping of swine and the keeping of animals of a wild and dangerous nature, such as lions or tigers, is prohibited with the town."

Now everyone hop on a mule and meet at the depot for a game of bandy!

Herndon's 1880 Census

The first home in Herndon was believed to have been built in the 1770s. The population growth was slow over the course of the next one hundred years, but that growth started to surge after the railroad track and train depot came to Herndon in the late 1850s. The year after the town's incorporation occurred, the 1880 national census was taken, counting the town of Herndon as a separate jurisdiction. There were only 422 people living in town that year.

The information shown on the 1880 census reflects a snapshot in time where one can read about the occupations, races, national origins, education levels and wealth of those people who lived within the town.

Of the eighty-eight heads of households that were listed in 1880, the vast majority were white males. There were nine female and fifteen black or mulatto heads of households. The female heads of households had no husbands. With the exception of two (a farmer and a house servant), all of the female occupations were listed as "keeping house."

All of the fifteen black or mulatto heads of households were either laborers or servants, except for Henry Simms, who had his own blacksmith shop. There was a total of twenty-three servants in town. Therefore, on average, there was one servant per every four households. Thirteen of those servants were teenage females, ranging in age from eleven to nineteen years old.

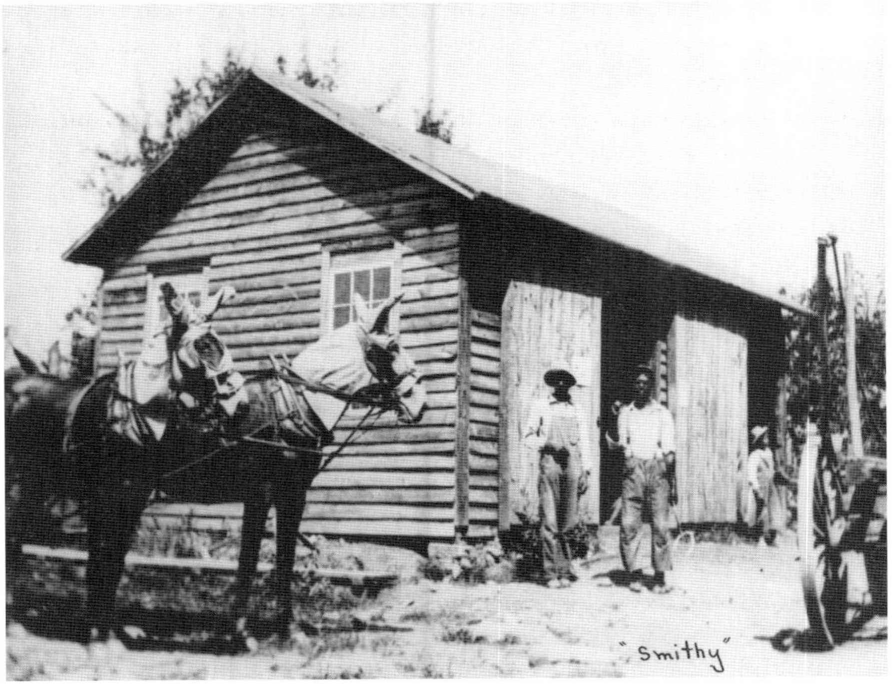

An early Herndon blacksmith. *J. Berkley Green Collection of the Herndon Historical Society.*

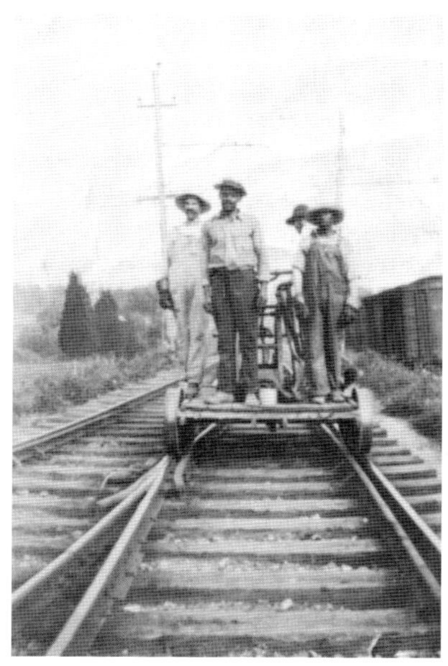

Herndon resident Thomas Wilson (*left*) and others worked on the railroad. *Doris Rosenberg.*

Most of the head of household occupations that year in Herndon were farmers (twenty-one) and laborers (twenty). The next most prevalent occupations were government clerks (nine), who were white men, and people "keeping house" (seven), who were all females. Other occupations included house carpenters (five), general merchants (four), clergymen (three), millwrights (two), wheelwrights (two), house servants (two), shoemakers (two), photographers (two), house painter (one), machinist (one), physician (one), blacksmith (one), huxter (one), railroad trackman (one) and railroad agent (one). A millwright was someone who built and installed machinery. A wheelwright was someone who built and repaired wooden wheels. A huxter was a term of that time that meant either a door-to-door salesman or someone who had a small ramshackle shop selling a variety of miscellaneous goods. Other miscellaneous jobs included an apprentice, a teacher, a farmhand, a confectioner and one who was "studying law."

Most of the heads of households were literate, but there were still several whom were not able to read (fourteen) or write (nineteen).

The remaining 334 people who lived in town, who were not heads of households, were either not employed or had a variety of other jobs. Some were listed as boarders, servants or laborers.

There were 187 children under the age of eighteen who lived in town. Many (103) attended school that year. The others were either under school age or simply did not attend school.

Almost half (forty) of the heads of households were born in Virginia. The rest came from a variety of states and countries. Most of those from Virginia were either farmers or laborers. Many others came from northern states: Pennsylvania (eight), Maine (four), New York (four), Connecticut (two), Maryland (two), New Hampshire (one) New Jersey (one), Ohio (one), Wisconsin (one), Michigan (one) and Washington D.C. (one). Most of those from northern states held skilled jobs, such as government clerks, machinists,

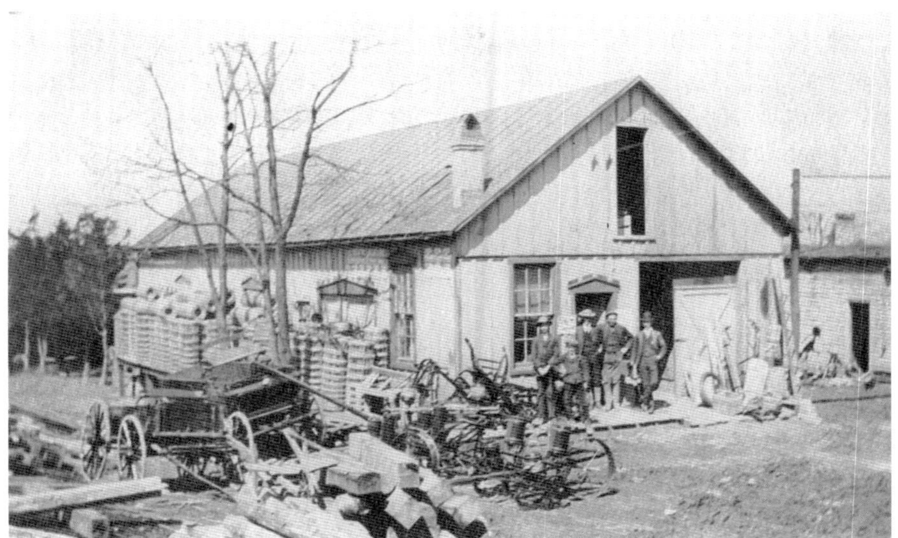

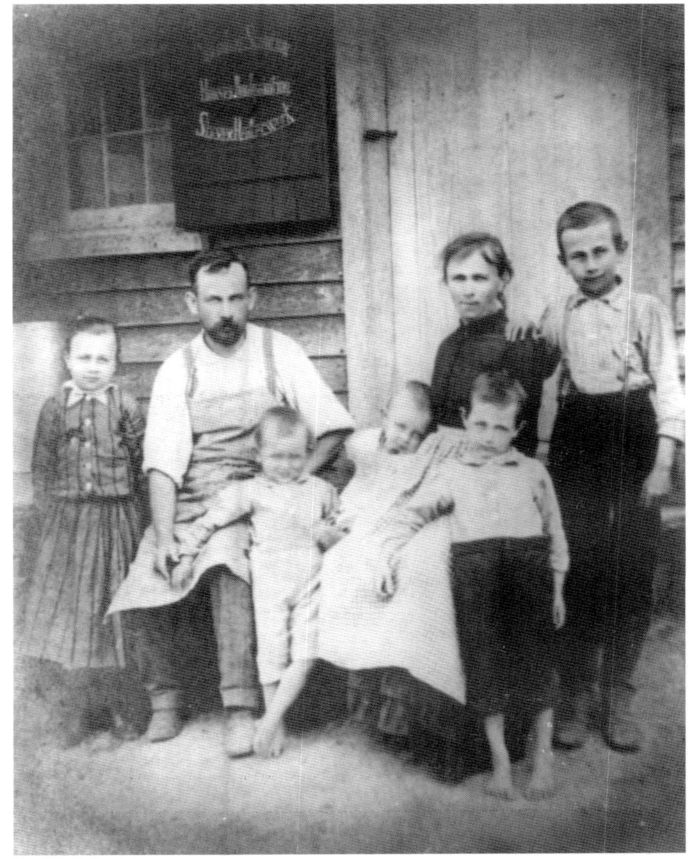

Above: Men conducting business at a utility railroad building near Station and Lynn Streets. *Herndon Historical Society.*

Right: A Herndon tinsmith, Paul Buchwald, and his family, circa 1892. *J. Berkley Green Collection of the Herndon Historical Society.*

photographers, carpenters and clergymen. Several of these northern men also became the Town of Herndon's first town councilmen.

Southern residents who were not born in Virginia were from South Carolina (three) and Kentucky (one). They held jobs such as laborers, blacksmiths and house painters. There were also a few residents who were born in other countries, including Ireland (two), Germany (two) and England (one). They were farmers and railroad men.

Although not expressly stated in the census, it is known that many of Herndon's southern farming families came from various parts of Virginia and had been in Virginia for a long time. Many of the northern families transplanted to Herndon after the Civil War, looking for warmer climates, buying affordable land, opening farms, establishing churches and commuting to government jobs in Washington, D.C.

When the railroad opened up, merchants and farmers were easily able to ship their milk and other goods into Washington and other surrounding areas, and Herndon residents were able to commute to their government jobs in Washington. Conversely, city dwellers were able to commute out to Herndon to take a vacation "in the country." As people and their respective businesses were attracted to the young town of Herndon near the train station, many other jobs in Herndon evolved to support those businesses and the town's growing economy. General merchandise storekeepers and shoemakers helped to feed and clothe the families. Carpenters built more homes and stores. Laborers supported the farmers. Wheelwrights took care of peoples' wagon wheels. And clergymen, servants and physicians cared for the growing number of Herndon families and their children.

6

The Evolution of Herndon's Early Schools

Schools from the 1860s to the 1960s

The Herndon School

In 1869, the Virginia General Assembly authorized a State Superintendent of Public Instruction and a State Board of Education. Fairfax County started opening public schools soon thereafter. Some of Herndon's earliest schools had private origins.

One early mention of a school in Herndon was made by Lottie Dyer Schneider in her memoir book *Memories of Herndon, Virginia*:

> *The first school in Herndon was probably a little building erected on property now owned by Dr. Meyers. The Younts owned this property and previously Mr. Downing was the owner. This little school was built in 1869 before I was born. W.D. Sweetzer and George Howard taught at this school and I knew both of these men. The building was burned down before I remember it.*

The property Lottie Dyer Schneider refers to is in the vicinity of 810 Monroe Street. Little else is known about that school, including whether or not it was a private school or a public one. It is believed that the school burned not too long after being built, and school operations may have temporarily been moved over to what is commonly called the Yellow House, then located on Elden Street.

Another school that was built at about the same time is commonly accepted as "the first" public school in Herndon, as it was also built in the 1860s and served as the town's public school for many years. It was called the Herndon School. It served only white students and was run by a Herndon School Association. This old school building still stands today and is located at 725 Center Street. It is a private home.

In the 1860s, Ancel St. John gave a half-acre of land to the town for a school. In 1868, he was appointed the president of the Herndon School Association. The deed for the land, signed by St. John and the school trustees, was rather explicit in its purpose: The land was "for the maintenance, support and perpetuity of a Public School for the diffusion of knowledge among the children of men…a Public School for the diffusion of knowledge among the progeny of men regardless of any particular religious faith."

The Herndon School was a three-room schoolhouse and was built in two sections in different years. The rear section, with an east–west axis, was built in 1868. A front section, perpendicular to the rear section and parallel to Center Street, is estimated to have been added around 1876.

In 1875, Herndon and Fairfax County agreed that the school would become part of the county's Dranesville District school system, and the

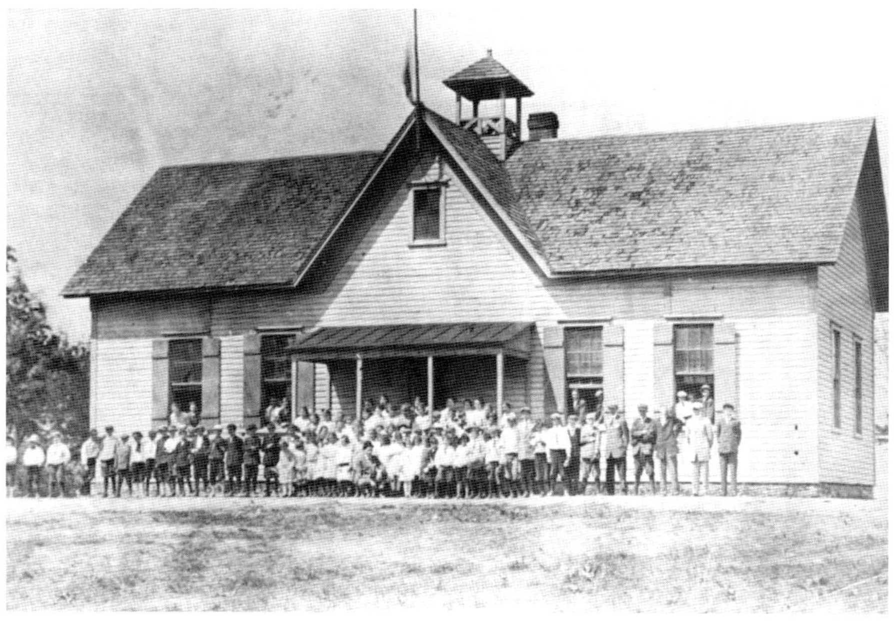

The Herndon School on Center Street, with its added front addition, circa 1905. *J. Berkley Green Collection of the Herndon Historical Society.*

Herndon School Association agreed to transfer its interest in the school lot to the district trustee.

Fairfax County auctioned off the land at the old Herndon School site on Center Street. It was purchased by Russell Lynn in 1912. In 1913, he sold the school building to the Chamblins, who intended to convert it into a residence as a wedding gift for their daughter. Orlin A. Chamblin made several changes to the building, including rolling the house forward so it would be closer to Center Street, building a fireplace and three new chimneys, making numerous changes to the windows and adding a front porch. At some point, the school's old bell tower was removed from the roof.

The building has had many occupants over the years. Inside the unfinished attic one can still see some signatures written in white chalk along the huge attic beams, signatures belonging to some of the students who attended the school in the 1890s.

Herndon High School

Around 1910 or 1911, Fairfax County decided that the school on Center Street was inadequate for the future needs of the town. The county bought several acres of land on Locust Street and began building a new school. The new school was dedicated in 1912, and it was named Herndon High School. It initially housed grades one through eleven, with the twelfth grade added later.

In a sad turn of events, that school was destroyed in a fire during the 1927–1928 school year, but it was quickly rebuilt. Each class moved to other locations while the school was being rebuilt.

Various current Herndon residents still remember their time at the school. One 1941 graduate remembered, "During my eleven years at Herndon High School I, like all students, carried my lunch. When the other buildings were built on, one area near the Home Economics cottage became a soup kitchen. If students brought their own bowl and spoon, they could get soup to eat with their lunch. I never tasted bean or potato soup as good as theirs."

Another student who attended the school from 1940 to 1952 recalled that Herndon High School was "the only school in town" at the time, with only four other high schools in the county. Although the building was small, about five hundred students attended the school. "It was a close knit group of students. You knew about everyone. Students who went to other elementary

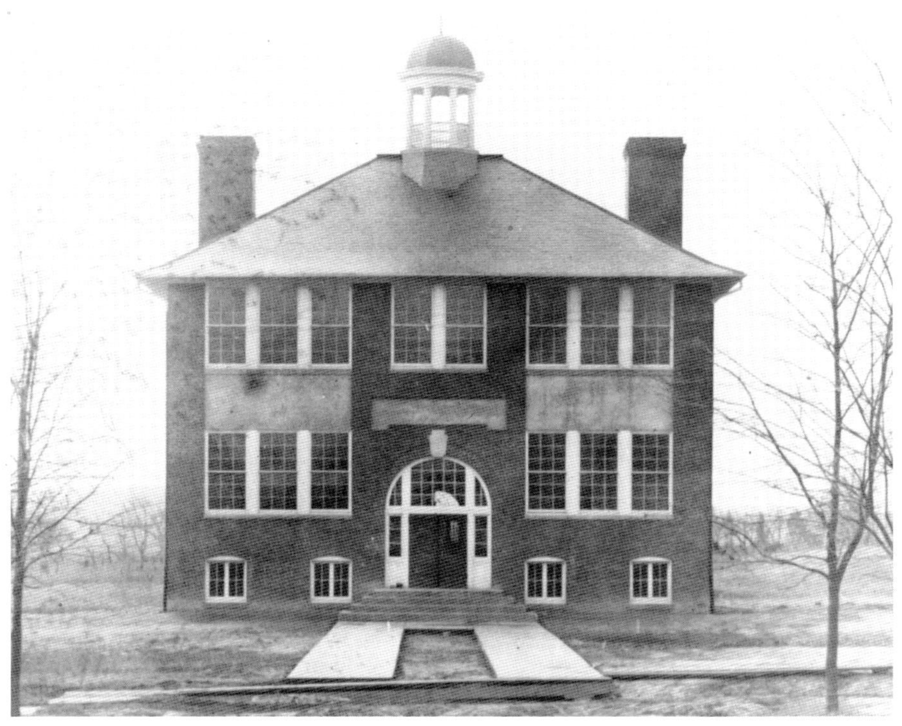

Herndon High School on Locust Street, 1912–1927. *J. Berkley Green Collection of the Herndon Historical Society.*

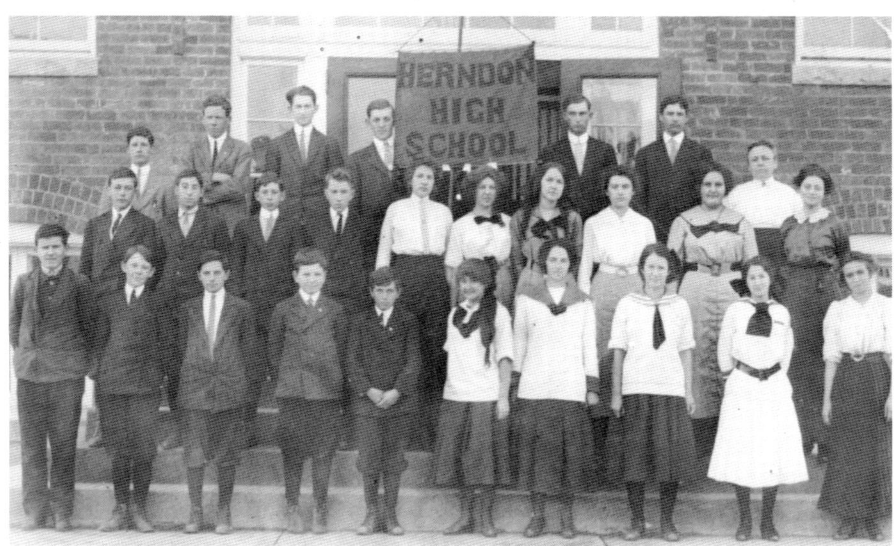

Herndon High School students, circa 1924. *J. Berkley Green Collection of the Herndon Historical Society.*

schools in the area—such as Floris and Great Falls—came to Herndon High when entering the 8th grade. There was no intermediate or middle schools at that time."

As the population of Herndon grew, more school space was needed. In 1952, a new school building was constructed next door on Locust Street, just east side of the older structure.

All grades continued attending the school on Locust Street until the 1960s. The elementary students were moved to Herndon Elementary School on Dranesville Road when it opened in 1961. And the high school students were moved to the new Herndon High School on Bennett Street when it opened in 1967. The school building on Locust Street remained as Herndon Middle School.

The 1927 building on Locust Street was torn down in the early 1980s. A new addition was added onto the west end of the 1952 building in the early 1990s.

OAK GROVE SCHOOL

Like many post–Civil War counties of that time, there were two sets of schools—one for white students and one for black students. Although the Herndon School on Center Street is commonly considered Herndon's first public school, the Oak Grove School for African American students also came about at approximately the same time.

According to the document *African American Landowners, Churches, Schools and Businesses in Fairfax County, 1860–1900,* one-room schools served African American children around Fairfax County, with enrollments as high as 408 in 1870 to 1,150 in 1890. The schools were commonly referred to as "colored" or "negro" schools. The average school served students up through grades six or seven. In the 1870s, a teacher's salary was about one dollar per day. High schools for Fairfax County's African American students did not come about until the 1950s.

Sometime after the Civil War, a Canadian couple, George and Cynthia Bell, moved into the Herndon area and bought many acres of land in the vicinity of the Herndon/Loudoun border. In a 2010 *Fairfax Times* newspaper article, Loudoun historian Eugene Scheel described how, in 1871, the Bells subdivided a large parcel of their wooded land into small one-acre lots. These small parcels of land provided an opportunity for many former slaves to own land and to subsequently settle in the community. A church was built in the community in 1868. The Oak Grove Baptist Church website indicated that the name "Oak Grove" was created in part due to the stately oak trees surrounding the church grounds. The growing surrounding community was subsequently named after the church. A 2007 *Washington Post* article said that by the 1950s, Oak Grove was a largely black community of more than three hundred people, many descendants of area slaves, close or distant cousins. The community was situated between Sterling Road (Route 606) and the Washington & Old Dominion Railroad track, near Herndon's western boundary.

A second area in the town of Herndon where black residents formerly lived was Cooktown, located at the north end of Monroe Street. The Herndon children who lived in Oak Grove and Cooktown, as well as some Loudoun children, attended Oak Grove School.

It is not clear exactly when the 1800s-era Oak Grove School was first established. It is possible that the earliest Oak Grove Church may have doubled as a schoolhouse. The first church was established around 1868. Early evidence of the Oak Grove School is documented in old Herndon Town Council minutes. Minutes from 1881 and 1882 show the town council approving expenses of $15.50 for wood and $15.00 for teacher Thomas Oden at "the colored school."

Additionally, an 1898 land survey conducted on a parcel of land that stretched east of Crestview Drive along the W&OD Railroad track made reference to the colored school that abutted the western edge of that lot. One longtime resident recalled via oral history that an earlier one-room school was once located just yards south of the current Oak Grove Baptist Church. Lastly, Ada Lee, who was interviewed in 1991 when she turned one hundred years old, remembered how she attended a one-room Oak Grove School, "up Crestview Drive, just before the railroad track near what is now the Tralee subdivision."

This school existed up until the next Oak Grove school building was constructed in 1930. A 1929 *Fairfax Herald* newspaper article described how Fairfax County received a letter from the Citizens Association of Oak Grove Colored School, stating that it acquired one and half acres of land, which was located next to the half-acre it already owned. The group was prepared to give the school board the title to the land, as long as the board agreed that a school would be erected. Knowing that many Loudoun students would also be attending the school that was located in Herndon, the board appointed a committee to discuss the question of Loudoun County paying tuition for

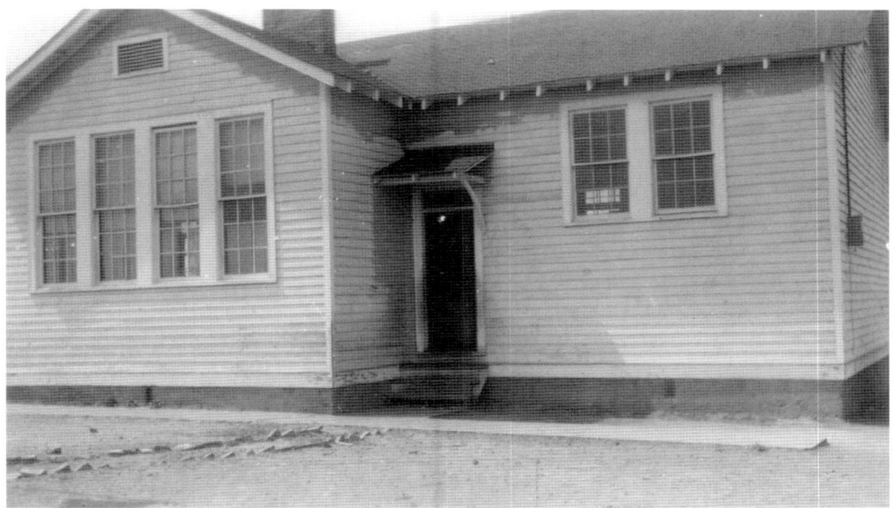

The 1930 Oak Grove School. *Fairfax County School Board.*

students who would attend Oak Grove School. That same year, the *Fairfax Herald* also announced that M.S. Robinson was named as a teacher at Herndon's colored school.

A hint about the demise of the older Oak Grove School may be indicated in a quote from a 1931 *Herndon Observer* article, which read, "The unused workshop at Floris and the school building at Oak Grove have been given [to] the Herndon School and it is now planned to sell the lumber in these buildings to house the gymnasium and the rooms for the class in home economics."

The 1930 Oak Grove School was built with some Julius Rosenwald funds. Rosenwald was a clothier and businessman from Illinois who once co-owned Sears, Roebuck and Company. He became interested in social issues, especially regarding education for poor, rural African American students. In the early 1900s, he befriended Booker T. Washington, leader of the Tuskegee Institute. As a philanthropist, Rosenwald endowed the institute and established a Rosenwald Fund in 1917. A rural school building program was administered by this fund, contributing over $4 million in matching funds to construct schools. Fairfax County received $400 from the Rosenwald Fund to go toward the total $3,670 construction costs of the next Oak Grove School.

Rosenwald schools were built in accordance to specific guidelines laid out in the Rosenwald Community School Plans. In the summer of 1930,

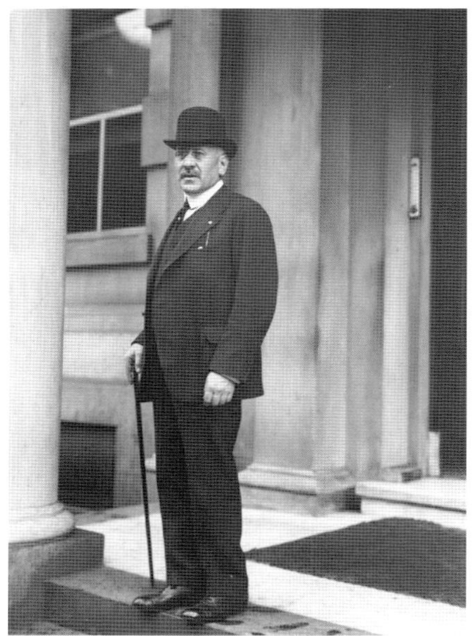

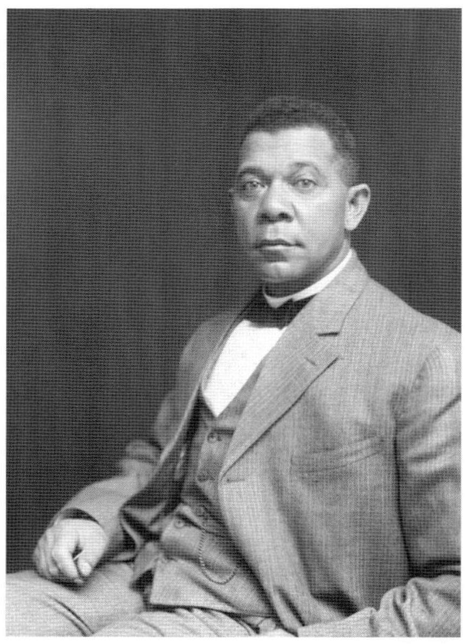

Left: Julius Rosenwald, 1917. Harris & Ewing, photographer. *Right*: Booker T. Washington, circa 1895. F.B. Johnston, photographer. *Library of Congress.*

Fairfax County's new school superintendent, W.T. Woodson, had received architectural plans from the state architect showing that the Oak Grove School would have two classrooms with two acres of adjacent land for privies, a well and a recreational area. The school board awarded a contract for the construction of Herndon's colored school to Edgar E. Gillette, a carpenter and home builder who had also been Herndon's mayor from 1925 to 1929.

The Oak Grove School building opened in September 1930. It was located about 150 yards southeast of the current Oak Grove Baptist Church, now the present-day location of the cul-de-sac at the north end of Artic Quill Road.

Some area residents still remember the school. Lucinda Brooks Gormes, who walked from her home in Cooktown to attend the school from 1947 to 1951, recalled that the building had yellow wood siding and was very primitive by today's standards. It had two classrooms with coal stoves. A third room in the center was unheated and was used either as a kitchen or a library. There were two outhouses and a pump for drinking water. (A bid was accepted in 1931 to sink a well at the school.)

The school housed students from kindergarten to seventh grade. There were two teachers, one who taught kindergarten through third grade and

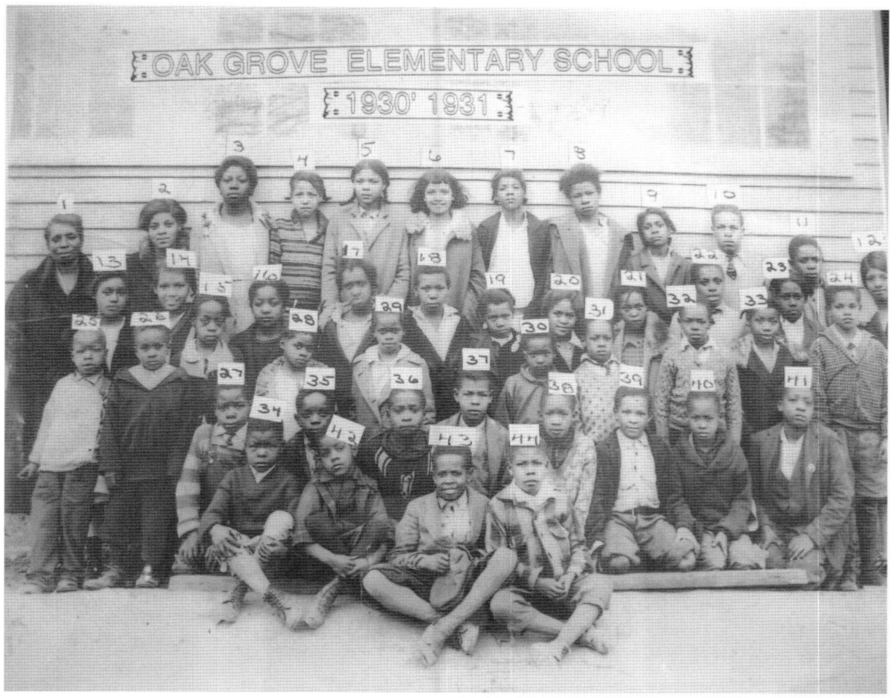

Students at the Oak Grove School in 1930. *Oak Grove Baptist Church.*

another who taught grades four through seven. Mrs. M.S. Robinson was one of the teachers at the school when it opened. One of the teachers acted as the principal. The books they had were used or obsolete.

Another former student, Thomas Payne, remembered the trees around the school, how they were used for bases when they played games. Payne remembered the steep embankment leading down to the railroad tracks, which served as a good barrier for playing cowboys and Indians.

James Johnson, who was born in 1921 and attended Oak Grove in his seventh grade year, remembers how the students had to bring their own sandwiches for lunch, but he also recalled that soup was sometimes served from the kitchen on cold days. The school often depended on donations for such food supplies. Johnson remembered that the school day ran from about 8:30 a.m. to 3:00 p.m. and recalled lessons in history, geography, civics, math and spelling. His teacher was Julia Hall; she lived in Chesterbrook (McLean) and took the train each day to work.

That school closed in 1952. In 1953, a new brick Oak Grove Elementary School was opened about one half mile away, at the intersection of Rock

Hill and Sterling Roads. Although the books in the new school were still out of date, the building's physical characteristics were greatly improved. The new six-room school building had indoor plumbing, central heating and a room that acted as an auditorium, lunchroom and clinic. The outdoor dirt play area was eventually blacktopped in 1957.

The 1953 Oak Grove Elementary School was built and administered by Fairfax County. At the time, Fairfax County had two separate supervisors for its elementary schools, one for white schools and one for black schools. Prior to 1954, high school students in Herndon's black community had to travel to Manassas or Washington, D.C., in order to attend high school. One former Oak Grove student said, "It was frustrating to ride by several schools in order to get to one." In 1954, Luther Jackson High School was opened on Gallows Road in Falls Church, the first all-black high school in Fairfax County.

The new Oak Grove School on Rock Hill Road served approximately 150 students from both Fairfax and Loudoun Counties. Both counties were still segregated at that time. The school was staffed by black teachers and had a black principal named Earl Pulley. Pulley, who was born in North Carolina, attended Virginia State College, moved to Washington, D.C., and became the principal of Oak Grove School at the age of twenty-nine.

Herndon resident Darryl Smith was born in the Oak Grove area and attended the Oak Grove School. Both Smith and Thomas Payne recalled

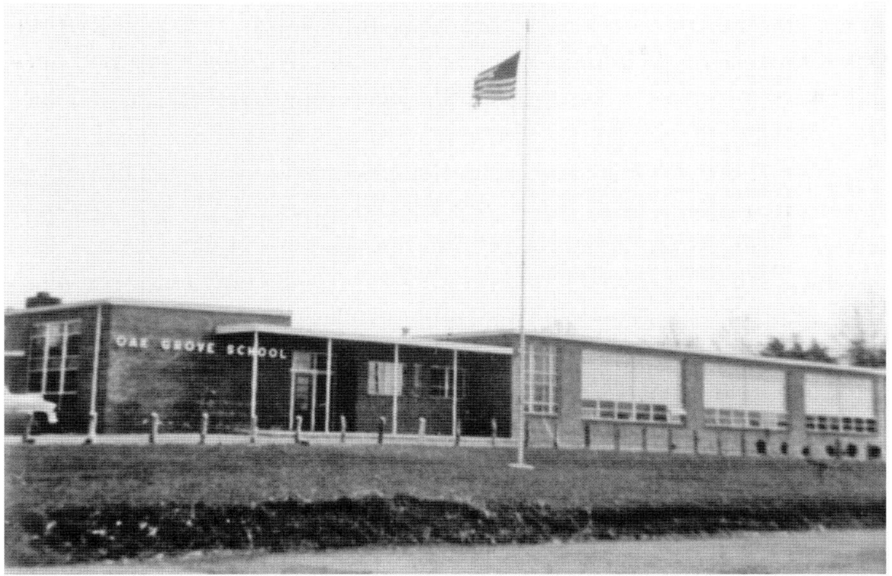

The 1953 Oak Grove School. *Herndon Historical Society.*

how Pulley would set students straight with either a stick or switch if they got out of line. Dwight Brooks, who started school at Oak Grove in 1953, recalled how the teachers would not spare the rod. He also remembered how teachers would check the students' teeth and other physical areas each morning to make sure they were clean. Regardless, the former students expressed their respect for Earl Pulley, the teachers and the life lessons the students were taught. Former students agreed that the quality of teachers at the old and new Oak Grove Schools outweighed any outdated facilities or books. The school served as one of the focal points of the African American community. The children not only attended school but also engaged in recreational and social activities, or just hung out.

Since 1930, Loudoun County made payments to Fairfax County to offset the cost of schooling Loudoun children at Oak Grove School. That changed in 1958 when Loudoun County built Frederick Douglass Elementary School in Leesburg, a segregated school for black students. Herndon's Oak Grove School was closed in 1964, and the Fairfax students who formerly attended the school were moved to Herndon Elementary School. Darryl Smith attended Douglass Elementary for one year. Sad to see Oak Grove close, Smith was especially disappointed to have to be bussed twenty miles away to Leesburg. For the Loudoun students of the Oak Grove community, the Douglass school was the closest black school available for them to attend until Sterling Elementary School started admitting black students in 1969.

Between the late 1960s and the late 1970s, Fairfax County utilized the Oak Grove School building for a variety of uses, including a senior center and nutrition site as well as a Head Start Program. Recreational activities were also held there. Smith remembers a gentleman named Forest Johnson who organized team sports for the area children, including baseball, softball and touch football teams.

The Town of Herndon bought the old school building from Fairfax County in the early 1980s. The town put a new façade on the structure and, in the mid-1980s, started using the building to house its police department. Darryl Smith, who served in the Herndon Police Department for many years, had his office in what used to be Principal Pulley's office. By the early 2000s, the police department started to outgrow the building.

In 2004, the Herndon Police Department moved out of the former school building and relocated to 397 Herndon Parkway. The former Oak Grove School building now houses the Town of Herndon's Zoning Enforcement Office.

7
Blacksmiths: The Unknown Stories of Herndon's Important Tradesmen

The Men Who Worked a Once Vital Profession

Blacksmiths were once important members of communities throughout America. As metal workers, they created objects by heating iron or steel and using tools to hammer, bend and cut the metal. Civil War armies used blacksmiths to shoe horses and repair things such as wagons, horse tack and artillery equipment.

Many small towns had at least one blacksmith. The Herndon blacksmiths provided a vital trade that dates back to Herndon's beginnings and extended up to the mid-twentieth century. They made important tools, machine parts and everyday items, including nails, hooks, hinges, bolts, locks, horseshoes, wagon parts and stove and fireplace utensils, just to name a few.

It is believed there were at least three blacksmith shops that existed in Herndon since the time the town was incorporated in 1879. They were run by Enos Garrett, Henry Simms and William Henry Moffett.

Enos Garrett

Enos Garrett, born in 1841, was a member of a very prominent Pennsylvania family who later came to Herndon. In 1863, when General Robert E. Lee's army entered Pennsylvania, Garrett answered the call for volunteers and was appointed as a second lieutenant in the 20th Pennsylvania Cavalry. Garrett came away from the war unscathed and ended his term of service in 1864.

Enos's brother Henry, however, was not so lucky. He successfully participated in the Battle of Gettysburg. But later, while serving as a Union army captain in the 8th Pennsylvania Cavalry, Henry sustained serious injuries in the Battle of Haw's Shop in Virginia and spent time in a hospital in Northern Virginia. By 1865, Enos moved to Virginia to help his older brother recover.

While in Virginia, Enos met Louisa Caywood. Louisa was the daughter of Benjamin and Philena Caywood, originally from New York, with strong Union ties, and owners of hundreds of acres of land in the Herndon area. Interestingly, according to Lottie Dyer Schneider, and confirmed by other Garrett family members, Louisa Caywood Garrett was in Ford's Theatre the night Lincoln was shot in 1865. After the shooting, she was picked up and placed on the shoulder of her brother Aaron Caywood so that she would not be trampled. Louisa remembered seeing John Wilkes Booth fall as he jumped onto the stage. About three months later, Louisa and Enos were married in Herndon's Methodist Church on Elden Street, and they went on to have several children.

Enos Garrett served as Herndon's postmaster in 1867. In 1868, Garrett purchased one acre of land for $350 on the southeast corner of Elden and Center Streets, the current location of the empty parking lot adjacent to the former Horn Motors NAPA Auto Parts store (vicinity of 771 Elden Street). Looking at an 1878 map of Herndon, drawn by cartographer G.M. Hopkins (see the map on pages 6–7), Garrett's lot can be seen, marked with the words, "Enos L. Garrett," "Res." (Residence) and "B.S.S. & W.W.Sh." (Blacksmith Shop & Wheel Wright Shop).

Most documents found about Enos Garrett—from his army registration in 1863 to a Herndon census in 1910—listed his occupations as a wheelwright, a wagon maker and a blacksmith. A wheelwright is someone who makes and repairs wheels. Early wagon and cart wheels were made of solid wood but increasingly had iron parts, such as hubs and rims. It would not be unusual for one man to be both a blacksmith and a wheelwright, for wheelwrights were sometimes described as a cross between a carpenter and a blacksmith. It seems Enos Garrett may have considered his primary occupation to be a wheelwright, but it is also known that he had a blacksmith shop on his land near his wheelwright shop and he did some blacksmithing as well.

Enos Garrett became increasingly involved in Herndon, in local business and in government activities. He served as the secretary of Herndon's Methodist Episcopal Church Sunday school in 1873. He served a short stint on the town council in 1880 after Councilman Ancel St. John resigned.

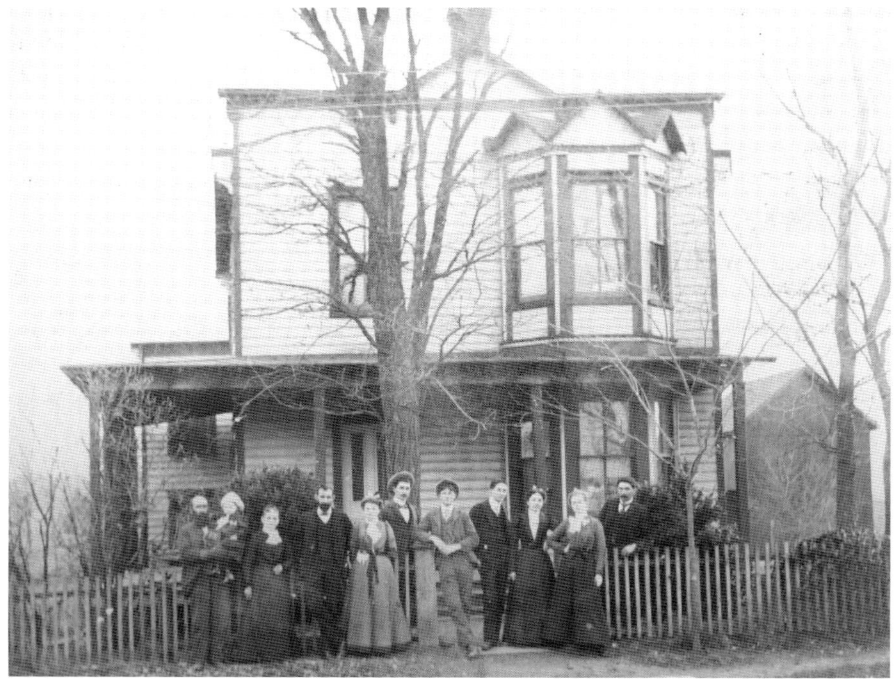

Enos Garrett (*left*) and family members in Herndon, 1903. *Benjamin Garrett.*

Shortly thereafter, he became the town clerk. Enos Garrett was elected as mayor of Herndon in 1891 after the previous mayor resigned.

Garrett's prosperity attracted his siblings—Henry, Benjamin and Tacy—all of whom eventually joined him in the Herndon area, as did their mother, Sarah, several years after their father died in 1870.

After the war, Enos's brother Captain Henry H. Garrett worked for the government and got into farming, initially living in Loudoun County. Sometime between 1880 and 1900, he moved to Herndon; he was elected mayor in 1903. He died of kidney disease in 1910 while living on Pine Street.

Enos's other brother, Benjamin Garrett, lived on Elden Street with Enos in the 1880s. Benjamin was known to be a machinist and a carpenter. In 1880, he bought piece of land across the street from the Garrett home, on the northeast corner of Elden and Center Streets. On the land he owned (or possibly co-owned with Enos) was a building called Garrett Hall, which was a center of social activity in Herndon at the time. Garrett Hall was rented out to various local groups and was sometimes used for town council meetings, for Masonic Lodge meetings and for school space.

Benjamin Garrett was elected to the town council in 1882 but was absent from several meetings. His seat on council was declared vacant and was later filled by another candidate. Benjamin and his wife moved to Florida, where he became a fruit farmer. He died in 1923.

Enos Garrett remained active in Herndon throughout the years. He became a land agent, a school trustee, an incorporator of the Herndon and Aldie Railroad Company and a delegate to the County Democratic Convention. In 1909, he was the Herndon registrar. And, although he accidently chopped off the tip of one of his fingers while using a hand axe, he became one of Herndon's checkers champions.

Enos Garrett later served again on the town council in 1911 and was again elected mayor in 1913. While on the council, he pursued the introduction of electrical lighting and power for downtown Herndon. However, he did not finish the final portion of his term due to a debilitating stroke, which left him partially paralyzed with his speech affected.

Garrett could no longer care for himself, so the family closed up their Herndon home and moved in with a son and his wife in Jetersville, Virginia. In 1915, the Garrett home on Elden Street was sold at auction, as were most of its contents. A letter from one of Enos's grandsons recounted the closing of the Elden Street home and the auction. Enos's Civil War sword brought five dollars, the highest bid of anything sold. The grandson wanted to keep the service pistol that Enos had carried during the Civil War but was told he was too young to have the gun. So he stole it, wrapped it in burlap and threw it under the house, intending to return to the house to retrieve it someday. When he returned in 1950, he could not find it. The whereabouts of the pistol are unknown. Enos Garrett died in 1926. The house was torn down sometime between 1957 and 1962.

HENRY SIMMS

Henry Simms (sometimes spelled Sims) was the only blacksmith listed in the Town of Herndon's first official census in 1880. He also happened to be the only African American in the incorporated Town of Herndon to own a business.

Simms was born in South Carolina, but his birthdate is not clear, possibly anywhere between 1832 and 1845. In 1867, Simms married Ann "Annie" Morton in Herndon. Annie would ultimately bear fifteen children.

Henry Simms most likely operated a blacksmith business elsewhere in the Dranesville District before he bought the land in what is now the town of Herndon. In 1878, he bought a parcel of land in Herndon for seventy-five dollars. The lot was located in the vicinity of the northeast corner of Jackson and Elden (then Washington) Streets, now the present-day location of 604 Elden Street (where Jiffy Lube is today). This parcel can also be seen on the 1878 Hopkins map of Herndon. The lot is marked on the map as "Hy. Simms."

In 1891, Simms recorded a declaration:

> *By and between Henry Sims of County of Fairfax, in the State of Virginia, who doth hereby declare his intention as a householder and head of a family, to claim the full benefit of a "Homestead" under Article XI, of the Constitution of Virginia, and of the act of the General Assembly of Virginia, passed June 27th, 1890, relating thereto; the same to be exempt from Levy, Seizure, Gameskeeping, or Sale, in the following property, viz.*

The property he listed was a house and one acre of land in the village of Herndon ($500), a set of blacksmith tools ($20), one horse ($25), household furniture ($25) and two hogs ($20).

Henry Simms and his family can be found on Herndon census documents up through the year 1900. At least three of his sons also practiced blacksmithing.

In the early 1900s, Frances Darlington Simpson frequently spent summers in Herndon at her grandfather's summer home, located near the intersection of Monroe and Van Buren Streets. In her book *Virginia Country Life and Cooking*, she recalled:

> *Just across the road lived Belle's Aunt Irene and Uncle Pete Simms. Uncle Pete, the village blacksmith, was known for miles around and enjoyed the respect of all who knew him. People came, bringing their horse to be shod and it was fascinating to sit by the hour in Uncle Pete's shop ad watch him hammering and shaping the red hot horse shoes on his anvil and then nailing them to the horse hooves. My sister and I never tired of watching him and were always thrilled and delighted when he made rings for us out of horse shoe nails.*

There are no Herndon census documents that list the name Pete Simms, although many longtime Herndon residents remember a town blacksmith

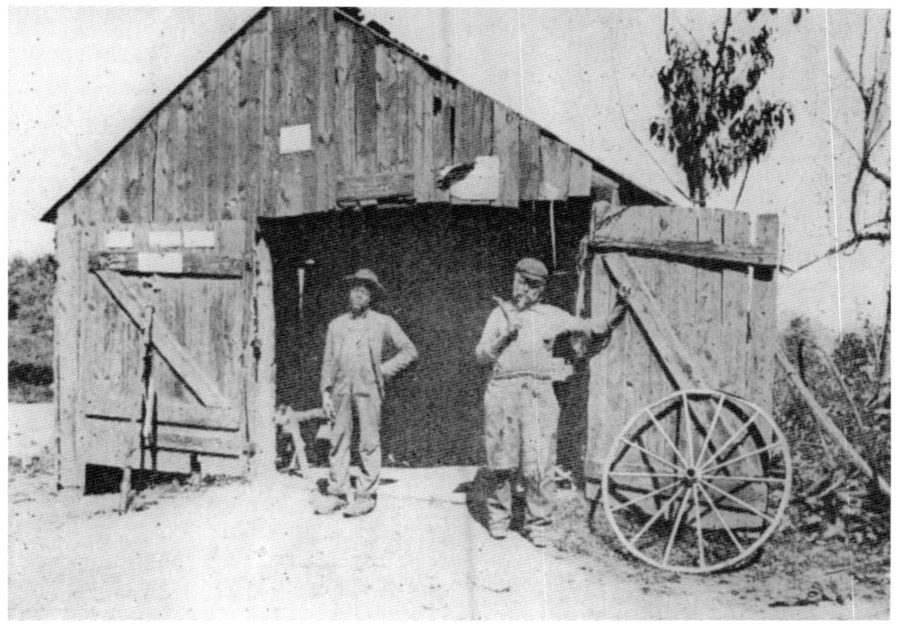

Simms family blacksmith shop. *J. Berkley Green Collection of the Herndon Historical Society.*

by that name. It is assumed that the name Pete was a nickname for Henry's son James, who carried on the family business in Herndon and had a wife named Irene.

Town council minutes from 1948 indicate that the chief of the Fire Prevention Bureau had prepared a report showing that the Pete Simms's shop at the corner of Jackson and Washington Streets was in very poor condition and was a highway hazard. (Elden Street east of Monroe Street was formerly called Washington Street.) The council directed that no action be taken at the time. But by 1949, the council voted unanimously to authorize the highway department to condemn the Simms property, with the town bearing whatever costs necessary.

WILLIAM HENRY MOFFETT

William Henry Moffett, born in 1897, was a fifth-generation blacksmith. His father and grandfather were blacksmiths in the town of Leesburg. In 1906, Moffett's father, Joseph Moffett, bought a three-thousand-square-foot piece of land in downtown Herndon and operated a blacksmith shop there. This piece of land was on the west side of Station Street, located at the end of an alley next to a concrete block gashouse. It was situated behind the town's livery on Station Street. The Moffett blacksmith shop burned down in Herndon's Big Fire of 1917. As an example of how important blacksmiths were to the community, the shop was the first structure to be rebuilt after the fire.

In his young adulthood, William Moffett worked for Bethlehem Steel in Maryland. In 1918, he registered for the army and went off to training at Camp Lee, Virginia, in September of that year. However, the war soon ended, and Moffett was discharged in December 1918. Afterward, his father, Joseph, urged him to go into the blacksmith business. By 1920, Joseph was back in Loudoun County running a blacksmith shop, while his son William, now married, ran the blacksmith shop in Herndon.

The location of Moffett's blacksmith shop near the town livery was perhaps a convenience to him, as Moffett was also known to have farrier skills, trimming and shoeing horse hooves. Virgie Wynkoop, who wrote her memories of Herndon in a manuscript called *Herndon–Etcetera*, recalled:

> *Mr. Moffett was a farrier by trade…he not only shod horses but* [did] *numerous repair jobs repairing broken down farm equipment for the many farmer of that time. Back in the 20's he had the distinction of being second in the world championship for shoeing horses. He said he did not know he was being considered for a contest the day he shod twelve horses in twelve hours.*

A 1933 article in the *Fairfax Herald* spoke about how Moffett was active in two different fields. He had been a blacksmith for about thirty years, and "his services have always been well-directed and his clientele developed to extensive proportions as a result." In 1930, Moffett entered the coal and wood business as a sideline, winning high acclaim in that business as well.

By the 1950s, the need for blacksmiths had diminished, as there were few horses to shoe or wagons to repair. Moffett, who also liked farming, decided to raise beef cattle after he closed the blacksmith shop in 1955 at the age of sixty-eight.

The old Moffett blacksmith shop was later bought by Fairfax County and moved to Frying Pan Park in 1975. Moffett's daughter and Herndon resident Elma Mankin said, "When Fairfax County bought the blacksmith shop, my father said he wanted to be there when they took it apart and he supervised the disassembly and reassembly. He marked every board."

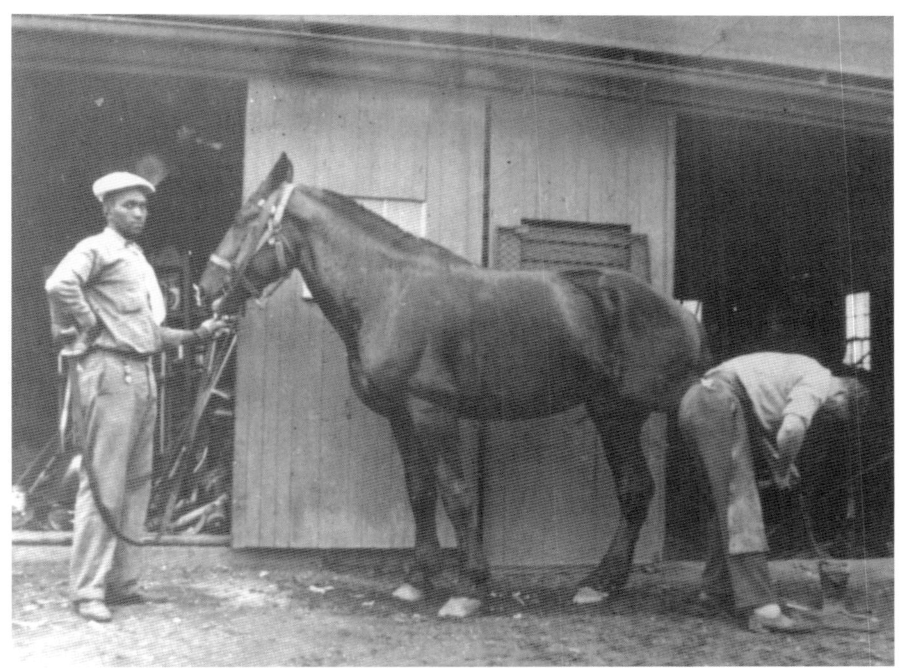

William Henry Moffett (*right*) at his blacksmith shop. *J. Berkley Green Collection of the Herndon Historical Society.*

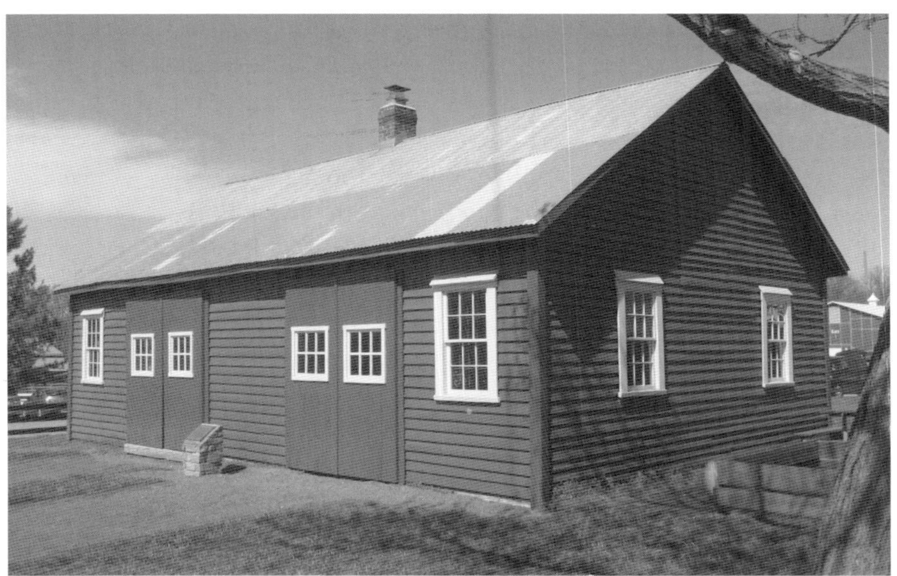

The Moffett Blacksmith Shop currently located at Frying Pan Farm Park. *Barbara Glakas.*

The remnants of the foundation of the old blacksmith shop can still be seen in Herndon, next to the old gashouse, now across the street from the Herndon Municipal Center on Lynn Street. The Moffett blacksmith shop still stands in Frying Pan Park on West Ox Road, with a plentiful display of many of Moffett's blacksmith tools. It is the last known original and operational blacksmith buildings left in Fairfax County.

The Fairfax County Park Authority noted that Moffett, like many blacksmiths before him, "served the needs of his rural community during a period of changing technology, from a time of horse-drawn wagons to automobiles, and from hand-operated machines and tools to devices powered by electricity."

8

The Yellow House: One of Herndon's Oldest Homes

The Home of Herndon's First Undertaker

Now sitting at the corner of Pearl and Oak Streets is a home commonly referred to as the Yellow House. Built approximately 150 years ago, the home has always been a shade of yellow, but it has not always been at its present location. The house was originally located at 721 Elden Street, where the Adams-Green Funeral Home now stands. This small plot of land, conveniently located at the southwest corner of Elden Street and the former railroad track, was held by a succession of different owners in its early years.

In the mid-1800s, the land where the Adams-Green Funeral Home now stands was part of a larger tract of land owned by James S. Purdy. In the late 1850s, this land was bought by Sumner and Sophoronia Coleman. The Colemans then sold the land, measuring about one acre, to Jacob M. and Electa Lester in 1859. Tax records from 1861 do not indicate any building on the lot. Records from 1862 to 1866 are missing, lost during the Civil War. The Lesters later defaulted on a lien. As a result, the property was bought by R.B. Norment at an auction. Norment then immediately sold the land and premises to Madison and Sarah J. Whipple in 1867. Madison Whipple was the Herndon postmaster in 1866. At the time of this sale, the 1867 tax records show a substantial building present on the lot, evidently built by the Lester family. Therefore, it is known that the Yellow House was built sometime between 1862 and 1867.

In addition to serving as a residence, the Yellow House was also used for other functions. Shortly after a small school building was constructed on

Monroe Street around 1869, it burned down, and classes were subsequently held at the Yellow House. One of the teachers was William D. Sweetser. Lottie Dyer Schneider recalled in her memoir that school had been taught "in a big yellow building which overlooked the railroad track and was property owned by Tom Reed in my childhood." The house also kept the books of the Fortnightly Club Library for a time.

The ownership of the house and the land continued to be complicated between 1867 and 1888. Records show that Elizabeth Sweetser had a claim to the land due to a debt Madison Whipple owed her. A trust was written to this effect, although Whipple and his wife still occupied the property. However, Madison Whipple sold the land and premises to Charles H. Moulton in 1873, pending the debt to Elizabeth Sweetser.

A deed in 1885 spoke of a pending court suit against Whipple in which the county court commissioner confirmed that Elizabeth Sweetser had bought the property and its premises in a public auction in 1880. The court presumably invalidated the sale to Moulton. The 1878 Hopkins map (see map on pages 6–7) shows that Whipple, not Moulton, was associated with the property where the Yellow House sat. In 1888, Elizabeth and Moses Sweetser sold the property to Thomas E. and Lillie L. Reed. Today, the Yellow House is widely remembered as the former residence of Thomas Edgar Reed (1856–1918), Herndon's first undertaker.

Herndon's Cemetery Association was formed in 1881, and the Chestnut Grove Cemetery was officially platted in 1882. Soon after came the town's first funeral home business, which Thomas Reed established in 1885. The Yellow House was Reed's residence. He and his wife, Lillie, were married in 1883 and had three children—Marjorie, Ralph and Thomas Edgar II—who were all born between 1891 and 1894.

Reed operated his funeral home business in some buildings along Spring Street, the block between Elden and Locust Streets. He used the small A-frame building that Jimmy's Old Town Tavern now uses for catering. He also used a barn that was formerly located at 681 Spring Street. It was in those buildings that Reed built caskets, stored caskets, garaged his funeral carriage and horses and possibly conducted some embalming. Unlike today, funerals were typically held in churches and private residences, not in funeral homes. In addition to being an undertaker, Reed was also a liveryman. Having two jobs helped make ends meet, as sometimes he would only have one funeral per month.

Thomas Reed died in 1918. In the 1920s, his sons had the Yellow House moved a short distance to the rear of the lot at 719 Elden Street. In its new

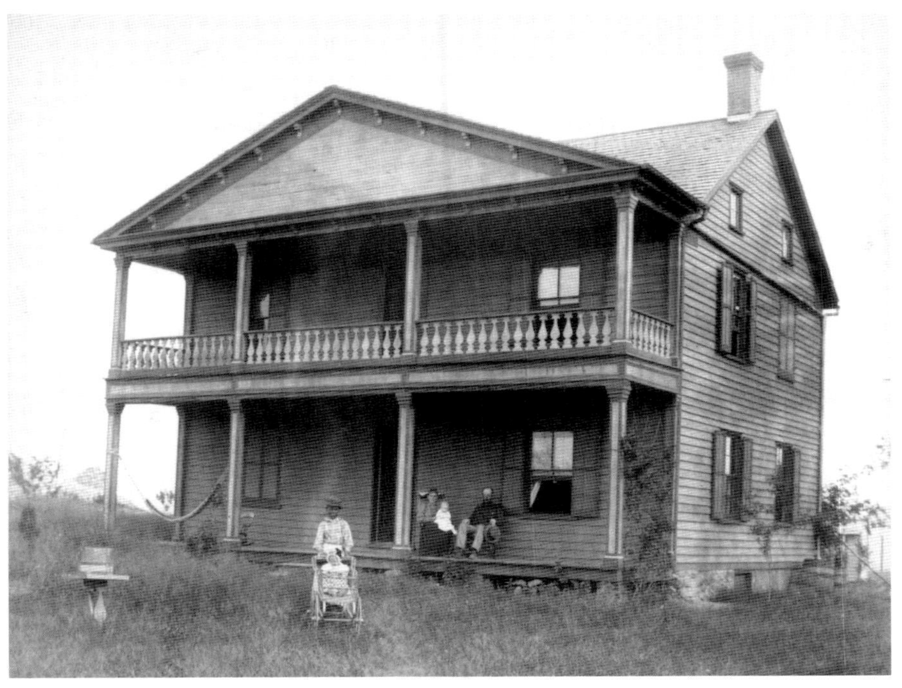

The Yellow House, circa 1893. *J. Berkley Green Collection of the Herndon Historical Society.*

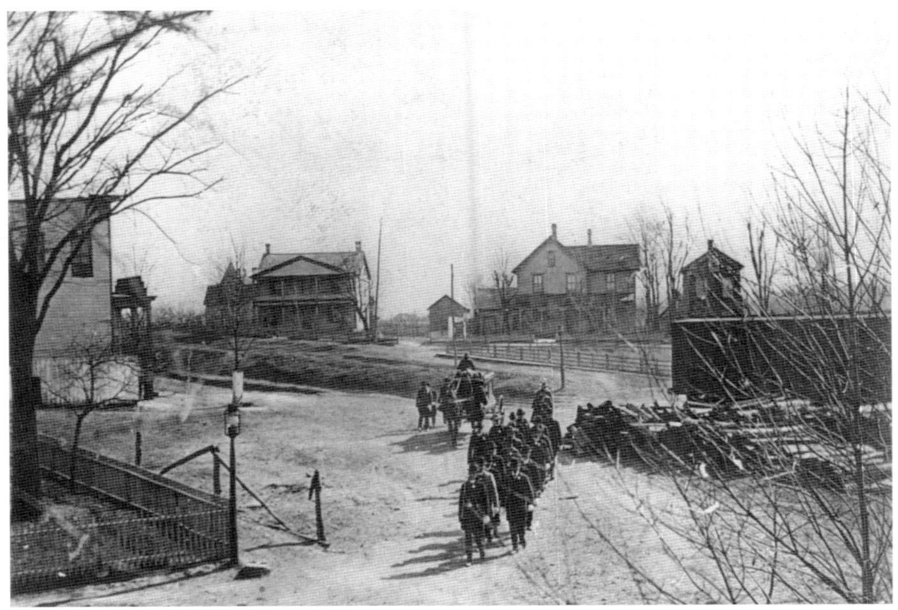

Yellow House is pictured at background left as a Masonic funeral crosses the railroad track, circa 1900. *J. Berkley Green Collection of the Herndon Historical Society.*

location, the Yellow House faced the Washington and Old Dominion Trail. For many years, it was a landmark to pedestrians and bikers who entered the town of Herndon along the trail. Ralph Reed built his mother a large brick home on the Elden Street lot where the Yellow House formerly sat.

Lillie Reed died in 1937, and the brick house at 721 Elden Street was turned into a funeral home. The funeral home business in the brick house continued to be operated through the years by T. Edgar Reed II until J. Berkley Green bought the business in 1954 and purchased the property in 1959. Green passed away in 1998. Eventually, Christopher and Kathryn Adams took over the business; the Green estate sold the property to them in 2000. The Adamses now operate the business as the Adams-Green Funeral Home.

For years, the Yellow House—which continued to sit on the lot behind the brick funeral home—was rented out to various tenants by the Reeds, Greens and Adamses. In 2003, the Adamses asked the town for a permit to remove the Yellow House in order to make room for needed parking for the funeral home. The Adamses agreed to work with the town to see if the

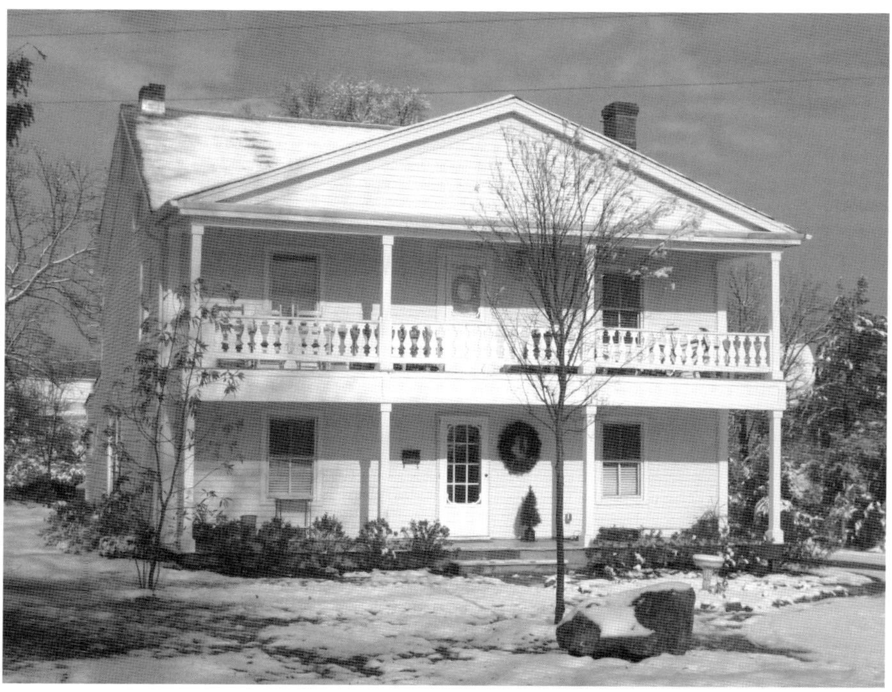

The renovated Yellow House at its current location on Pearl Street. *Barbara Glakas.*

house could be saved. The Herndon Historical Society played an active role in advocating for saving the house.

Mayor Mike O'Reilly appointed a committee to determine what could be done to save the historic Yellow House. A new location for the house was identified at the corner of Pearl and Oak Streets. The adjacent property owner agreed to subdivide her large lot to accommodate the relocation of the Yellow House. The builders who were in the process of redeveloping the adjacent Darlington Oaks subdivision set up the necessary utilities for the new Yellow House property.

The Yellow House was moved a second time to its new location in 2006 and was sold at auction in 2008. Some proceeds from the auction paid for the move of the house. In order to preserve the historic attributes and significance of the house, a condition of the sale was that it be preserved and maintained in accordance with the town's heritage preservation guidelines.

The new owner renovated the house, and it is once again a single-family residence.

9

A Chronicle of Lynn Street Family Businesses

The Nachman Building and Schneider's Hardware Store

The St. John-Corey-Hindle-Robey Years

The building located at 718 Lynn Street has a long history in the town of Herndon—almost 150 years. It is commonly referred to as the Nachman Building, as the Nachman family owns the structure and occupies office space on the second floor. The bottom floor is currently occupied by a retail business called Green Lizard Cycling.

In the 1860s, this land where the Nachman Building now sits—as well as the adjacent land that now has a small parking lot—belonged to Ancel St. John. This was a twenty-thousand-square-foot lot. In 1869, St. John sold this land to James W. Corey.

Corey was a Civil War veteran who served with the New York Volunteers. As the result of a wound he suffered at the Battle of Chancellorsville, his left arm was amputated. After the war, he obtained a law degree from the Columbian College of Law in Washington, D.C. He got married in 1864. His wife's family was from the Herndon area.

Corey started constructing the structure on Lynn Street that is known today as the Nachman Building. It was to be two stories tall, with nine-foot ceilings, and was planned as an office, store and dwelling, with a storehouse in the rear. Charles W. Kitchen, a local carpenter and builder, worked on the structure.

James Corey never finished the building. Instead, in 1871, Corey sold the property and the unfinished building to Lawrence Hindle (who would later become one of Herndon's first town councilmen in 1879). At the time Hindle bought the property and building from Corey, the final parts of the roof still need to be completed. The building also still needed the flooring, windows and doors, and some plastering work needed to be done. In an odd legal twist, it was later discovered that Corey had previously sold at least part of this land for one dollar in trust for his wife and young son. When Hindle realized he did not have clear title to the property, he sued Corey. The courts eventually declared Hindle full owner.

Hindle started work on the building about six months after purchasing it. It was completed by 1874. The building can be seen on the Hopkins map (see map on pages 6–7). It is marked "L. Hindle Store." Early residents often referred to it as "Hindle's Store."

In the 1880s, William I. Robey operated a general grocery store out of Hindle's building. Robey was renting from Hindle. Robey was also a Civil War veteran who had served with Virginia's 8th Infantry Regiment. Like Corey, Robey had also been injured in the Battle of Chancellorsville. In the late 1880s, Robey and his son Ernest started a drugstore on Pine Street called Wm. I. Robey & Son.

The Schneider Years

After Lawrence Hindle died, Suzanna Hindle sold the lot in 1898 to Robert Schneider, who became a longtime hardware store owner in downtown Herndon. The deed said the sale involved the land with "all buildings." Again, this land included what is now known as the Nachman Building as well as the land on the west side of it, which had other small structures on it at the time. One of those small buildings housed Perez Barnum Buell's real estate agency. A small parking lot is on the property now.

Born in Germany to German parents in 1852, Robert Schneider came to America in 1868 on a six-week voyage at the age of sixteen. While living in Pennsylvania and repairing bicycles, he decided to move in order to look for greater business opportunities. He read a letter from a subscriber in a German newspaper. A tinsmith named Paul Buchwald (sometimes spelled Buckwald) wrote about how the opportunities were great in Herndon, Virginia. Schneider moved to Herndon and made a one-year partnership with Buchwald, operating a combination tinsmith and hardware store. Learning that Buchwald was of questionable character, which negatively

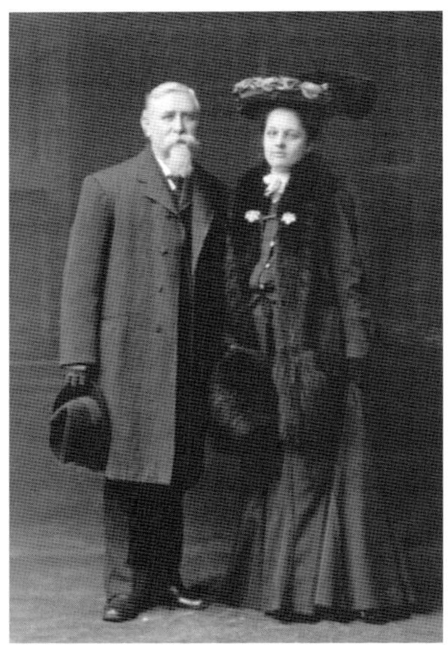

Robert and Lottie Schneider, circa 1903. *Robert J. Schneider.*

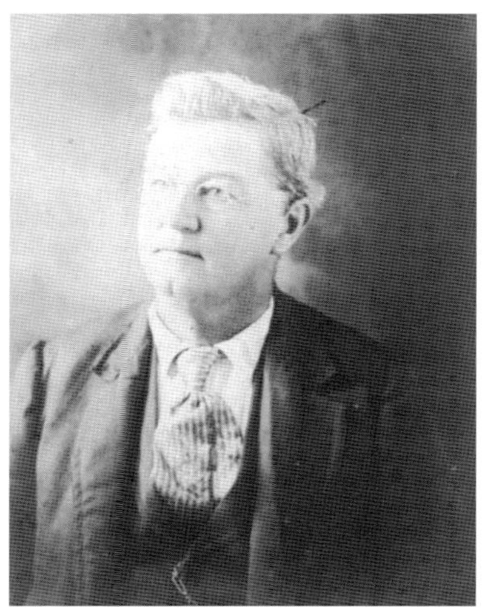

Elisha Dyer. *Robert J. Schneider.*

affected business, Schneider bought him out at the end of the one-year contract. Schneider started adding more goods to his store and grew a successful business, drawing trades from Alexandria to Bluemont. He bought the house he once rented.

Robert Schneider married the mayor's daughter, Lottie Dyer, in 1903. Despite a significant age difference, Robert and Lottie lived happily together and had two children.

Lottie Dyer was the daughter of Elisha and Mildred Dyer. Elisha was a prominent and well-respected man in town. Born in Fairfax County, he was known to have joined the Confederate army before deserting to the Union army. He enlisted in the Confederate army in North Carolina's 62nd Infantry Regiment in 1862 and later—after going absent without leave—joined a Union unit, the 21st Pennsylvania Calvary Volunteers, in 1863. Elisha was known to have been involved in the Battle of Cold Harbor and the First and Second Battles of the Wilderness. He once reminisced to his son that he would switch sides to go "wherever the action was."

Elisha and Mildred Dyer lived in a house on Monroe Street, across from the current Pines Shopping Center, in the vicinity where the Junction Square development now sits. They had seven children. Elisha served as Herndon's mayor and as town sergeant over the course of several years in the late 1800s and early 1900s. Despite some missing town records, archived *Fairfax Herald* newspapers show that Elisha was reelected as mayor in 1891, indicating that he must have served as mayor in a previous term. Elisha resigned later that year, explaining he had "too much to attend to." The newspaper described his resignation as "a calamity." Later, the *Fairfax Herald* reported that Elisha Dyer was elected mayor again in 1907.

One of Elisha's daughters remembered him studying large law books and enforcing the law in Herndon with great vigor. He sometimes wore a pistol in his belt, as he once received a threatening note after he impounded someone's cattle that was roaming the streets in Herndon. Elisha enjoyed checkers, fishing and taking trips to old battlefields. He also apparently had a good sense of humor. A story in a book entitled *A Chronicle of the Dyer-Johnson Family* indicated how one of Elisha's neighbors would sometimes let their chickens wander into his garden. In response, Elisha "scattered some corn with labels fastened securely to the grains. So the chickens went home with the string and labels hanging out of their mouths, bearing such messages as, 'Please keep me home' and 'I've been in the neighbor's garden.' "

Like her father, Lottie Dyer—who was born the year the Town of Herndon was incorporated—enjoyed education and made it her life's work. She attended the Herndon School on Center Street. Prior to marrying Robert Schneider, Dyer taught in Princeton, Massachusetts, and in Falls Church, Virginia. She became one of the first supervisors of Fairfax County schools.

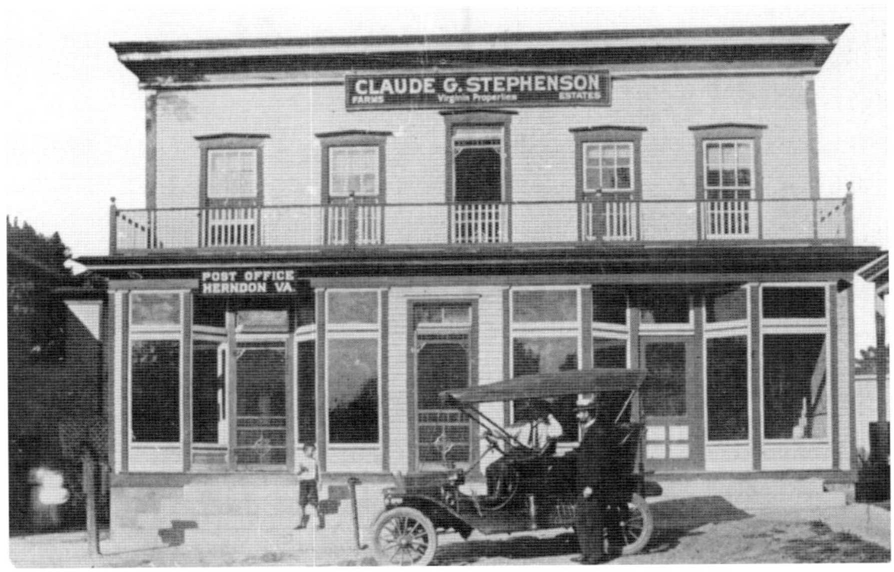

The Nachman Building during the time it belonged to the Schneiders and Cohens, circa 1909–1913. *J. Berkley Green Collection of the Herndon Historical Society.*

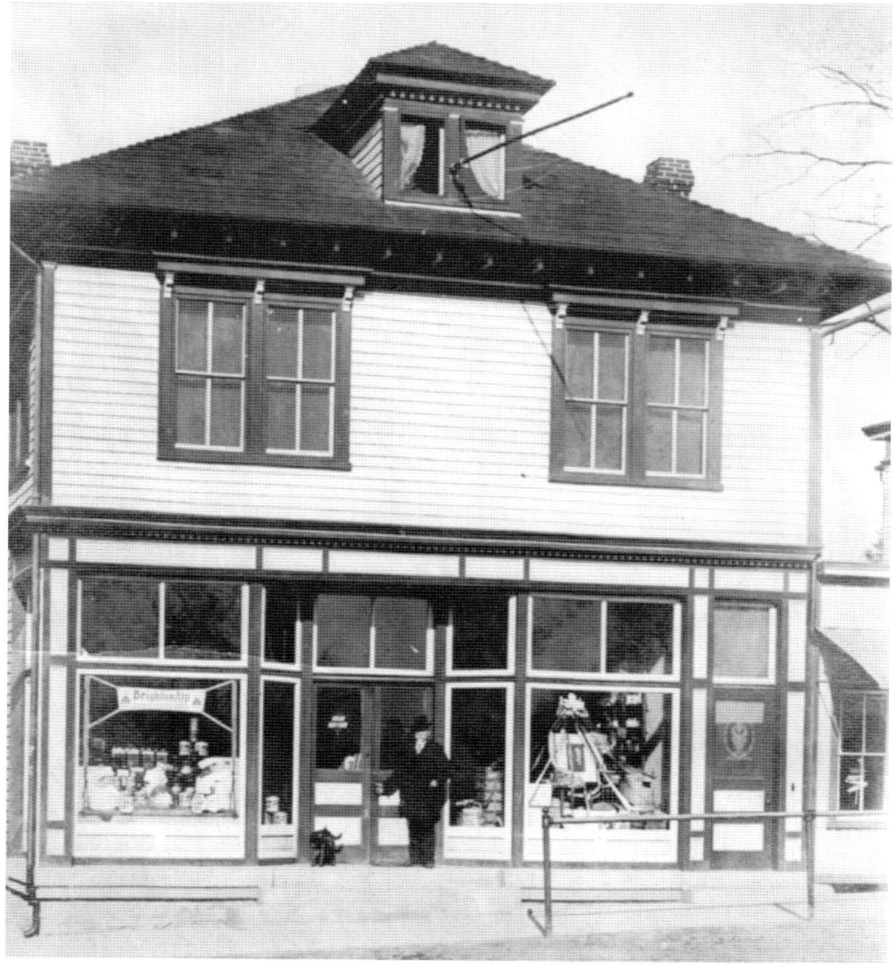

Robert Schneider standing outside his hardware store on Lynn Street, circa 1909–1919. *Robert J. Schneider.*

In 1909, Schneider made an agreement with the U.S. postmaster general to house the post office in a section of the first floor of the two-story wooden frame building on Lynn Street, then known as Schneider's Building (formerly Hindle's Store). At one point, Claude G. Stephenson, Herndon mayor from 1909 to 1911, operated a real estate office out of the Schneider's Building.

It was about this same year (circa 1909) that Schneider opened a new store on Lynn Street, moving his business from his former building into a new structure that was constructed next door (on the adjacent lot where the small parking lot is now located). The new Schneider Hardware Store was a large building and sat on the northeast corner of Station and Lynn Streets. It was built by a Herndon carpenter, Charlie Reed. Lottie recalled, "I have never seen such heavy timbers as he used." Schneider's Hardware thrived.

THE SCHNEIDER-DUDDING-COHEN-NACHMAN YEARS

In 1913, Robert Schneider sold "5980 square feet of land plus a building" on Lynn Street to Marcus and Celia Cohen, according to Donald LeVine's *Herndon, The Land: 1649–1900*. This is the older structure that Schneider vacated, which is now known as the Nachman Building, at 718 Lynn Street. The Cohens were from Baltimore, Maryland. After they purchased the building, they opened a clothing store that bore their name. It was during this time that the Cohens were operating their clothing store in one building, while Schneider continued to operate his hardware store next door.

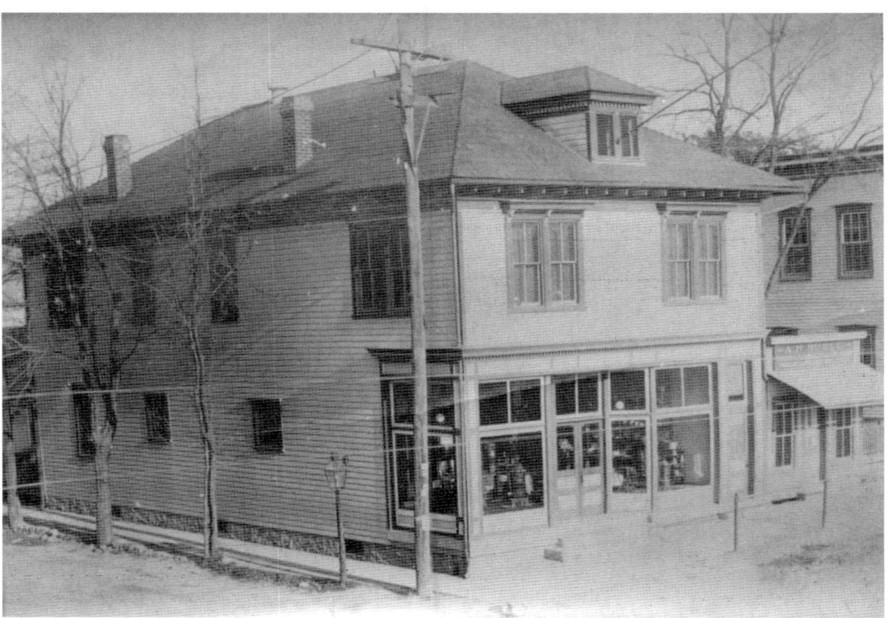

Schneider's hardware store. *Herndon Historical Society.*

At about the same time, in 1911, sixteen-year-old Julius Nachman emigrated from Russia with his family. They settled in Baltimore, where Nachman worked in various general retail stores that carried clothing and dry goods. In 1919, through a family connection, Nachman bought an interest in the Cohen's store in Herndon. The store was subsequently renamed Cohen and Nachman.

Once World War I began, anti-German sentiment abounded. In his memoir, Robert Schneider wrote:

> *I often wondered what happened to the generous, friendly American people, for whom I had always had a deep admiration. How could they become so quickly hysterical and narrow in their thinking? Customers that had traded with me for more than 20 years withdrew their trade. I received threatening letters, predicting what would happen to me if I did not show more patriotism. As it was I was buying all the Liberty Bonds I could possibly afford. They did not consider that I had been a citizen of this country before many of them were born, for I had voted in every presidential election since Grant's second term....I loved America as fervently as did these enthusiasts for war.*

As a result of distress and protracted worry, Robert's health failed. The Schneiders sold their hardware store to Charles and Belle Dudding in 1920 and then moved to Shepherdstown, West Virginia. Lottie taught at Shepherd's College. Back in Herndon, Charles Dudding died in 1924, but his wife continued to run the hardware business. Robert Schneider died in 1937, and Lottie died in 1967. They are buried at Herndon's Chestnut Grove Cemetery.

In 1920, Julius Nachman married a second cousin named Anna, whom he had met in a Baltimore synagogue. She had been a department store employee in Winchester, Virginia.

In 1928, the Cohens sold their property and the remaining interest in their clothing store to Julius and Anna Nachman. The name of the store was again changed, to Nachman's. The Nachman family lived on the second floor of the building and operated their clothing and dry goods store downstairs.

The Herndon Post Office was moved out of the Nachman Building and into Herndon's new Town Hall building when it was constructed in the late 1930s. This enabled Julius Nachman to expand his business to occupy the entire first floor of his building. Prior to that, the post office had still occupied

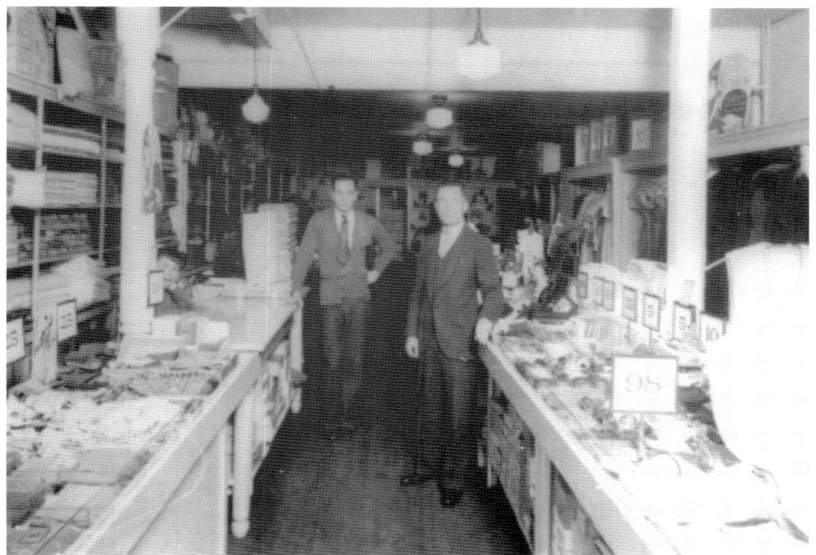

Julius Nachman *(right)* shown in his store, 1934. *Herndon Historical Society.*

part of the first floor of Nachman's building. Nachman made another major change. The store originally had steps and horse hitches in front of the building. Around 1936, the building was lifted, a basement was dug out for a furnace and other utilities, the front steps were removed and the building was lowered down to ground level so that customers could walk right into the front door without having to climb steps.

Julius Nachman's son Philip "Melvin" Nachman, wanting to modernize the building, enclosed the front of the upper porch with a modern metal grating in 1966. Immediately below that, a horizontal strip of black ceramic tile was added that reflected the Nachman name. In 1979, Melvin added a 2,200-square-foot cinderblock addition to the rear of the original 2,600-square-foot frame building. This provided more storage area for the business, as well as a space for a tuxedo section, an alterations section and a receiving area.

Julius Nachman passed away in 1969. Grandsons Howard and Arthur Nachman continued to run the family business. The store merchandise changed over time as Herndon evolved from a rural to a suburban area. In the earlier rural years, the store carried overalls, rubber boots, house dresses and sewing fabrics. Later, the store carried Dickies brand work pants and shirts as well as children's clothes. Later still, as the town continued to evolve and become more suburban, the store carried ready-to-wear career clothes.

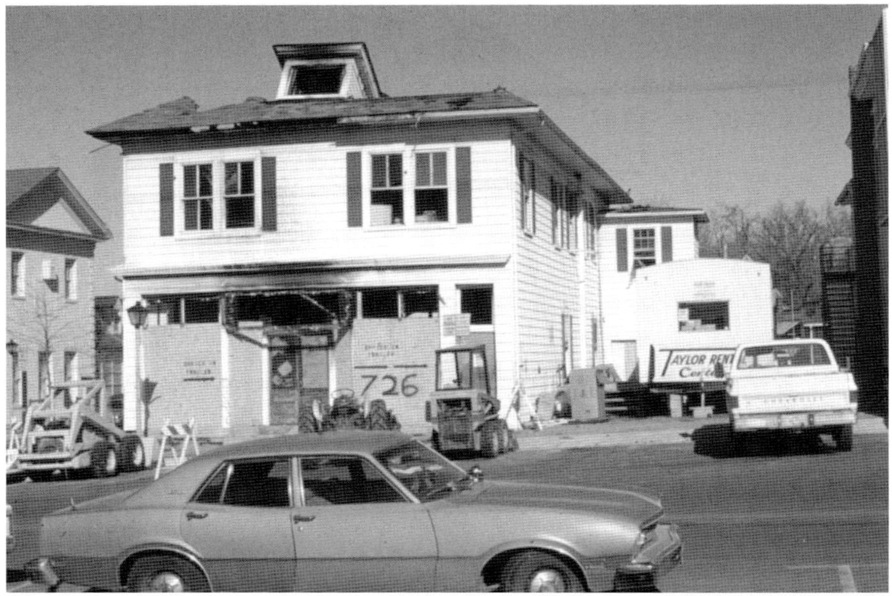

The former Dudding's Hardware Store after its fire, 1980. *Richard Downer.*

Belle Dudding continued to operate Dudding's Hardware Store next door until the 1960s. In 1967, she sold the store. It became the Herndon Farm and Garden Center and later the Taylor Rental Center. In 1980, the building had an accidental fire and was subsequently torn down. Today, there is only a small parking lot where the Schneider Hardware Store once stood.

Melvin Nachman passed away in 1991. Howard and Arthur Nachman closed the clothing store in 1994. It had been in operation for seventy-five years. The brothers both went on to work in commercial real estate and ran their business out of the former store. The metal grating on the upper porch was removed, and a large "The Lynn Street Exchange" sign was placed on the front of the building to reflect the property management company that they owned. Spaces within the building were also rented for other businesses, many arts related.

A memorable mural was painted on the exterior western wall of the Nachman Building in 1996 by local artist Patricia Macintyre, with the help of some Herndon High School art students. The mural was a historic depiction of the Nachman store during the early 1900s, showing customers arriving to the store in their horse-drawn wagons with the Nachmans greeting them inside. That mural was replaced by a new one in 2012 that depicted scenes from Herndon's history, including representations of the Nachman family.

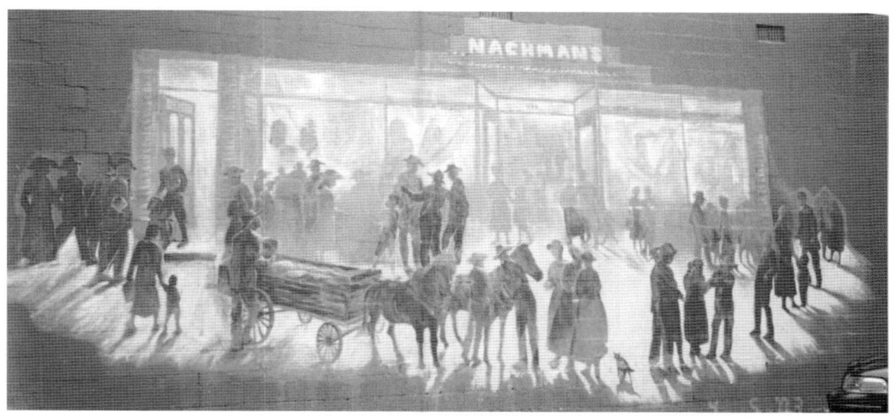

The former mural on the west wall of the Nachman Building, circa 1993. *Patricia Macintyre.*

In 2013, Green Lizard Cycling—a busy bike shop with a coffee bar—moved into the ground floor of the building. The previously cordoned-off office walls were removed from the first floor, taking the interior back to a wide-open floor plan with its original wood floors, reminiscent of the original Cohen and Nachman clothing store. The Nachman brothers still maintain an office space upstairs. Additionally, the owners of the cycling shop live in a residential space upstairs. The building is still used as it was originally intended in 1869—as a store, an office and a residential dwelling.

10

Gypsies, Street Entertainers and Medicine Men in Early Herndon

Odd and Amusing Visitors in Turn-of-the-Century Herndon

Lottie Dyer Schneider and her younger sister, Ruth O. Dyer Williams, wrote of their observations of early Herndon in their memoirs *Memories of Herndon, Virginia* and *Lest We Forget*. The sisters lived on Monroe Street in the late 1800s and attended the Herndon School on Center Street. Their father served as town sergeant and as mayor in the late 1800s and early 1900s.

Their recollections include the interesting visitors who would sometimes wander into town during their childhood years, visitors they would describe as either amusing or odd.

One such visitor was "the medicine man," a gentleman who would occasionally come into town to sell bottles of dark liquids that supposedly had miracle qualities, made for aches and pains. Crowds would gather around him, and the children enjoyed watching the medicine man as he stood on top of a box, yelling out the miraculous qualities of the products he had to sell.

Another man brought a brown bear into the village on a chain. The bear would dance on his hind legs as the entertainer sung a merry tune. The children were curious and fascinated but also fearful of the animal, which Lottie Dyer Schneider described as having a fierce face and powerful looking claws.

Yet another fun visitor was a "little foreign looking man with the hand organ and a monkey." Lottie Dyer Schneider described the sight as being "thrilling." The small monkey was dressed in a bright suit and a red cap and sat on his owner's shoulders. The man played happy tunes as the monkey

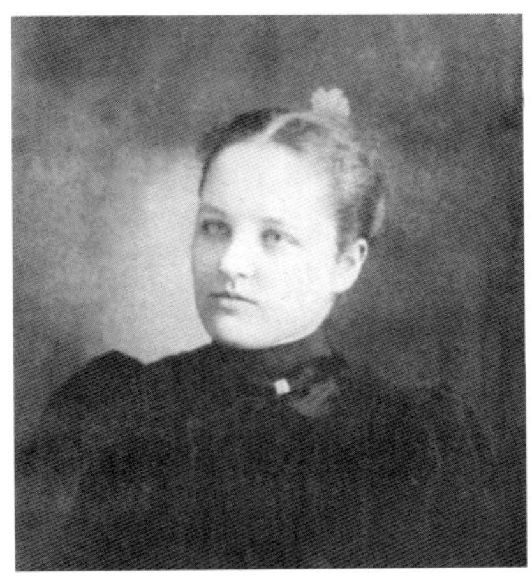

Lottie Dyer Schneider. *From* Memories of Herndon *by Lottie Dyer Schneider.*

hopped onto the organ. It would hold out its cap to collect pennies and nickels from the fascinated onlookers.

Bands of gypsies would also occasionally come into town. In his role as mayor, Elisha Dyer would not let them camp in town, but sometimes local residents would allow them to stay on their land for a few days. Lottie Dyer Schneider described them as having happy dispositions but also having a reputation of stealing things. They wore "gay but dirty" clothes and were often pushy, working their way into people's homes and town businesses in an effort to tell fortunes in order to get money or food. They would occasionally spit on people when they became angry. The townspeople appeared relieved when the gypsies left town.

Beggars also frequented town. They would come with a small pack of belongings they would have bundled together and would attach to stick, which they rested over their shoulders. They often came asking for food. Some would offer to pay for their food by doing such tasks as cutting wood. Others would just take the food and leave. Lottie Dyer Schneider thought that some of the beggars would notch marks on some fences or gates, indicating to other beggars where food could be easily obtained or where ferocious dogs resided.

Ruth Williams recalled peddlers in town, describing these wandering people as having suitcases filled with useful wares such as needles, thimbles, jewelry and fans that supposedly came from the Orient. She watched with delight as the peddlers would display their wares on the front porch of her house. She said, "Mother always bought something from them to encourage them, but if father was around he would scare off the poor fellow, for he felt that all people who led a wandering life were evil."

Another unusual peddler came to the Dyers' door with a note from an aunt who lived seven miles away. The note explained that the stranger was "a worthy person. Give him all the help you can." The man stayed for a few days. Ruth Williams said the man was not educated but had "a very active mind and was noted for his splendid memory." She was impressed with the stranger's ability to recite every president from George Washington to Grover Cleveland (who was the president at the time). But Williams also added, "I do not recall that he ever told us his name."

All the visiting gypsies, street entertainers, medicine men and beggars added to the flavor of early Herndon life.

11

From Wilkins Store to Jimmy's Tavern

A Historic Building, a Herndon Mainstay

As Herndon's farming community grew in the latter half of the 1800s, so did the businesses that supported the farmers and families who lived there.

In 1897, Magnus T. Wilkins married Cora Laws, of Catlett, Virginia. Wilkins moved to Herndon, where he started operating a general store. Wilkins's father-in-law, Harlon Waite, was a skilled carpenter and cabinetmaker. He and other local help built the Wilkins family residence at 637 Oak Street. The Waites eventually sold their Catlett home and came to Herndon, where they lived with the Wilkinses until they passed away.

The Wilkins and Bro. Herndon Bargain Store building is believed to have been constructed around 1899, at the southwest corner of Elden and Spring Streets. It is believed that Magnus Wilkins's brother James may have been initially involved in the business, but for what length of time is unknown. James died in 1928.

By 1911, Herndon had about 750 residents. Wilkins's store was one of several general stores in the area. Herndon's commercial district depended on, and revolved around, the train station. Farmers within several miles depended on Herndon's business district for services and supplies.

During that same period, the Herndon Town Council was made up of both farmers and businessmen. Magnus Wilkins had served on the town council since the early 1900s and was acting mayor from 1913 to 1915, due to the sudden illness of Mayor Enos Garrett. He was again appointed as acting mayor in 1918, this time due to the illness of Mayor William Ayre.

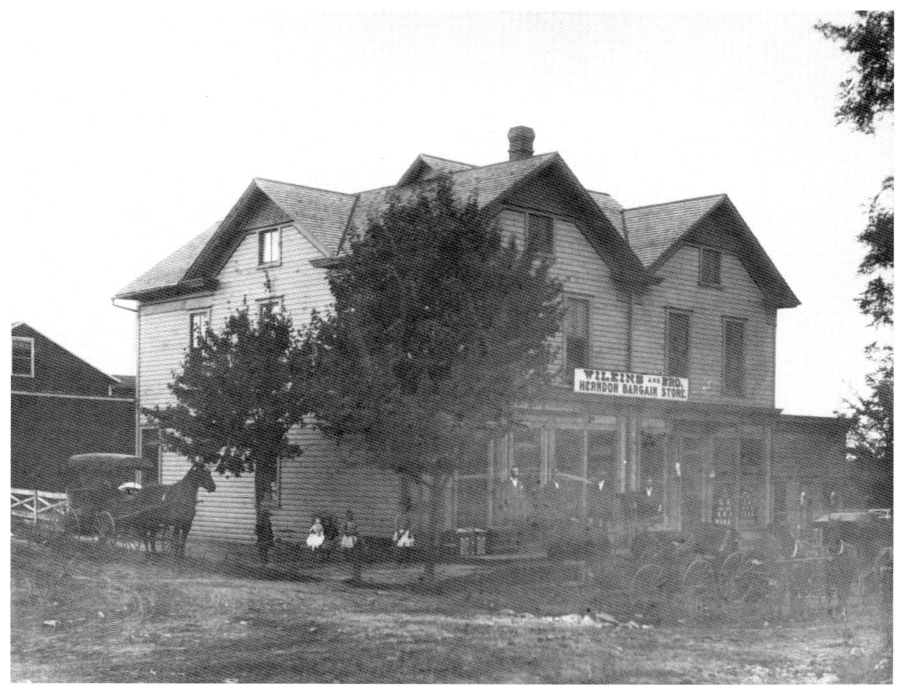

Wilkins and Bro. Store, circa 1900, at the corner of Elden and Spring Streets. *J. Berkley Green Collection of the Herndon Historical Society.*

A 1932 news story in the *Fairfax Independent* newspaper explained how the Wilkins store had been in business for thirty-five years. (The business possibly started in another location prior to moving into the building at Elden and Spring Streets). The news story described the business as an outstanding general merchandise store, saying it could be in a mythical "Hall of Fame" of businesses. The article went on to say the following about the store:

> [It] *enjoys a wide clientele, particularly of housewives, and has served so consistently that it is known as one of the foremost members of the commercial section in Herndon. The store had a complete stock of the finest merchandise found here at all times and is priced in keeping with the modern economic trend. Mr. Wilkins and his clerks constantly ensure prompt and accurate services and personal attention to every patron and are ever increasing in popularity of this concern in this community. Mr. Wilkins is quite popular in this section, being greatly interested in the general welfare of the whole community, and has always been found ready and willing to do everything in his power to insure its future development.*

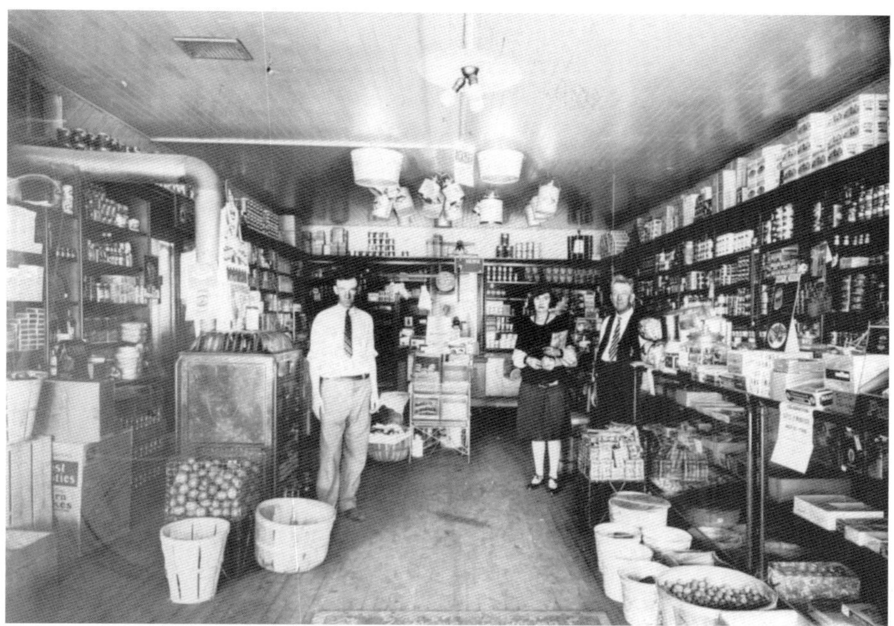

Inside Wilkins store, in 1928, with Magnus T. Wilkins at right. *J. Berkley Green Collection of the Herndon Historical Society.*

After the era of the Wilkins store, many tenants and businesses occupied the building, including a grocery store, a sporting goods store and a butcher shop. According to an index of captions of the historical society's J. Berkley Green Collection:

> *Wilkins and Bro. Herndon Bargain Store is now Jimmy's Old Town Tavern at 697 Spring Street. In the 1940's it was a pub run by Grafton Debutts, and then it became a General Merchandise Store owned by Anne Feldman. When she moved next to the fire station, it became Western Auto, then an Army Surplus Store, and Robert's Carpet until he moved across from the firehouse in the old Safeway Building on Spring Street.*

By 1990, Herndon's population was over sixteen thousand. That same year, Doug and Pam Roach opened their antique store on the upper level of the old Wilkins building. A dart bar called Foot Anakin's occupied the downstairs area.

In 1996, Jimmy Cirrito heard from a friend about a restaurant for lease in downtown Herndon. He came to Herndon to look at the property—the

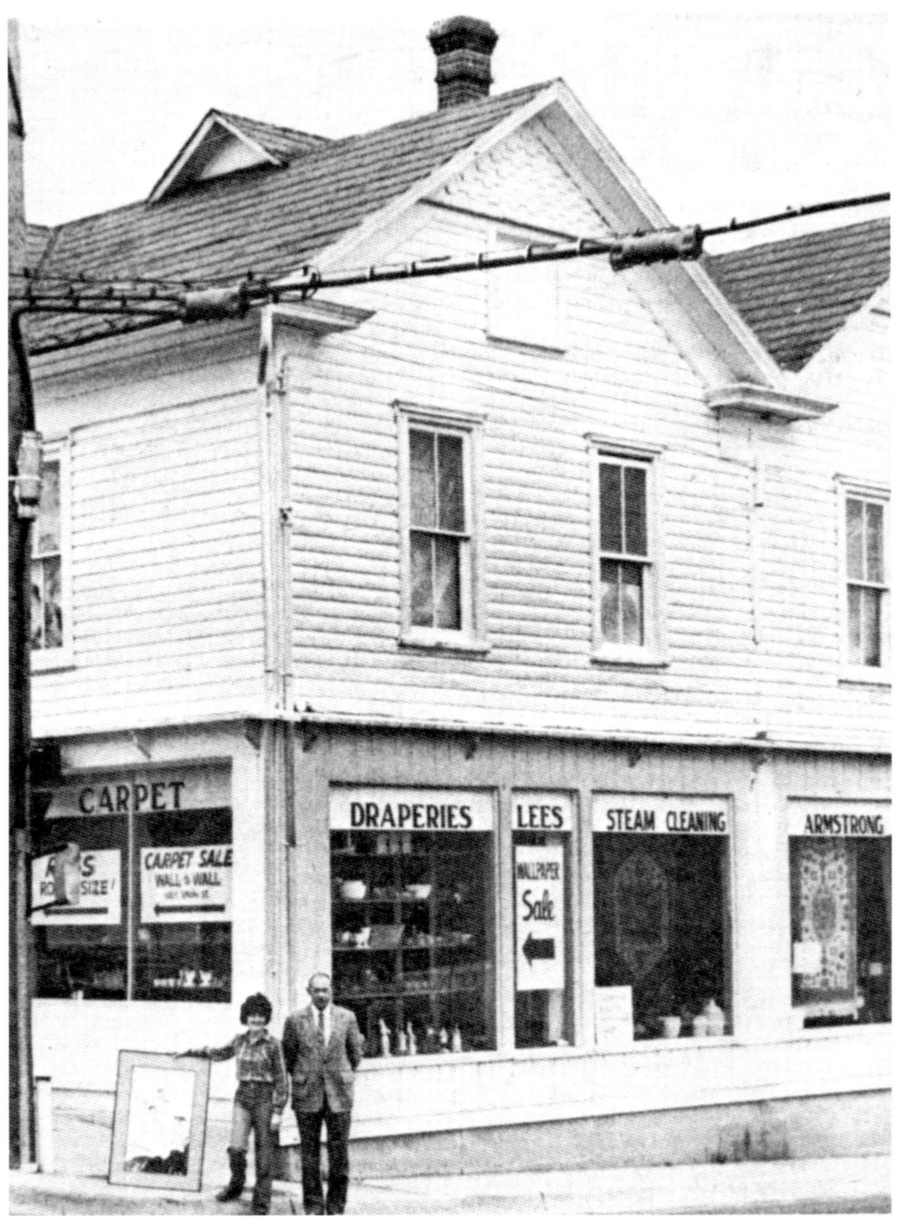

The former Wilkins store building, 1983. From the *Herndon Observer.*

old Wilkins store. He fell in love with the old building, the town and the historical atmosphere. He signed a lease in November of that year. After months of planning and renovating, the Cirritos opened the doors of their new restaurant and bar—Jimmy's Old Town Tavern—in May 1997.

Much like Magnus Wilkins's store, Jimmy Cirroto's tavern has also garnered many accolades for the well-loved business, becoming one of the most popular hangouts in town, "where everyone is treated like a regular." In 2017, Jimmy Cirrito expanded his business by having an addition constructed onto the south side of the old building, where Wilkins once had a porch.

From Wilkins store to Jimmy's Old Town Tavern, the building at the southwest corner of Elden and Spring Streets has maintained a history since 1899, housing popular community-oriented businesses, whose proprietors cheerfully serve their Herndon customers.

12

From Ashes Arose a New Herndon

The Impact of Fires on a Growing Town

Herndon's Historic Fires

By 1910, the population of the town of Herndon was about eight hundred people. Many buildings lined the downtown area of the town. The area immediately surrounding the train depot now included a jewelry store, a livery stable, a harness shop, a furniture store, a telephone building, a carpenter's shop, a drugstore, a shoe shop, a bank, a post office, a clothing store, churches and several homes. There were additional industrial and commercial buildings such as sawmills, lumberyards, general supply stores and a blacksmith shop. Many of these buildings were made of wood frame construction, making them highly susceptible to fire.

This chapter describes some of the significant twentieth-century fires that once ravaged Herndon's downtown area and their aftermath.

The Big Fire of 1917

One of the most horrific fires that occurred in downtown Herndon took place in March 1917 and is commonly referred to as "The Big Fire." The fire started in Harrison's livery stable on the west side of Station Street, just north of Pine Street, in the vicinity of 845 Station Street, currently the location of The Closet thrift store building. A 1917 article in the *Herndon News-Observer* newspaper reported that the fire was quickly discovered at 10:30 p.m., but within a few minutes, the two adjacent buildings on Station Street were also "blazing like a furnace." Pieces of burning wood and embers floated out into other areas of town, causing small forest fires and endangering nearby homes. The heat and embers from the burning buildings was so intense that the fire quickly jumped across the road and started igniting structures on the north side of Pine Street. The fire continued to creep up Pine Street.

There was no Herndon Fire Department or any fire alarm system at the time. Many townspeople attempted to pour water out of windows and over roofs to save buildings. When the fight to save one building was considered a lost cause, efforts were abandoned and were shifted to another structure.

In an effort to save the Congregational Church, formerly at the northeast corner of Pine and Monroe Streets, it was decided to dynamite the home next to the church in order to create a fire break. The blast from the dynamite broke many windows of buildings across the street, but it also kept the fire from spreading, which saved the church. According to the *Fairfax Herald*, the town was aided by a chemical apparatus from Cherrydale, Clarendon and elsewhere until the fire was finally extinguished.

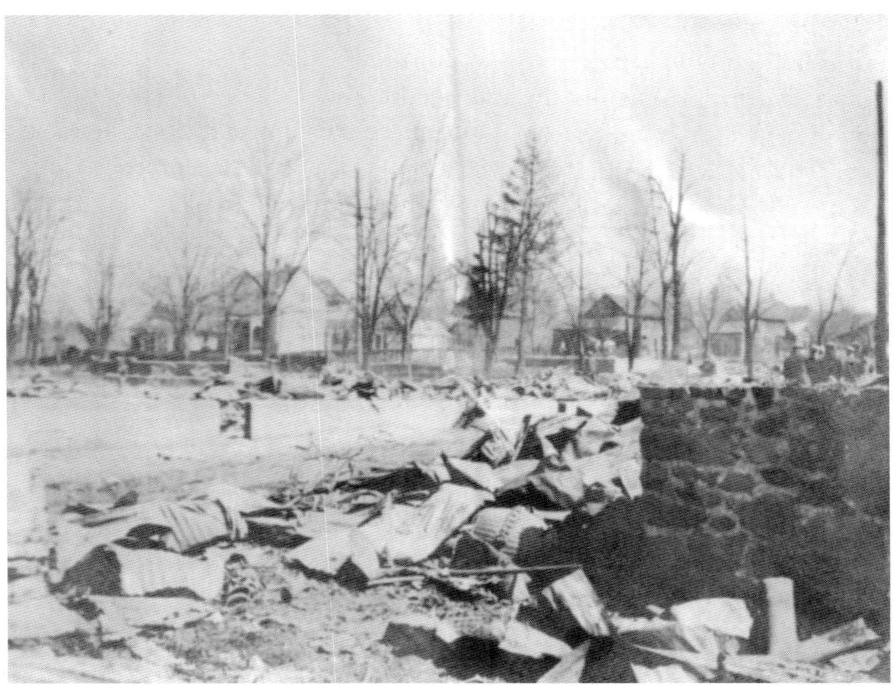

Scene from Herndon's Big Fire of 1917. *J. Berkley Green Collection of the Herndon Historical Society.*

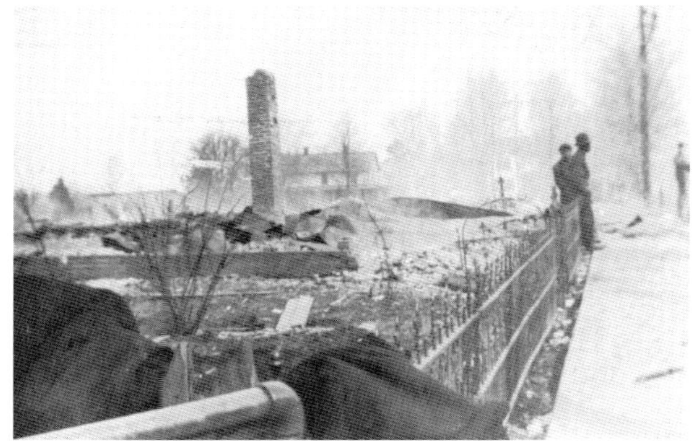

Scene from Herndon's Big Fire of 1917. *J. Berkley Green Collection of the Herndon Historical Society.*

Resident Bill Moffett once recalled a story about his father when interviewed by Kate O'Connor. He said, "During that fire [1917] our father was 19 years old and they got the call by word of mouth—there weren't any telephones—that there was a fire that was threatening the bicycle shop. Dad jumped on a mare that he used to have that you could ride without a bridle. So he swung up on the bare back." Moffett said he got up to Park Avenue and added that all the streets were gravel and dirt back then with depressions and mud holes. He continued: "So before he could lean which way he wanted the horse to go, it hit the mud hole and fell and threw him. [It] knocked him out and broke his collar bone."

The next day the local doctor set his collar bone, but two days later one of the local papers wrote that "young Henry Moffett broke his collar bone jumping from the third story of the Walker building during the fire." He never even got to the fire. The Walker Building—then considered the largest structure in Fairfax County—was formerly located at the corner of Station and Pine Streets and was destroyed in the fire.

In the end, the fire destroyed a good portion of the downtown business district, burning fourteen stores and homes along sections of Station Street and Pine Street. No one was killed, but the losses were estimated at $60,000. Lottie Dyer Schneider, who was living in Herndon at the time, said in her memoir, "It is difficult to imagine what a nightmare we endured that night unless you lived through it."

The Herndon Milling Company

Another large-scale fire that threatened downtown Herndon occurred in March 1936. A feed mill known as the Herndon Milling Company caught fire due to an explosion of a blow torch when a person attempted to light an oil-burning furnace in the mill. The mill was located at the northwest corner of Elden and Station Streets. In addition to the feed mill, the fire also destroyed an adjacent house and a barn. Ironically, it also damaged the roof of the firehouse, then located nearby on Station Street.

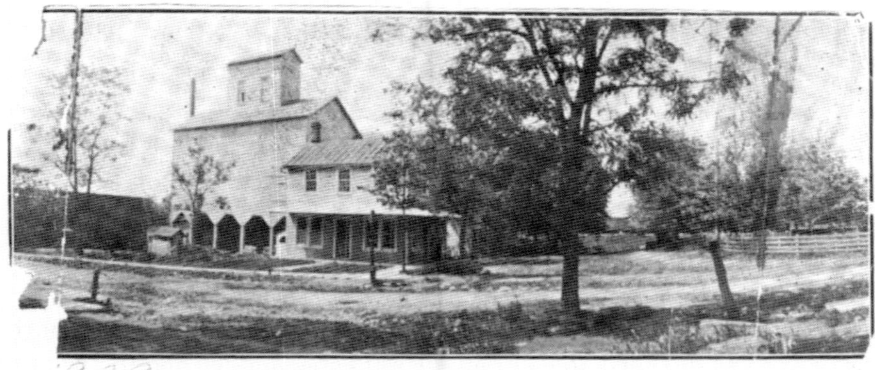

The Herndon Milling Company, pictured around 1909, near the intersection of Elden and Station Streets, prior to it being destroyed in the 1936 fire. *Mary Rosonet.*

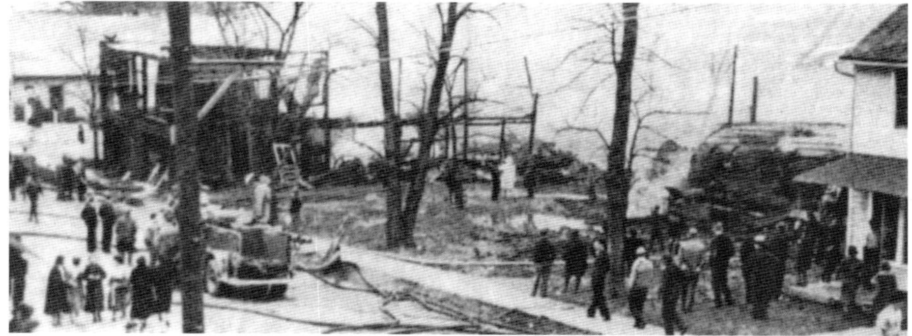

The 1936 fire at the Herndon Milling Company and a nearby home. *J. Berkley Green Collection of the Herndon Historical Society.*

The furnace in the mill exploded, and like in the Big Fire, hot embers flew high in the air and endangered nearby businesses, including Horn Motor Company. Robert Horn put out a fire on a nearby loading platform near a gas tank, saving the town from another potentially large explosion. Luckily, at this point in time, Herndon had its own volunteer fire department. Other nearby fire companies also responded to the blaze. No serious injuries occurred.

Chamblin's Pharmacy

Chamblin's Pharmacy formerly stood on the south side of the Cushman Insurance Company and Maude Hair Salon building at the northwest corner of Station and Lynn Streets. The building dated to late 1800s or early 1900s. Bert Sasher bought the store from the Chamblins in 1934, and the Sasher family ran the pharmacy until the 1960s. It was later sold and became the Pet and Hobby Shop.

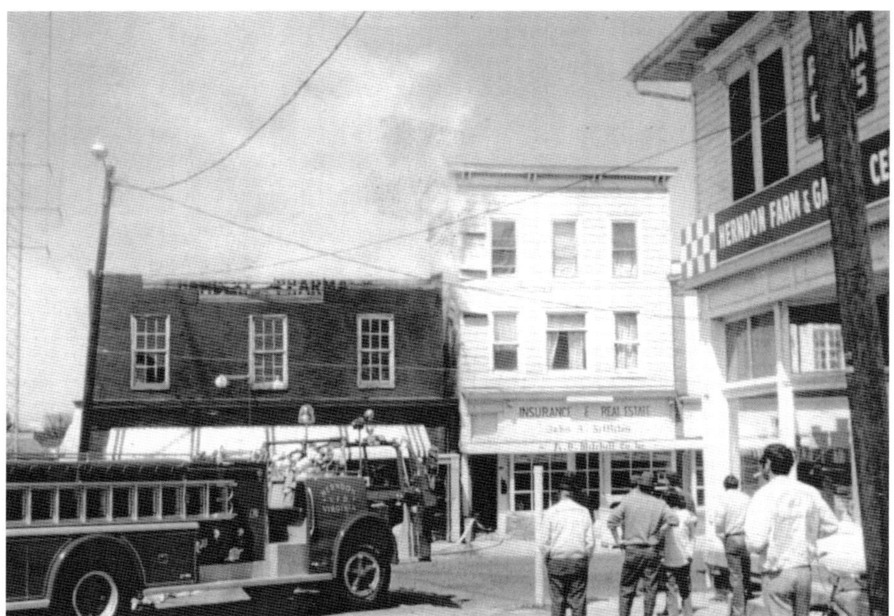

The former Chamblin's (later Sasher's) Pharmacy after the fire, 1971. *Richard Downer.*

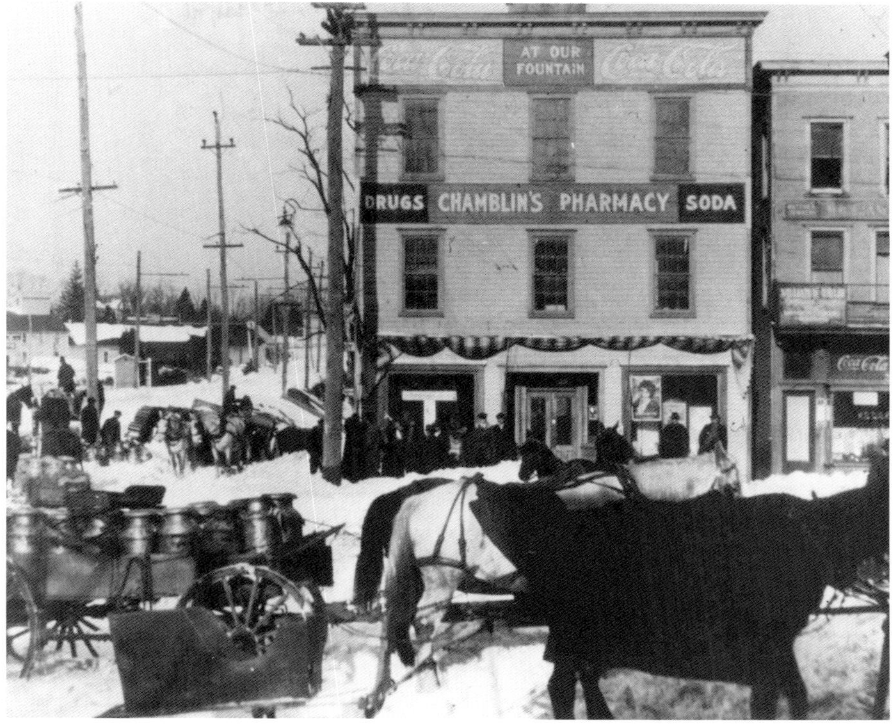

Chamblin's Pharmacy on Station Street. *J. Berkley Green Collection of the Herndon Historical Society.*

Fire heavily damaged the store in 1969. It was later discovered that the store owner had removed all the animals from the building prior to the fire occurring. Some in town thought the fire may have been arson, but charges were never brought against the owner for lack of strong evidence. The building was eventually torn down in 1971. Lynn Street was later extended westward toward the new Herndon Municipal Center, through the property where the drugstore used to stand.

The Larro Mill

The Larro Mill and Starlight Room Dance Hall were part of a partially vacant General Mills Granary, which had stopped operations in the 1960s. The mill was located on the property that is now the town green behind the current Herndon Municipal Center. This mill burned in 1971, threatening surrounding businesses such as the nearby Murphy and Ames Lumber Mill building, Sterling Concrete and the Citizen's National Bank.

According to the *Herndon Tribune*, the fire resulted from Charles Guilford leaving his food cooking on an old wood stove while he went out for a visit. Guilford was the former owner of the General Mills store and resided in part of the building. One longtime town resident remembered that Guilford "ran his form of a 'car rental agency' out of the building, along with raising chickens and ducks in the building while he also lived there...chickens and ducks were often seen wondering on Station and Pine Streets and the junk cars he collected/rented, about 100+, were strung along the creek bed from the General Mills building down to Willow Street [near Center Street]."

The old mill building had no electricity, and the stove had been the cause of three or four earlier fires. Two years prior to the 1971 fire, Herndon's fire chief had demanded that Guilford get an estimate to bring the building up to code. A county inspector had attempted to inspect the building several months prior to the fire, but he was met with locked doors.

The fire resulted in a total loss of the building.

DUDDING'S HARDWARE STORE

The hardware store that used to stand on the west side of the Nachman Building at 718 Lynn Street had an accidental fire in 1980 and was subsequently condemned and torn down. Prior to the fire, it had housed the Herndon Farm and Garden Center and the Taylor Rental Center. Originally constructed around 1909, the building had been the home of Schneider's Hardware store, run by Robert Schneider, a former town councilman and

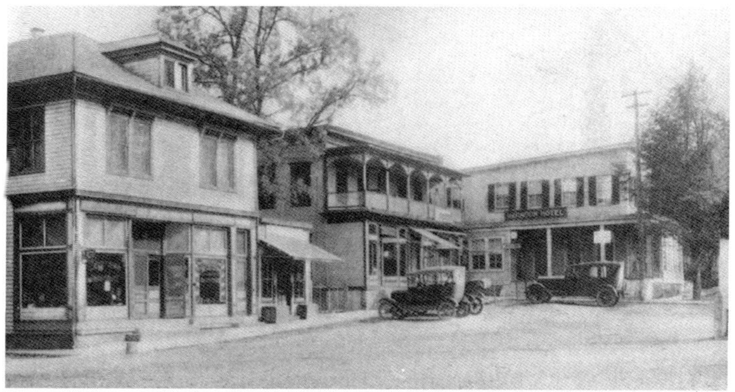

Dudding's Hardware, Buell Insurance Agency, the Nachman Building and the Herndon Hotel on Lynn Street, circa 1920s. *J. Berkley Green Collection of the Herndon Historical Society.*

popular businessman. Between 1920 and the 1960s, it had been Dudding's Hardware Store.

The fire started in a kerosene space heater. Damage was estimated to be $250,000. After the fire, the building was taken down, and it was never replaced. Today, the land where the store once stood is a small parking lot.

THE HERNDON CONGREGATIONAL CHURCH

Built in the 1870s, Herndon's Congregational Church had been saved from the Big Fire in 1917, but it later burned down in a fire that occurred in March 1980. According to the *Herndon Observer*, the church had been in use until 1968, when it was sold and the congregation moved to a new location. At the time of the fire, the building was occupied by a business called the Swap Shop.

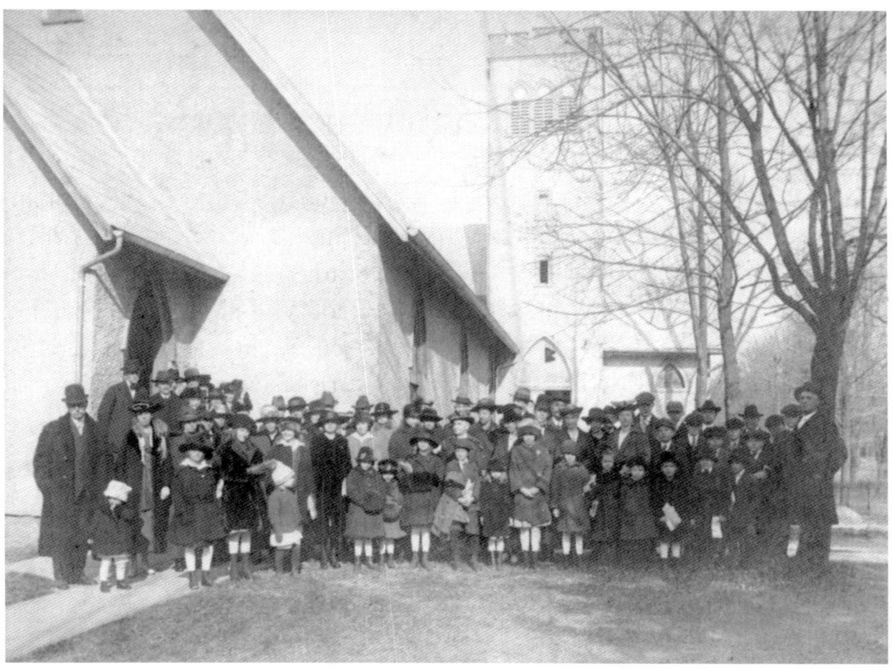

Herndon Congregational Church, circa 1913. *J. Berkley Green Collection of the Herndon Historical Society.*

The fire was discovered after midnight by a passerby who saw flames through the first-floor windows. Flames quickly spread to the steeple. Firefighters responded quickly, but they were hampered by low water pressure when six hundred feet of hose had to be run from three different fire hydrants. Additionally, the heavy church bell was suspended directly over the fire's origin, making it dangerous for firefighters to enter the building. Documentation on the cause of the fire was not found. The piece of land where the church once stood is now occupied by the Pine Street Plaza, a small office complex.

HERNDON'S VOLUNTEER FIRE DEPARTMENT

Herndon has one of Fairfax County's oldest fire departments. The impetus for the town starting to make serious fire prevention plans was the 1917 Big Fire. The Herndon Town Council quickly went to work, holding special meetings to talk about rebuilding the town, establishing new building construction regulations and buying fire apparatus.

After the Big Fire, the town sergeant reported to the town council that he had found fifty fire buckets but could not find any fire ladders. Two councilmen were appointed to a committee to procure fire ladders. (It was later discovered that a ladder and some buckets were being used by someone to paint his house.)

The council started developing building codes that would require using fireproof materials for new construction. The clerk was ordered to notify representatives of fire engine manufacturing companies that the town council wanted to meet with them the following month.

Four manufactures came before the council to describe the merits of their particular chemical fire engines. Mayor Ayre appointed three councilmen to select a fire engine. By January 1918, the council agreed to a maximum budget for the purchase of two trucks and ten three-gallon chemical fire extinguishers.

The town council minutes remained silent on any progress until October 1920. By this time, Mayor Wrenn was in office. The town government and a group of town residents called the Citizens Association collaborated to fund the fire department's needs.

The town council pledged a sum of $500 as the initial payment on a chemical fire engine, which would cost approximately $2,000. The council agreed to a covenant for assuming the obligation for the fire apparatus, providing that the Citizen's Association would agree to furnish the money, or the balance to be paid, on the fire apparatus. Three councilmen were then appointed to a committee to cooperate with the Citizen's Association to investigate the merits and price of different fire engines.

In December 1920, the fire engine committee reported some progress on a location for a firehouse. "The Park," adjacent to the Herndon Depot, had been offered as a site for the new firehouse, but committee preferred to own the lot and building for the prospective station house.

The council then unanimously elected R.S. Crippen as Herndon's first fire chief "with full power to appoint all his aids." Roscoe Swan Crippen was born in 1877 and grew up in Herndon. Born to a farming family, he worked in the farming industry for most of his life. However, in 1920, he was living with his wife and two teenage children on the south side of Pine Street, earning his wage as an auctioneer. Although his home survived the Big Fire, there were two other "Crippen buildings" on Station Street that burned alongside the livery.

By February 1921, the *Fairfax Herald* reported that Herndon had its new fire engine, a chemical pump on a Model T chassis that was touted to have enough capacity to take care of any blaze. The town council authorized a $1,300 note to pay for a fire engine from the American LaFrance Fire Engine Company. A lean-to type of structure was attached to the side of the Murphy and Ames Lumber Company building on Station Street, across from the depot, as a temporary shelter for the new vehicle. The fire engine would reside there until a firehouse could be built.

The Citizen's Association devised a fundraising plan whereby schoolchildren would sell bricks at a price of thirty cents each to help pay for a new building. Those who sold the most would receive a handsome prize. Fireman's carnivals were also organized in the railroad park next to the depot to help raise money to pay off the fire department's debts.

In 1923, the year Clarence Mills was fire chief, a one-garage, wood-frame firehouse was erected as a more suitable temporary shelter for the fire truck. The location of this temporary firehouse was on Elden Street, on the west side of the former Herndon Theatre (now The Upholstery Shop), in the vicinity of 761 Elden Street. At the time, the land belonged to the family of Thomas Reed.

The year 1927 was another particularly difficult year for fires. Herndon High School, on Locust Street, burned down during the 1927–1928 school year, and shortly afterward, yet another fire occurred downtown.

An editorial in a 1927 *Herndon Observer* newspaper characterized the mood and doled out some advice to the people of Herndon:

> *It has been truthfully said that fire is a faithful servant but a terrible master. No locality in the county has had more opportunities to observe this fact than Herndon. Some years ago the business section was pretty well wiped out. Only a few months ago the high school was burned and on Tuesday night fire again menaced the town and but for the fact that there was no wind and the account of ready assistance from neighboring towns, appalling catastrophe might have occurred. In view of these facts and the ever present possibly of another Herndon holocaust, the citizens of the town should take the matter of adequate fire protection under careful and intelligent consideration.*

Another new fire chief, Walter Farr, was appointed in 1927 and served until 1942. Farr, with the assistance of prominent resident George Harrison, reorganized the firefighting volunteers. In 1929, a new American LaFrance 500 pumper was purchased. Its large size required a larger firehouse. That same year, a new permanent brick fire station was constructed on Station Street, next to the former Murphy and Ames Lumber building, across the street from the train depot. Local newspapers initially reported that the new firehouse was to have two stories and measure thirty-five by forty-two feet. However, once built, there was not a second story, other than an attic. The Herndon Volunteer Fire Department was officially chartered with the Commonwealth of Virginia in October 1929.

Soon after, the Herndon Volunteer Fire Department's Ladies Auxiliary group was formed with Eudora Armfield acting as president. The ladies were responsible for fundraising in order to pay off the debt for the new firehouse and its equipment. For many years, social activities in the town revolved around the activities that were planned by the Ladies Auxiliary. The funds it raised not only paid for fire trucks and large equipment but also for things such as helmets and boots. In addition to carnivals, the Ladies Auxiliary sponsored other town events such as dances, vaudeville shows, plays, card parties, dinners and food sales.

The Ladies Auxiliary was appreciated not only for its fundraising efforts but also for its care of the firefighters. When the ladies became aware that the firemen were out on a long-term call, they would go the site of the fire and provide the firefighters with sandwiches and drinks.

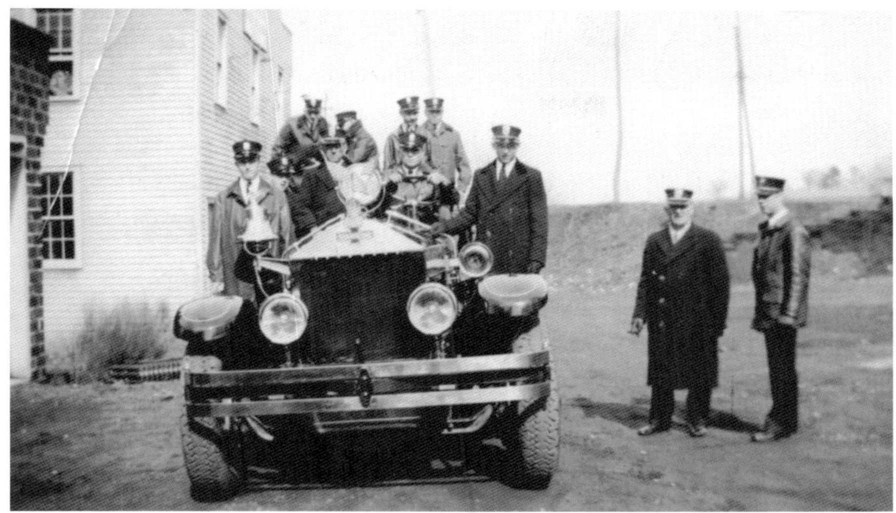

Above: The Herndon Volunteer Fire Department, circa 1933. Chief Farr is second from right. *Herndon Historical Society.*

Right: Herndon Volunteer Fire Department members and Ladies Auxiliary group, 1957. *Doris Rosenberg.*

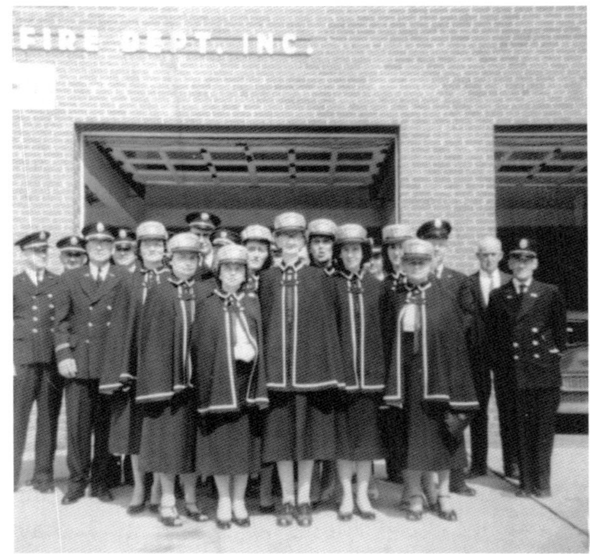

Luckily, the Herndon Volunteer Fire Department was established prior to the serious fire at the Herndon Milling Company in 1936. Herndon's fire department and other nearby fire companies kept the fire from spreading farther.

For many years, the Herndon Volunteer Fire Department was the only fire department between Leesburg, Fairfax, McLean and Vienna. In 1937, Chief Farr reported that the Herndon fire department had responded to five fires in Loudoun, five fires in Herndon and fourteen fires elsewhere in Fairfax County. An average of ten men responded to each call.

Early firefighters recall that the doors to the fire station were often left open. When fires occurred, the firefighters got a call and the siren on the building would blare, which would bring all the volunteers in. The siren would frequently be activated by the town's telephone operator, who was located on Pine Street. When residents picked up their phones to report a fire to the switchboard operator, the operator would flip a switch in her office to activate the siren at the station and then would call the firehouse to report where the fire was located.

In 1940, the Ladies Auxiliary presented the fire department with its first ambulance. The volunteers were trained in first aid.

During the years of World War II, from 1941 through 1946, the volunteer fire department suffered a shortage of manpower, as many of the men were called into the armed services. As a result, the fire department lowered the minimum age to become a volunteer fireman from eighteen years old to sixteen. It continued to operate, albeit with a smaller crew.

After the war, Oscar Costello—one of the volunteers—was hired in 1947 as the first full-time paid fireman. His salary was paid by the Town of Herndon and by Fairfax County. Another new fire truck was purchased that year. By 1949, the Herndon Volunteer Fire Department had approximately 150 members.

In 1950, a new fire department building was constructed on a lot at 680 Spring Street, between Elden and Locust Streets. The land was purchased from Raymond and Mamie Printz, who lived nearby on Elden Street. Individuals and businesses from all around the Greater Herndon area contributed to the effort.

The new brick building on Spring Street had two stories and fit all of the firefighting equipment and ambulances. Later, the second floor was sometimes used for town council and Fairfax County District Court meetings. The space was also rented out for dances and other social events and used for dinners and bingo sponsored by the fire department to raise money.

In 1977, the Herndon Volunteer Fire Department was incorporated into the Fairfax County Fire Department. An agreement was made between Jack Herrity (chairman of the Fairfax County Board of Supervisors) and Howard Nachman (president of the Herndon Volunteer Fire Department). The county was to receive the land and all the other assets of the volunteer fire department except for the cash. The cash was maintained by the volunteer fire organization to help pay for any fire station needs that the county might not finance. The agreement also stated that should the fire department ever leave the Spring Street location, the title to the land would

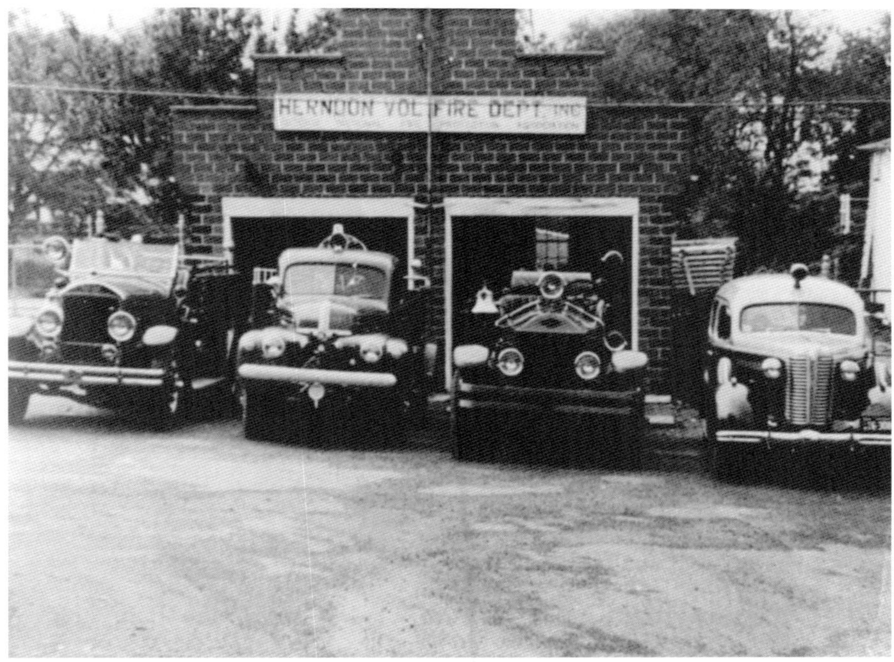

Above: Herndon Volunteer Fire Department building on Station Street, 1948. *J. Berkley Green Collection of the Herndon Historical Society.*

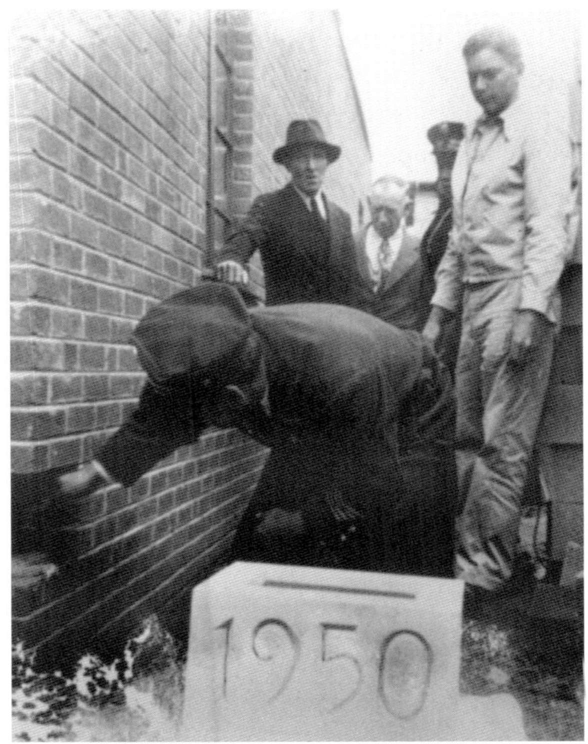

Right: The cornerstone of the Spring Street fire department building being laid in 1950. *J. Berkley Green Collection of the Herndon Historical Society.*

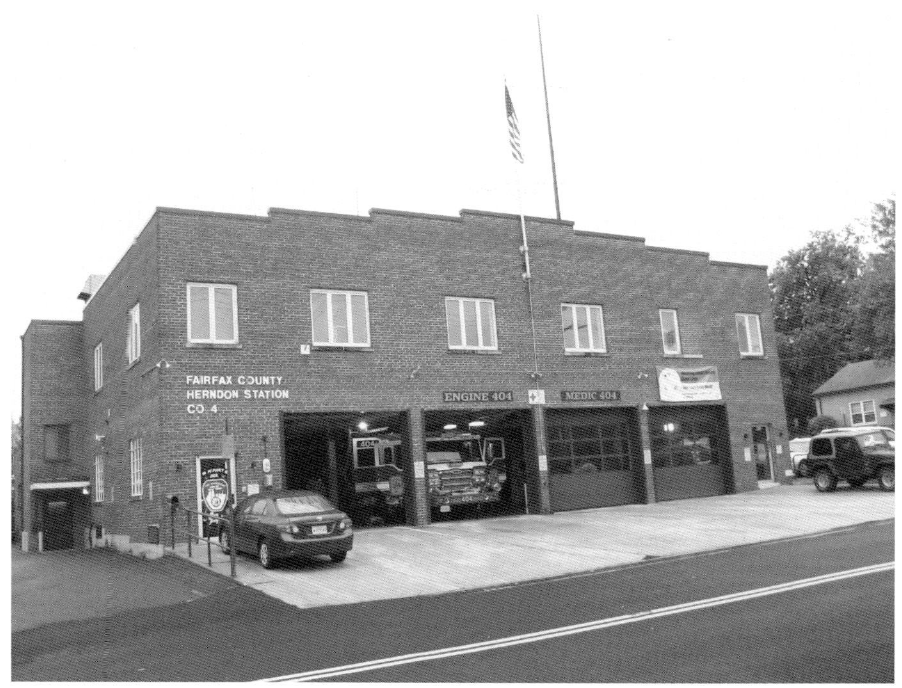

Herndon Fire Department, Station No. 4, 2014. *Barbara Glakas.*

revert to the Town of Herndon. The county also agreed to provide a certain amount of equipment and personnel at the station to ensure that the town was adequately covered. The second floor of the building was now used as sleeping quarters for the county's paid firefighters. The volunteers remained active, conducting fundraisers for Herndon's fire department, Station No. 4.

The Herndon Fire Department eventually outgrew its building, and it needed to be updated. In the early 2000s, studies and searches were conducted for a location for a new Herndon fire station. Many public meetings were held. Potential alternate sites that were considered included next to the police station on Herndon Parkway or near Stanton Park on Third Street. Each location had its difficulties, whether it was space, cost or public discontent. It was ultimately decided that the old fire station on Spring Street would be torn down, and the new fire station would be rebuilt on the same lot.

In 2014, a temporary fire station was erected in a parking lot located at the corner of Center and Locust Streets. In 2015, the old fire station was torn down. Many townspeople wanted a piece of history and requested individual bricks from the old station to save as souvenirs. Once the old fire station was torn down, construction of the new fire station began. The grand reopening of Herndon's new fire station, Station No. 4, was held in March 2017.

The new fire station has a larger footprint of approximately 14,500 square feet. The station has two stories with underground parking, larger facilities for female firefighters, increased space to accommodate larger ladder trucks, decontamination facilities, fitness facilities for the firefighters and upgrades to meet all the standards of the Americans with Disabilities Act. The new fire station also displays historic photographs and artifacts having to do with the history of Herndon's fire department, including the original brass fireman's pole and the 1950 cornerstone of the former building.

One of the oldest fire departments in Fairfax County, Station No. 4, is steeped in history, starting as a volunteer force out of need, with many Herndon residents allowing themselves to be called on day and night to help protect their neighbors' lives and property.

CONCLUSION

As devastating as the many Herndon fires were, they also spurred new beginnings in town. The Big Fire motivated the town to establish the Herndon Volunteer Fire Department. The town council created building regulations and fire protection plans. New buildings were required to be constructed with fireproof material. This led to replacing the former wooden buildings with the many brick and stone structures that are seen in downtown Herndon today.

The spot where Larro's Mill used to sit is now the expansive town green, surrounded by the Fortnightly Library and the Herndon Municipal Center. New businesses and a municipal parking lot were constructed where the Herndon Milling Company once stood.

A reporter at the *Fairfax Herald* said it best in 1917 when he explained that those who lost property after the Big Fire intended to immediately rebuild, claiming, "Herndon will arise from its ashes, better and more handsome than ever."

13

The KKK in Herndon

A Dark Chapter in Herndon's History

Activities of the Ku Klux Klan (also known as the KKK or the Klan) first appeared in Virginia in the mid-1860s but were short-lived due to the U.S. Congress passing a series of laws that limited those activities, including the passing of the Fifteenth Amendment, which granted African American men the right to vote.

However, a resurgence occurred in the early 1900s. Kleagles—or KKK officers—were tasked to recruit new members and were dispatched across southern states, including the small towns of Virginia. In the 1920s, the group used a professional public relations firm to develop an improved public profile.

A decline in Klan activities was reported in the *Washington Post* in 1930. In 1944, the national Klan was sued by the U.S. Treasury Department for unpaid taxes. The Klan settled by agreeing to disband.

A third resurgence of the Klan occurred in the mid-twentieth century as a reaction against desegregation and the civil rights movement.

The town of Herndon—like many other small towns in Virginia—did not escape the touch of the KKK. The book *Fairfax County, Virginia, A History* described Herndon as being "another center of Klan activity" in the county. Growth of the KKK was attributed in part as a post–World War I reaction to the formerly dominant farmers losing local political control to town merchants and to Herndon businessmen who worked in Washington, D.C. In some cases—at an attempt to preserve their lifestyle, reassert their influence or vent their frustrations—some vulnerable farmers would either join or tolerate the activities of the KKK.

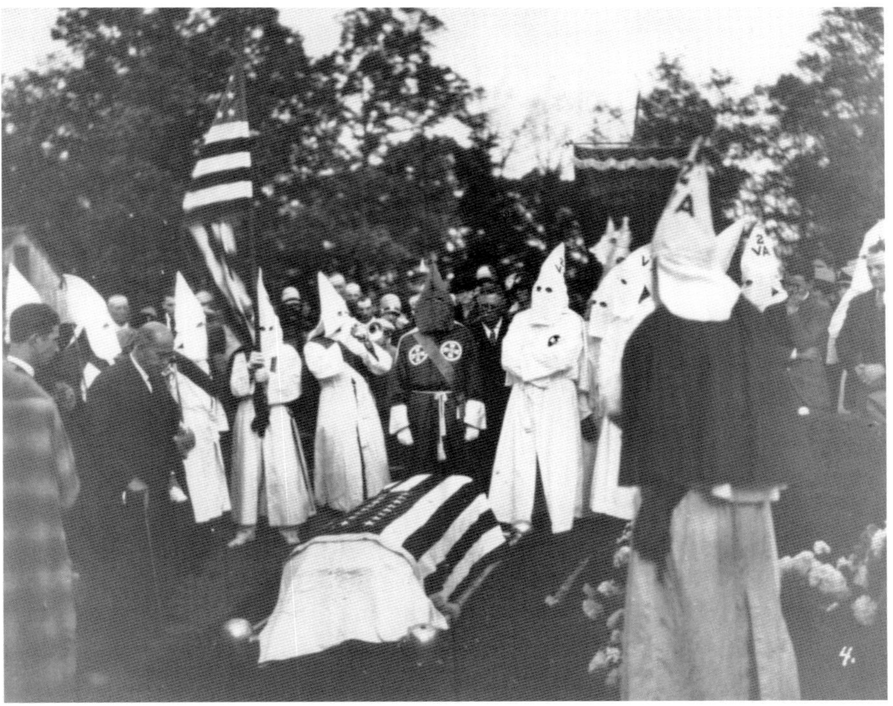

A Ku Klux Klan funeral at the Fairfax Cemetery, circa 1920s. *Fairfax County Public Library Photographic Archive.*

Rita Schug, author of a study called *The Town of Herndon*, described interviews conducted in 1973 with three Herndon residents. Schug explained how one of these men told her that he had been visited by "these hooded Americans who sought to initiate him as a member. He recognized some by voice and others by their shoes. Although he did not join the Klan, claiming the pressing needs of his family and business, he did enjoy a free showing of *The Birth of a Nation*," a 1915 silent film set in the Reconstruction period that glorified the KKK, depicting them as noble warriors.

The 1920s seemed to be a difficult time for Herndon as the KKK made an attempt to become more mainstream in small-town society. Membership in the Klan was normally a closely guarded secret, but its visibility eventually began to grow. In 1923, the town council discussed segregating the races in Herndon and passed an ordinance that said, "No property within Corporation limits shall be sold to any other person or persons other than one of the white race, without the sanction of a majority vote of the Town Council."

There were several newspaper articles, published in the Herndon edition of the *News-Observer* from the years 1925 to 1928, that described the Klan's activities in town. The "Klansman's Creed" was printed on the front page of a 1925 issue of the newspaper. Immediately below the title it stated that the creed was "published by request," but it did not specify who made the request.

The creed outlined the Klan's belief system, describing how it believed in God, church, separation of church and state, the Stars and Stripes, just laws and liberty, the Constitution, free schools, free speech, the protection of pure womanhood and law and order. It also purported not to believe in mob violence, but it did not believe in making laws to suppress the causes of mob violence. The creed concluded by saying, "I am a native born American citizen and I believe my rights in this country are superior to those of foreigners."

Schug said that some of the Klan's activities were directed as justification for upholding morals. She learned from locals that one white man was "tarred and feathered for deserting his wife and 'running around.' A burning cross warned others of his ilk."

The Klan had a baseball team that participated in many Herndon events, such as in local tournaments and Fourth of July celebrations. In various newspaper articles, the team was referred to as the "Crimson Ku Klux team," "The Kleagles," "The Red-Robed Ku Klux team" and the "Mystic Knights." The team played against Herndon teams as well as teams from Leesburg, Waterford and Round Hill. When scores were published, the Klan teams were usually on top. One newspaper reporter noted, "The hooded men have a very fast club."

Other places where the Klan made their presence known was at the town's Herndon Day event and at town carnivals, two large community events. One Herndon Day advertisement printed in a 1925 *News-Observer* touted the many activities and attractions that would occur at Herndon Day, including how the Ku Klux Klan would be "in full force" in the evening.

In a subsequent issue, the *News-Observer* reported how the Klan had participated in Herndon Day:

> *About 9 o'clock the Knights of the Invisible Empire assembled in front of the school, accompanied by the band of the Ballston Klan. The standard bearer led the Knights to the band pavilion which they entered while the band was playing, "Onward Christian Soldiers."*

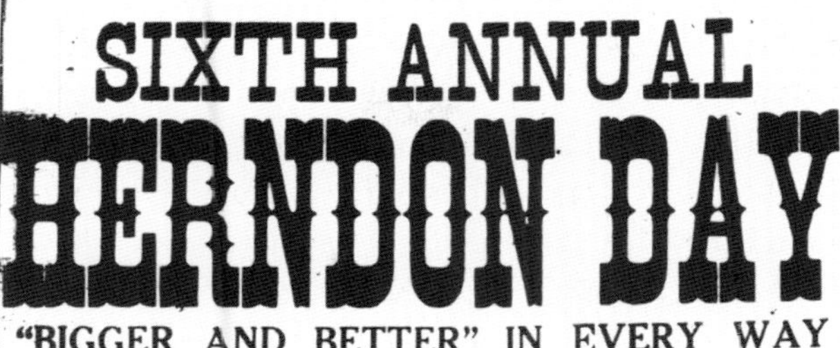

SIXTH ANNUAL

HERNDON DAY

"BIGGER AND BETTER" IN EVERY WAY

SATURDAY SEPT. 5 1925

ALL ✦ DAY

BASEBALL

Forestville vs. Fairfax, 10:30 A. M.

Alex. Cardinals vs. Herndon, 3:30 P. M.

TENNIS TOURNAMENT

Upperville vs. Leesburg } . . 10:00 A. M.

Alexandria vs. Herndon }

U. S. Band; Agricultural and Mechanical Exhibits; Tug of War, Forestville vs. Floris.
Ku Klux Klan in Full Force in Evening.

BABY SHOW: Prizes for Prettiest Baby Boy; Prizes for Prettiest Baby Girl
Barrel of Flour for Largest Family on the Grounds
$1.00 for Most Freckled Boy $1.00 for Most Freckled Girl

Minstrel Troupe Horse Shoe Contest Gypsy Fortune Tellers

Herndon Musical Club Will Furnish Musical Program from 7:30 to 8:30 P. M.
Refreshments: Pies, Cakes, Sandwiches, Ice Cream, Soft Drinks.

DANCE IN AUDITORIUM 9:00 to 11:30

ADMISSION: 25c and 15c.

The contractor advises that the new macadam road will be open from pike to pike and ready for use on "Herndon Day."

Right: A 1925 promotional advertisement for Herndon Day shows Ku Klux Klan participation. From the *Fairfax Herald* newspaper.

Below: A public outdoor event in Herndon in which Ku Klux Klan members can be seen in the foreground. *Fairfax County Public Library Photographic Archive.*

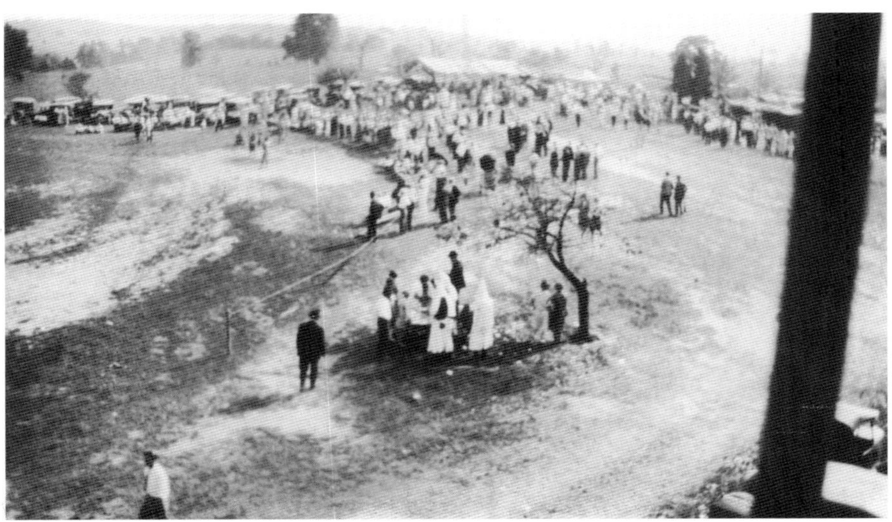

> *After a brief ceremony, the Knights moved southward to the field where the cross had been erected. While the Cross was burning, a class of four was duly initiated into the mysteries of the Empire.*
>
> *Following the burning of the cross, the Knights returned to the pavilion where some excellent speaking was had. Thereupon the Knights disbanded, leaving their hearers apparently well satisfied with the demonstration.*

Klan activities in Herndon—and throughout Virginia—appeared to wane after the 1920s. By the late 1960s, Virginia governor Mills Godwin reacted against the Klan, which had started holding rallies in cow pastures. He offered monetary rewards for information leading to arrests of those who engaged in cross burnings, a felony in Virginia. He also threatened to use the National Guard to break up Klan activities. Arrests were made and some were imprisoned, influencing a downturn of KKK activities.

14

Herndon's First Movie Theater

A Center of Herndon Entertainment in the Early 1900s

Today, the building at 757 Elden Street is occupied by a longtime Herndon business, Designs & Interiors by The Upholstery Shop. However, many years ago, this building was the town of Herndon's first movie theater.

According to a member of the Reed family and Virgie Wynkoop, who was one hundred years old when she wrote her memories of Herndon in 1979, Thomas E. Reed built Herndon's first movie hall in 1921 and ran it for a number of years. Lillie Reed worked in the ticket booth. The Reeds owned much of the land on the block where the theater was located. A man named Henry Lego, who was knowledgeable about movies, eventually came to Herndon. Lego owned another movie house in Purcellville. Thomas Reed rented the Herndon movie house to Henry Lego and then eventually sold it to him.

There were advertisements and articles written about Herndon's movie theater in the *News-Observer* and the *Fairfax Herald* newspapers, which date back as early as the 1920s. The earliest advertisements range from 1924 to 1927 and referred to a Herndon movie house as "Elden Hall" or "Elden Street Hall." Movies cost twenty-five cents for children and fifty cents for adults. Thomas E. Reed was listed as the proprietor. The advertisements included showings of *The Ten Commandments*, *The Big Parade* and *Birth of a Nation*. A vintage movie poster displayed in the Herndon Depot Museum advertises the showing of the 1923 silent drama film *The Trail of the Lonesome Pine* at Elden Hall.

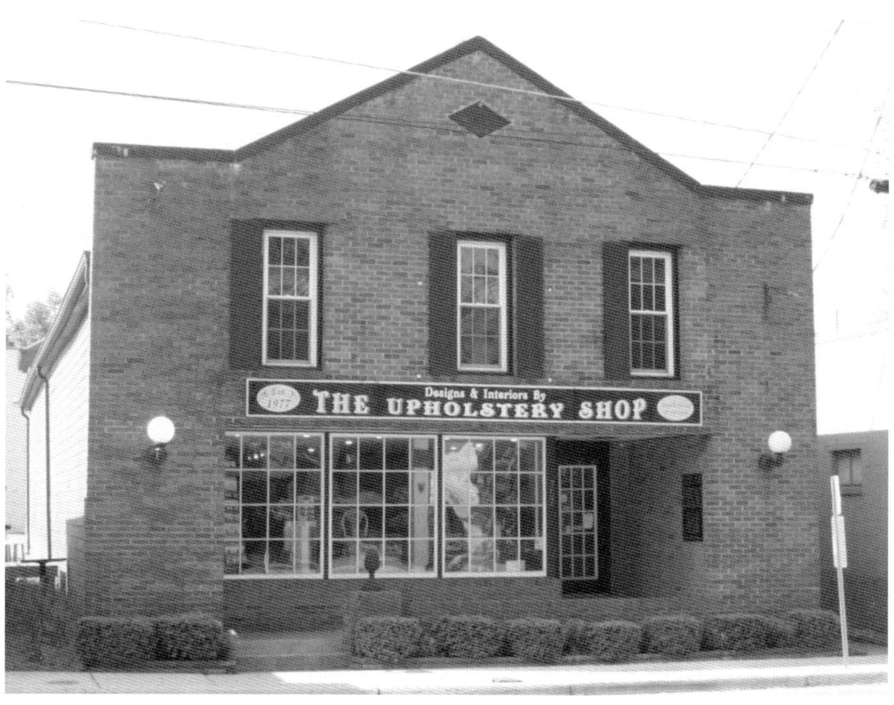

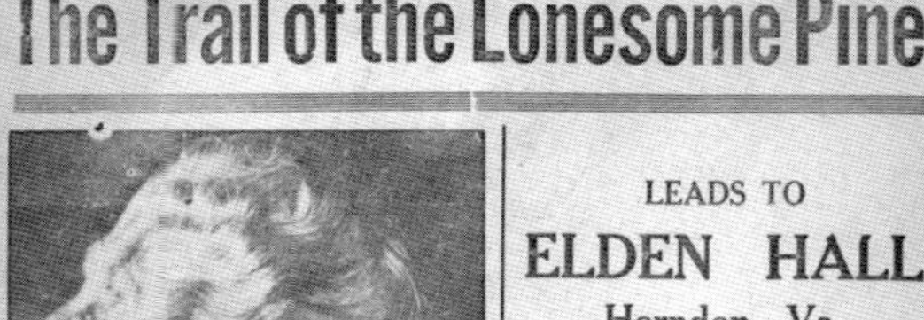

Above: The building that originally housed the Herndon Theatre. *Barbara Glakas.*

Left: A 1923 poster for a silent movie shown in Herndon's Elden Hall. *Herndon Historical Society.*

By the 1930s, newspaper advertisements that spoke of Herndon's movie house started referring to it as the "Herndon Theatre." Elden Hall and the Herndon Theatre were no doubt the same movie house that had simply changed names when ownership changed.

Census records show that Henry J. Lego was born in 1885 in Illinois, where he lived through his teen years. He served in World War I as a sergeant in the U.S. Army, from 1918 to 1919. He completed four years of college. In 1941, while in Herndon, he became one of the charter members of Herndon's American Legion Post No. 91.

A 1930 census showed that Henry Lego was living in Washington, D.C., and was a "moving picture salesman." A 1940 census showed that he was a movie theater owner, living on Elden Street in Herndon and boarding with Roberta Detwiler. Detwiler became a widow after her husband, Dr. Ben Detwiler, died in 1931. Her house at 825 Elden Street was just two blocks from the theater. Lego indicated in the census that he had been boarding at the Detwiler house since at least 1935. Also living in the house were Roberta's daughter and granddaughter. The daughter, Beulah Anderson, was listed in the census as a movie theater ticket seller. The granddaughter, Helen Anderson, was listed as a motion picture stenographer.

Advertisements that appear in several 1932 editions of the *Fairfax Independent* newspaper boasted that the Herndon Theatre had "the latest improved sound equipment." It had "high class feature pictures, comedies and selected cartoons." That year, movie tickets cost twenty-five cents for adults and fifteen cents for those under twelve.

Frances Darlington Simpson, who spent summers in Herndon during the early to middle 1900s, recalled her memories of the theater in her 1963 book *Virginia Country Life and Cooking*:

> *Across the railroad tracks is the* [railroad] *station and beyond that a little way is the theatre. What a fascination was that theatre or "movie hall" as it was called. Today it is used for dances and meetings as the Herndonians are very much au courant with television and not concerned with movies, but when we were children, it was a real treat to go with our friends to the movies at the "movie hall"—not that we always saw one when we got there. Sometimes the reel would break, other times a tremendous storm would come up and the electricity power would be shut off, leaving the player piano to carry on alone in the darkness while we crept home with flashlights and once more an angry skunk sought refuge in the movie hall, causing the audience to disperse in three minutes flat. Still it was great fun.*

A 1935 news article reported that a case of "infantile paralysis disease," or polio, had been reported in Herndon, as well as in other areas of Virginia. The County Health Officer suggested suspending all gatherings of children until the danger of the disease had passed. As a result, Henry Lego decided to temporarily close the theater until the health officer said the danger had passed. The Herndon Theatre was reopened about twenty-five days later.

Many people who still live in Herndon today have vivid memories of the theater. One longtime Herndon resident, who attended movies at the theater in the 1930s and 1940s, recalled that it cost sixteen cents to see a movie at this one-screen movie house. She said that theatergoers had to go up a few stairs as they entered the movie house to get to the ticket booth. Inside the theater was a small balcony in the back, near where the projector was located. She said the shows usually started with a war news reel, a cartoon, a movie short and then the main feature.

In a document called *The Town of Herndon Oral History Project, 1999–2001,* another early resident recalled how her husband used to play the piano in the theater so that people would have music while the picture was going on. "It was like a roller so all you'd have to do was pump it. And that was the music and everyone thought that was wonderful."

Another person recalled that they showed "lots of western movies and double features on Saturdays." She also recalled that on Saturdays "they not only showed news and a cartoon they also had a serial [movie], which you had to keep going to on Saturdays to find out what happened next." Some of her favorite westerns featured Randolph Scott, Roy Rogers, Gene Autry and Hopalong Cassidy. Love stories were also popular with memorable actors such as Tyrone Power and Clark Gable.

Other theatergoers from the 1950s remember the movie house having dark red velvet curtains. In the early days, the seats were all wooden, but some people recalled that the seats were later cushioned. The floor was flat, so anyone who had a tall person sit in front of them may have had a hard time seeing. The theater was not air-conditioned but had big fans in the basement under the stage that blew cool air.

The Herndon Theatre not only showed movies but also later hosted many other activities. One resident recalled attending high school dances on the stage at the theater.

Another resident who grew up in Herndon in the 1950s and 1960s described how a small snack bar was built on one side of the theater, with a few booths and stools at the counter. It was called the Hornet's Nest, as the high school team was known as the Herndon Hornets. The Hornet's

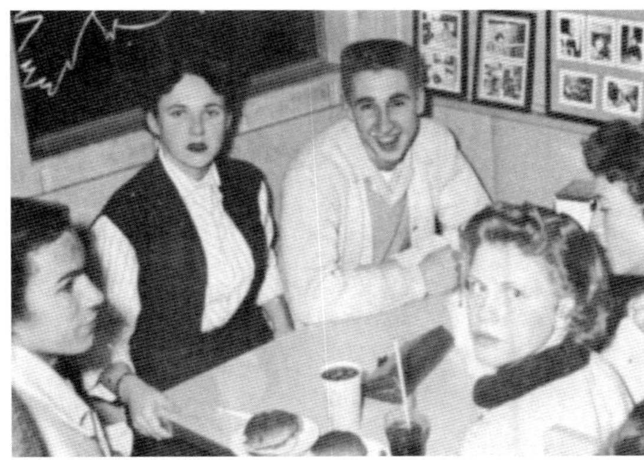

Students gather at the Hornet's Nest snack bar in the Herndon Theatre. *Herndon High School yearbook, 1956.*

Nest had mugs there for all the high school football players, and it sold burgers, hot dogs and milkshakes. The theater is where everybody went after the games.

Henry Lego later married and lived with his wife on Spring Street, across from Wood Street. Neighbors remember his backyard being filled with azaleas and magnolias. Lego died in 1960 and is buried at Herndon's Chestnut Grove Cemetery.

A 1992 *Herndon Times* newspaper said the Herndon Theatre closed its doors around 1965. At one point, Mike and Ruby Martin owned the building and had taken the seats out. The townspeople enjoyed special entertainment in the building, including teen dances. Ruby once recalled how her husband came home one night excited about a performer he had just seen in the theater. "I've just heard a little hillbilly gal from Winchester," he told Ruby. "Her name's Patsy Cline, and I just know she is going to be famous!"

According to the memories of other Herndon residents and local business owners, there were several other businesses that occupied the old theater building after the movie house closed. Some of those businesses included a pool hall called Rack & Cue Billiards and an antique furniture store called Touch of Europe. The Moose Lodge occupied the building for a few years in the 1970s before moving over to the former Burger Cabinet Shop on Center Street.

One longtime Herndon resident remembers that Rack & Cue Billiards opened sometime in the mid-1960s. In addition to having pool tables, it also had several pinball machines and served sandwiches. Indeed, advertisements in 1968 and 1969 editions of the *Fairfax Herald* newspaper described the pool hall as having "Family Fun for Everyone," boasting the "finest and largest sandwiches in the area."

The family-owned Upholstery Shop, which was established in 1977, moved into the old theater building in 1996 and has occupied it ever since. If one goes into The Upholstery Shop today, the front stage where dances were held and the balcony that used to be located in the rear can still be seen.

The interesting brick façade seen on the front of the building today was not part of the original construction but was added on later, possibly in the 1960s. Like many old structures in Herndon, the old Herndon Theatre building has wooden frame construction. The original wood siding has since been replaced by HardiPlank, a material that has a wood-like appearance. It has a cellar and a tin roof. The foundation was once improved due to the erosion caused by the creek that runs underneath Elden Street.

Another movie theater later opened in Herndon at the Dulles Park Shopping Center. Later, the Worldgate Theaters opened. Despite the plush and high-tech movie theaters of today, many lifelong residents still have fond memories of Herndon's original movie house at 757 Elden Street.

15

Prohibition in Herndon

The Evolution and Impact of the Temperance Movement in Herndon

Prohibition was a national ban on the manufacturing, sale and distribution of alcoholic beverages, a ban that was in place from 1920 to 1933. Prohibition impacted Herndon much like it did many other cities and towns around the country. However, the anti-alcohol trend began long before national prohibition laws went into effect.

The temperance movement started in the early 1800s, advocating against drunkenness and excessive use of alcohol. An American Temperance Society formed in the 1820s. Its membership grew to approximately1.5 million by the mid-1830s. A significant amount of its membership was composed of women. Methodist and Baptist groups were also very active in the temperance movement.

According to the Great Falls Historical Society, Virginia's opposition to liquor began in Charlotte County in 1826, where the Virginia Society for the Promotion of Temperance was formed. This movement toward prohibition continued through the mid-1800s, led by religious denominations. Temperance conventions held in the 1840s resulted in resolutions to enact laws prohibiting the sale of liquor in counties that adopted the law by vote.

After the distraction of the Civil War, the prohibition movement was revived. An 1866 local option act provided that each local jurisdictional could vote to issue liquor licenses within its own boundaries.

It was during this period that the town of Herndon was coming into its own. A little village started forming around the railroad depot in the 1850s and 1860s, with the first organized churches popping up in the 1870s. Incorporation followed in 1879.

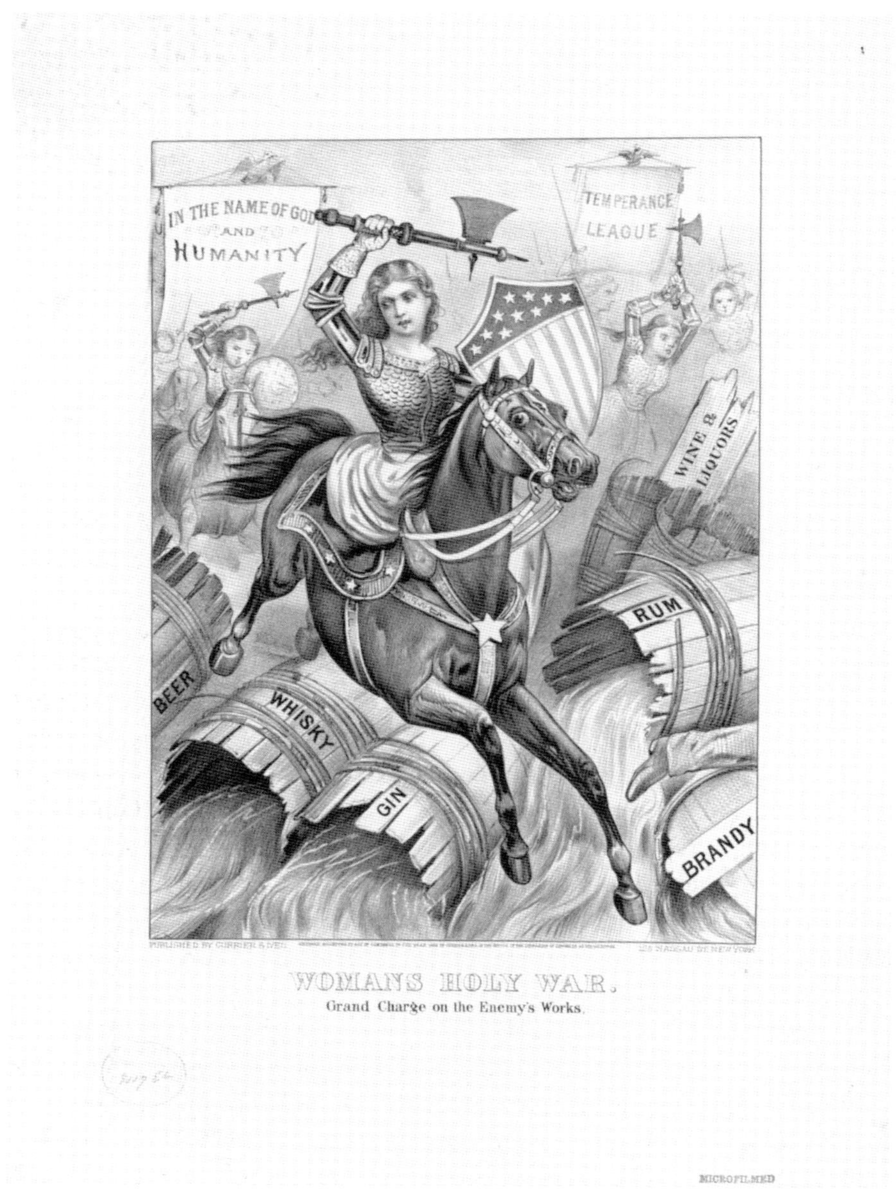

Womans Holy War temperance lithograph, circa 1874. Published by Currier & Ives. *Library of Congress.*

Map and land record evidence shows that a Good Templar group existed in Herndon the 1870s and 1880s. As part of the temperance movement the Independent Order of Good Templars was a fraternal order that accepted both men and women and promoted the total abstinence from alcohol. In 1878, Herndon residents Thomas VanDeusen, Howard Blanchard and Benjamin H. Bready—all trustees of the Sweet Home Lodge No. 12 of the Independent Order of Good Templars of Herndon—bought a piece of land on the west side of the intersection of Station and Pine Streets. The 1878 Hopkins map of Herndon shows the Good Templar Hall location. (See map on pages 6–7.) The nearby Willow Street was sometimes called Temple Street.

Coincidentally, the same year the town was incorporated was also the year that each district in Fairfax County voted on the question of whether or not to license the sale of liquor in their respective districts. The residents within Dranesville District, of which Herndon is a part, voted against the sale of liquor by a 146–117 vote.

According to Marilyn McGinty in a 1968 *Sun* newspaper article, a group of prohibitionist women in Herndon disapproved of the wild nightlife and lawless atmosphere that was created by men who drank and gathered around the town's train depot. They hoped that this disorderly behavior would stop when the town was incorporated and a law could be created banning the presence of saloons within the town limits. McGinty said these women were apparently successful in influencing the establishment of the 4.3 square miles as the town's boundaries. Since saloons were not allowed within the town, the 4.3-mile boundary would establish a difficult walking distance to the train station, thus deterring drunken nuisances around the station.

However, the first ordinances that were passed after the Town of Herndon's incorporation seemed to moderate the ever-growing push for full prohibition. The town's ordinance established that any person who applied to the county for a liquor license to sell liquor within the town limits must first submit to the county a certificate from the town council that verified that the applicant was a "suitable person."

Still, the impact of the temperance movement continued to be very influential, as reflected in an 1886 editorial of a Herndon newspaper called the *Weekly Comet*. During a special election for the Fairfax representative to the Virginia House of Delegates, the editors noted how the Republicans put up a candidate who was "a Christian gentleman who is also a prominent Good Templar, Jacob M. Thorne." The Democrats nominated a man named Enoch Lowe. The editors said "everyone knew Lowe was for free whiskey." Thorne was elected by a good majority, and "all decent people rejoiced…Fairfax has a good temperance man for a judge and a temperance man in the House of Delegates." The editors concluded, "The people of Fairfax when aroused declare themselves for temperance every time."

By 1902, there were no licensed bars in about one quarter of Virginia's counties. In several other counties, the recorded liquor license fees were very small, suggesting that each of these counties may have only had one or two barrooms.

National Prohibition began in 1920, when the Eighteenth Amendment to the U.S. Constitution became law. The Great Falls Historical Society noted that during Prohibition, doctors were allowed to grant their patients legal access to a pint of whiskey by writing prescriptions for one or two dollars. Herndon doctor Charles Russell reportedly wrote many such prescriptions in the last years of his practice for his "ailing" patients. The doctor died about two years before the 1933 repeal of the Eighteenth Amendment, creating speculation that his death must have caused a mass transfer of his patients to find an alternative source of "medicine."

Bootleggers were known to operate all around Fairfax County. Alcohol was hidden under brush piles and in hollow tree stumps. Some residents kept milk can or wash basin stills. Jails became overcrowded with Prohibition violators. Newspapers in 1924 reported that the majority of the inmates in the county's jails were those who had violated liquor laws.

In 1933, the Twenty-first Amendment repealed the Eighteenth Amendment, which had created nationwide prohibition on alcohol. State by state, the Twenty-first Amendment was ratified, with Virginia being the twenty-ninth state.

In October 1933, the Herndon Town Council issued a permit to H.B. Horn to allow him to sell wholesale beer in Herndon. Soon after, the town council made the sale of beer allowable in Herndon, with certain restrictions. In March 1935, Councilman Gibson made a motion that would make it unlawful for anyone to sell beer for consumption on premises each weekday after 10:00 p.m. or on Saturday after 11:00 p.m. It also provided that beer was not allowed to be sold on Sundays or on election days. It passed unanimously.

Establishing Herndon laws regarding the sale of liquor was a more difficult process, however. In January 1936, the Herndon Town Council considered a resolution that would allow the Virginia Alcohol Beverage Control (ABC) Board to open a liquor store in Herndon. Many, including the majority of town merchants, supported the resolution, believing it would bring increased trade, as people would no longer have to go outside of town to buy liquor. The vote passed four to two in support of the resolution, with Councilmen Robb, Linkins, Gibson and Wiley voting yes and Councilmen Wilkins and Wrenn voting no. Mayor Kirk signed the resolution.

This vote caused much uproar in town and was met with stiff resistance, including from the Herndon's Woman's Christian Temperance Union, which met in local churches and members' homes well into the 1940s. By the end of January, a citizen delegation was organized to go to Richmond in an effort to lobby legislators to stop the proceedings.

At the following town council meeting, a petition was presented that opposed the establishment of a liquor store in town. This petition had also been sent to the ABC Board in Richmond. Councilman Wiley offered a revised resolution that would have rescinded the town's request to establish a liquor store. After some discussion, the council decided to table the resolution until the next meeting.

The following month, at the February meeting, the town council voted on Councilman Wiley's revised resolution, and it passed. Only one councilmember, Councilman Robb, voted against the new resolution. Councilman Robb then resigned, saying that he felt his "efficiency as a member of the Council is now useless. I have no wish to remain as a member under these conditions."

The strong feelings about the liquor store are exemplified in an old photograph from the Herndon Historical Society's J. Berkley Green Collection, which shows how Councilmembers Gibson, Linkins and Wiley

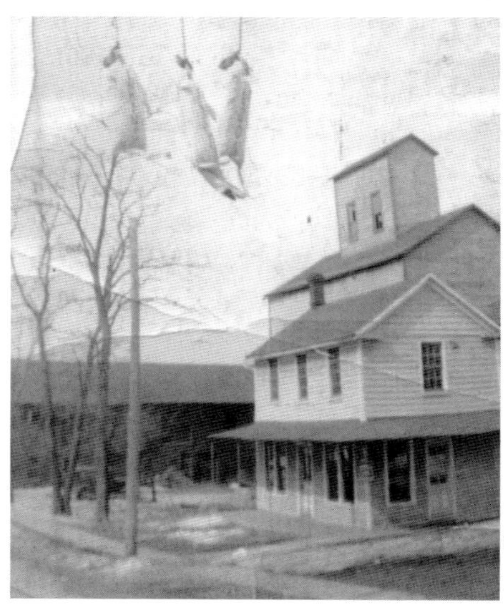

Town councilmen hung in effigy on Elden Street after an unpopular vote on liquor. *J. Berkley Green Collection of the Herndon Historical Society.*

were hung in effigy across Elden Street in the center of town, using sandbags with their names marked on each. These three men had voted in favor of liquor sales in January and had reversed their votes in February.

Herndon resident Henry Grafton De Butts (1876–1953), a local business owner and a former town councilman—who also had a penchant for writing poetry—wrote a poem that described the effigy episode when it occurred. The poem was called "The Sad Death of Three Councilmen":

Herndon's in a terrible fix,
Someone has raised its ire.
They have hung our three best councilmen,
On an electricity wire.

It really hurt our feelings,
And we tried to get them down.
And with the help of Mr. Electric man,
We brought them safely to the ground.

But boy it was really awful,
And was sure a bitter cup,
When they nailed them to 3 big oak trees,
And then burned them up.

By July 1936, Councilman Gibson made a motion to rescind the ordinance that had been passed in March 1935, which regulated the sale of beer in town. That passed unanimously. However, he then immediately proposed another ordinance that regulated not only beer but also wine and ale. It would be unlawful to sell these items in town after 11:00 p.m. on weekdays as well as on Sundays and election days. Again, this passed unanimously.

There is no other discussion of an ABC liquor store in any of the town council minutes for the remainder of 1936. However, the establishment of a liquor store in the town of Herndon was somehow miraculously accomplished later that year.

A 1936 Annual Report of the state ABC Board indicated that ABC store No. 170 opened in Herndon on June 18, 1936. This location is confirmed by a July 2, 1936 issue of the *Herndon News-Observer* newspaper, which described how an ABC inspector was in town, training personnel. Two people would be appointed—one as manager and one as clerk. The article stated that an ABC store was located on Elden Street in a building formerly used as the business office of the Horn Motor Company, later the location of the Stohlman Subaru dealership at 770 Elden Street, near the intersection of Center Street. A subsequent 1959 lease document confirmed this location as well, saying the store was located in the left (west) side of the building.

Virgie Wynkoop, who was one hundred years old in 1979, recalled that the town's first ABC store was located in a small building on Elden Street and later moved into the Dulles Park Shopping Center, built in 1965.

Today, the town of Herndon has two ABC stores. Alcohol may be bought in licensed establishments any day of the week with no restrictions on what hours it may be consumed.

16

The Herndon Community Cannery

A Cherished Community Amenity for Forty Years

One unique amenity in Herndon was the Herndon Community Cannery, which operated behind Herndon Middle School on Locust Street from 1944 to 1984.

In June 1944, the *Fairfax Herald* newspaper announced that the community cannery was being built on the Herndon High School grounds (which later became the Herndon Middle School) and was almost complete, inviting residents to come see the new facility. The cannery was a public service supported by state and county funds. Any family could use the cannery to can food for their own use.

The purpose of the cannery was to encourage food production and Victory gardens in order to conserve foods during the period when there was rationing during World War II. A Victory garden is a home garden planted to increase food production during the time of war. This would help prevent food shortages, ensuring that the U.S. War Department had enough food for our soldiers fighting around the world and save money that could be spent elsewhere for the military.

During the 1940s, rationing became necessary to support the war effort. Rationed items included things such as gasoline, aluminum, steel and electricity. Food products were also rationed, such as sugar, fruits, meat, cheese and butter. The cannery influenced residents to grow and can their own food supplies so that they could have enough food throughout the winter.

Initially, the cannery was run by school employees. Home economics or agriculture teachers were employed to supervise the cannery. These

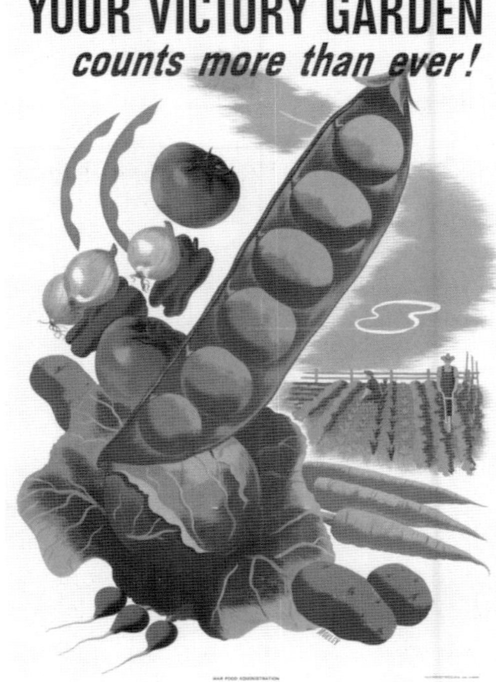

Left: American World War II–era poster promoting Victory gardens, 1945. Morley, artist. *Wikimedia Commons*.

Below: Herndon High School students standing outside the cannery. *Margaret Cyrus.*

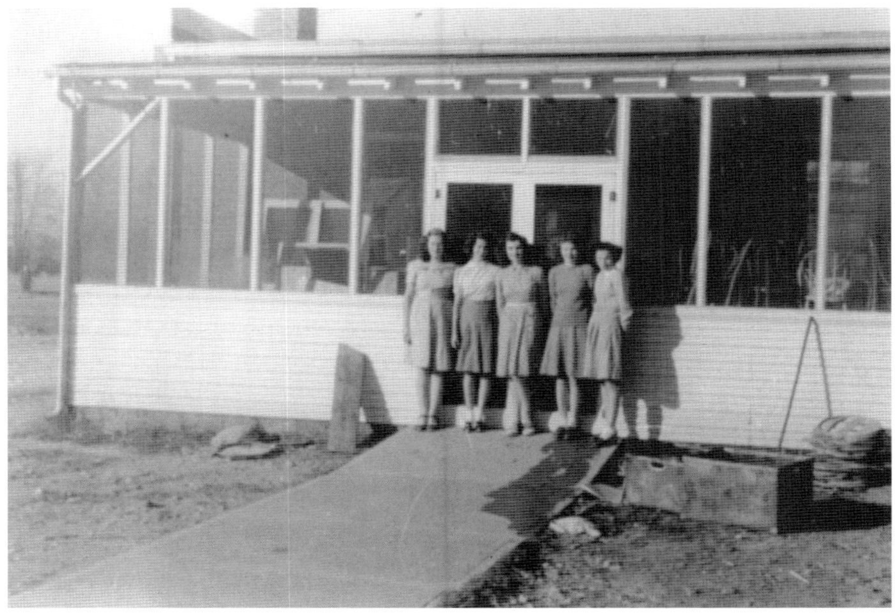

teachers may have done this as a sideline job for additional income. As time went on, local residents who were not teachers were hired to supervise the cannery.

The cannery was open to the public. Any person who used the cannery had to pay for each can they used. The cannery usually provided two different size cans. In 1948, number two cans cost five cents each, while number three cans cost six cents each.

The cannery was open three days per week, usually Monday and Friday mornings and Wednesday evenings. It was a seasonal operation, opening in the summer after the school year was over and closing at the end of November until the next summer. Articles were regularly published in newspapers to announce the seasonal opening and closing dates of the cannery each year. Those announcements included the hours of the cannery, the price of the cans and the telephone number that could be used to make an appointment. Postcard announcements were also used. An example of one such postcard with a Herndon postmark dated July 8, 1948, was found, addressed to "Box Holder," announcing the cannery's hours and prices for that season. These postcards were placed in each Herndon resident's mailbox in the post office formerly located in Herndon's Town Hall.

In the early years, residents were encouraged to bring their own salt, sugar, vinegar and any special spices that they might want to use with their fruits or vegetables, if needed. Canners were also encouraged to bring their own paring knives as well as dish towels and soap. As the years went on, the operation became more efficient, with most utensils and supplies being available at the cannery.

Those who wanted to use the cannery had to call ahead for an appointment. At the appointed time, residents would bring in their food. The cannery supervisors provided instructions on how to prepare the food and how to use the cannery equipment. The cannery supervisors provided advice and assistance while the residents provided their own food and labor.

An article in a 1976 *Reston Times* newspaper described one resident's initial experience in the cannery:

> *A few days before my arrival at the cannery, I called the manager to set up an appointment. At that time she asked what vegetables were to be canned and in what quantity. Had there been special preparation necessary, she would have given me instructions.*
>
> *At the appointed hour I arrived with my little sack of green beans. It was somewhat overwhelming to find that there were some customers there with as*

HERNDON COMMUNITY CANNERY
CANNERY HOURS

Tuesday and Friday - 8:30 to 4:30) Daylight
Wednesday - 4 - 10) Time

Cost of cans - No. 3 - 6¢; No. 2 - 5¢

Call 259 for appointment
Bring all utensils necessary for canning your products and please plan to clean all cannery equip,ment used by you.

Remember, if you want to can,
make an appointment

A 1948 postcard announcing the reopening of the cannery for the season. *Herndon Historical Society.*

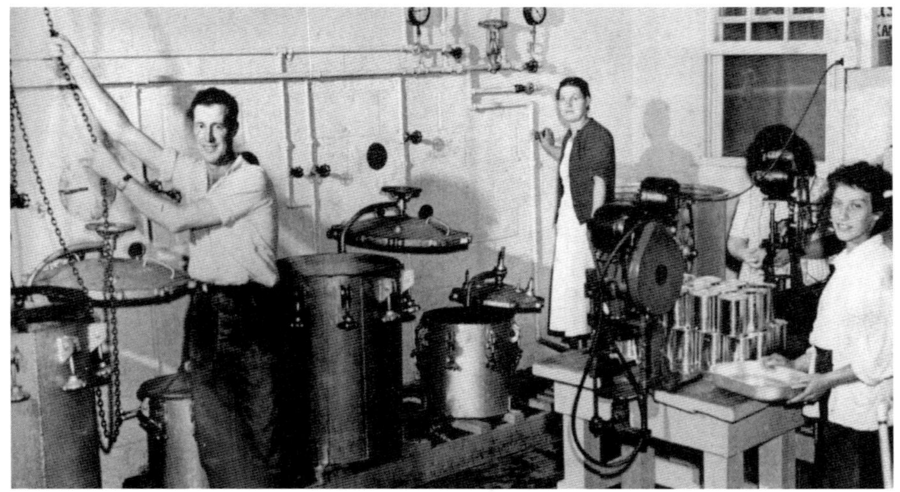

Inside Herndon's community cannery. *Herndon High School yearbook, 1950.*

many as six bushels of produce to be processed. This was not the first visit for a couple of the patrons.

The initial preparations were carried out on a screen porch built into what once was the kitchen when the intermediate school was a high school.

The air was decidedly friendly and there was a feeling of camaraderie between the peelers, shuckers and slicers as they readied their peaches,

> *tomatoes and beans. A breeze brought pleasant relief from the heat of the kitchen a few steps away.*
>
> *The first step was to wash the beans and snap the ends....Next, the beans went into a cauldron and were cooked in water until they reached a rolling boil. Then the vegetables were put into cans and were placed in a steam bath until the temperatures of the contents reached 160 degrees, the temperature necessary for safe sealing.*
>
> *My sealed cans were lowered into a mesh cage into one of three enormous pressure cookers.* [I saw the manager help a lady] *operate the heavy hydraulic lift and the locks on the pressure cooker. The beans were cooked at 240 degrees for 25 minutes.*
>
> *While this step was being carried out I had an opportunity to chat with other canners. Four women, all sisters-in-law, were busy peeling and quartering* [four bushels of] *tomatoes. They were having a marvelous time catching up on each other's gossip.*

Indeed, the cannery was also a social place where friendships were made and where neighbors could meet, chat and exchange recipes. Residents from all around the area used the cannery, from Floris to Reston to Great Falls.

One Great Falls resident who had used the cannery for over thirty years recalled:

> *Remember that day that we packed 500 cans of tuna? Spent a week on a tuna boat off Montauk, N.Y., some years ago. Caught fish all day long, and each night we'd clean 'em and freeze 'em. At the end of the week I loaded my pickup, a layer of ice and a layer of fish, like that. Started out from Long Island at 9:00 at night and got home at 6:00 in the morning. Spent the whole next day at the Cannery puttin' that tuna in pint cans.*

At some point in time, the cannery came to be operated under the supervision of the Fairfax County Department of Extension and Continuing Education. The annual budget was between $10,000 and $12,000 per year, which was partially offset by the fees the patrons paid for each can. By the 1970s, county residents paid twenty-five cents per can, while nonresidents paid thirty cents per can. By 1982, nonresidents paid forty cents per can.

Many current and former Herndon area residents still have fond memories of the cannery. One longtime resident, who taught home

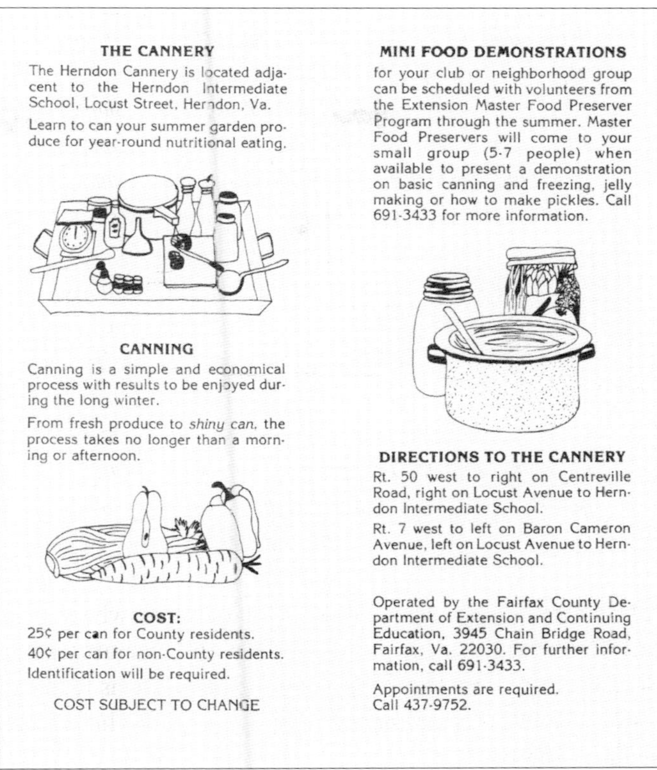

THE CANNERY

The Herndon Cannery is located adjacent to the Herndon Intermediate School, Locust Street, Herndon, Va.

Learn to can your summer garden produce for year-round nutritional eating.

CANNING

Canning is a simple and economical process with results to be enjoyed during the long winter.

From fresh produce to *shiny can*, the process takes no longer than a morning or afternoon.

COST:

25¢ per can for County residents.

40¢ per can for non-County residents.

Identification will be required.

COST SUBJECT TO CHANGE

MINI FOOD DEMONSTRATIONS

for your club or neighborhood group can be scheduled with volunteers from the Extension Master Food Preserver Program through the summer. Master Food Preservers will come to your small group (5-7 people) when available to present a demonstration on basic canning and freezing, jelly making or how to make pickles. Call 691-3433 for more information.

DIRECTIONS TO THE CANNERY

Rt. 50 west to right on Centreville Road, right on Locust Avenue to Herndon Intermediate School.

Rt. 7 west to left on Baron Cameron Avenue, left on Locust Avenue to Herndon Intermediate School.

Operated by the Fairfax County Department of Extension and Continuing Education, 3945 Chain Bridge Road, Fairfax, Va. 22030. For further information, call 691-3433.

Appointments are required.
Call 437-9752.

A Herndon cannery information flyer from 1982. *Herndon Historical Society.*

economics at Herndon High School in the 1960s, said she would sometimes help with food preparation at the cannery. She said, "People would come from as far away as the Blue Ridge Mountains. Some would back their pickup trucks to the cannery and unload bushels of tomatoes and beans." In addition to fruits and vegetables, she recalled that some people also canned things like venison and sausage. She also noted that the last thing that was canned at the cannery was water by a religious group. "These were the days before you could buy bottled water," she noted.

Virginia Clarity, who grew up in Herndon, remembers how her father worked as one of the managers at the cannery. As a young girl, she—along with her mother—would help out at the cannery, doing food preparation on the hot screened-in porch.

Dallas "Porter" Hutchison, who grew up in Chantilly and attended Herndon High School as a young boy, once recalled how he and his school chums were sometimes conscripted to help work in the cannery. As an adult, he and his wife, Libby, were regular patrons of the cannery. Libby once said, "It beats messing up your own place."

By 1982, the future of the Herndon Community Cannery seemed uncertain. In April 1982, the *Reston Times* reported that the Fairfax County Board of Supervisors approved enough money to keep the cannery open for a while but acknowledged that its future was in doubt.

In May 1983, as a result of the passage of the 1984 fiscal year county budget, it was reported that the cannery would no longer receive county money and, as a result, the cannery would be forced to close.

17

"This Town Needs a Good Party!"

Herndon's Tradition of Public Festivals

Herndon Day

Long before there was the Herndon Festival, there was another large town-wide celebration that dates back to 1919: Herndon Day. Much like the current Herndon Festival, Herndon Day was a large-scale outdoor event that involved many individuals, groups and businesses in town, attracting people from all around the county.

Frances Darlington was the granddaughter of J.J. Darlington, a prominent Washington lawyer who owned an estate in Herndon. Frances often spent her summers in Herndon and described the Herndon Day event this way:

> *Every year, usually in July, "Herndon Day" was held in the school grounds. This was the highlight of the summer and a red letter day! There were contests, prizes, a poor greased pig to be caught, a baseball game and rows and rows of booths selling the most mouth-watering things, all home made from fired chicken, country ham sandwiches, potatoes salad and pies of all kinds and sizes, shape and flavor of homemade cakes imaginable.*

The school grounds she referred to were that of the old Herndon High School, formerly located on Locust Street.

There are many articles and advertisements in the *Fairfax Herald* and *Herndon News-Observer* from the years 1919 to 1933 that described Herndon

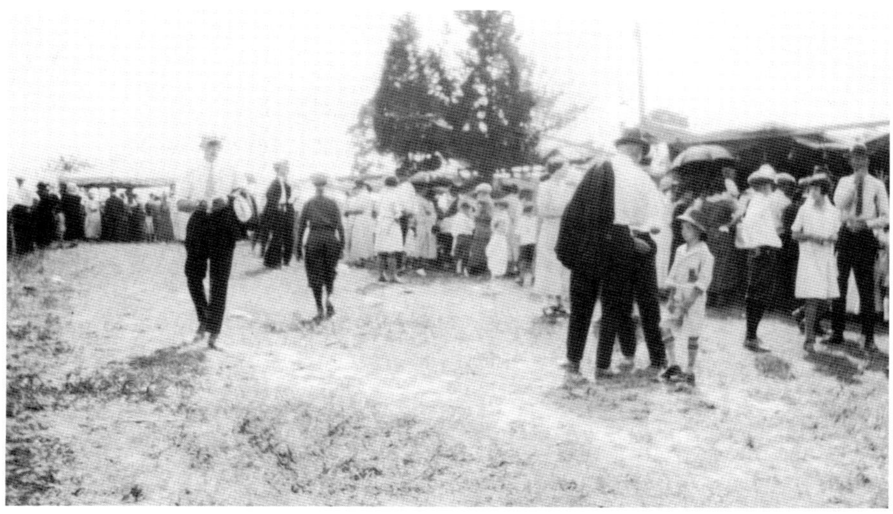

Herndon Day, circa 1925. *Fairfax County Public Library Photographic Archive.*

Day. Advertisements boasted that there would be "Something Doing Every Minute" and that Herndon Day would be "Bigger and Better in Every Way."

Many activities and attractions were planned for the big day. It included baseball and tennis tournaments, agricultural and mechanical exhibits, a band, a minstrel troupe, a musical club, a fortune teller and a horseshoe contest. A barrel of flour would be given to the largest family on the grounds. There would be evening dances and prizes for the prettiest baby and for the boy or girl with the most freckles. Additional articles showed that other attractions at Herndon Day would include bingo, gypsy tents, clowns, trap shooting, races, tug o' war, beauty pageants, wrestling matches, vaudeville sketches, horseshoe contests, baby carriage shows and a callithumpian parade.

One 1925 advertisement said admission to the Herndon Day event was twenty-five cents for adults and fifteen cents for children. In 1924, the Herndon Town Council paid $4 for police duty for Herndon Day that year, as the town only had one police officer at that time. Herndon Day typically netted between $800 and $1,200.

Herndon Day was sponsored by the Citizen's Association and the Community School League, a group that supported Herndon schools and later became the Parent-Teacher Association (PTA). It raised money to pay for school bonds. A 1924 *Fairfax Herald* article said the Herndon Day money would be "used to aid in the erection of the addition to the school

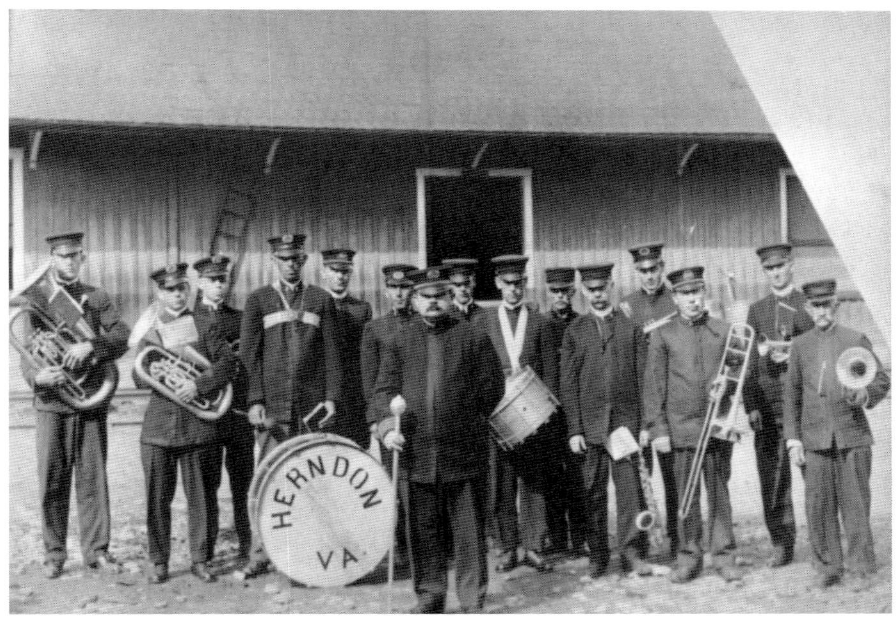

The Herndon band from the 1910s and 1920s most likely played at Herndon Day events. *J. Berkley Green Collection of the Herndon Historical Society.*

building." One *Herndon News-Observer* article encouraged everyone in town to participate in the festivities:

> *Everyone in town and vicinity is urged to co-operate and make this day a success from all standpoints. Two bonds on the school building were paid last year by the Citizens' Association and Community School League and this year it is hoped to do even better. To work for Herndon Day and retire bonds will prevent another bond issue for school purposes.*

FIREMAN'S CARNIVAL

In addition to Herndon Day, another big event that happened in Herndon during that time was the Herndon Carnival, which was held in the fall and sponsored by the Herndon Chamber of Commerce. A 1925 news article said the third annual carnival would be a "very enjoyable affair" and would be held in October. It too had a variety of attractions, including a trade parade, a kiddie parade, dancers, music, wholesome amusements and good eats.

Former resident Ruth Updike, who was once interviewed by Kate O'Connor, recalled:

> *The Firemen of Herndon had a fireman's carnival or fireman's day; it must have been in the mid-1920s. It was held where the Town Hall is now, that was a park, and it was Halloween at the time. There were contests for businesses and for people. I remember one time there was one for costumes and Mom won because she was dressed as a bride—that must have been '23 or something like that. There was a contest for the store or business house decorated for the keeping of the holiday and it seemed Daddy did because he won a prize of twenty dollars.*

Carnivals were common throughout the 1930s. Herndon's fire station was built in 1929, and the Herndon Volunteer Fire Department was chartered that same year. It held carnivals to raise money to pay off the debt for Herndon's first permanent firehouse on Station Street as well as to raise the funds they needed for other fire equipment.

THE HERNDON FESTIVAL

Fireman's carnivals eventually waned but were supplanted by a new event in 1981: the Herndon Festival, a throwback to Herndon Day.

Flashback to 1980: Jimmy Carter was president, and the town of Herndon's population was a little over thirteen thousand. At that time, the town had a small annual arts and crafts show near the Town Hall, but a Herndon resident named Arno Randall wanted more. Randall had just been elected as an officer in the Herndon Jaycees, a civic organization that was very active in town at that time. Trying to think of an activity that would bring local businesses, civic organizations, residents and shoppers together, he recalled a festival that he had once seen in his travels. A festival was something that he thought would work in Herndon.

Randall went to see Herndon's director of the Parks and Recreation Department, Art Anselene, and pitched the idea to him. Anselene mulled over the idea for a few months. He eventually agreed to the idea of trying to merge together the town's arts and crafts show with Randall's festival idea.

The small Parks and Recreation Department, along with the Jaycees, started planning the first festival. As they planned, the initial thought was

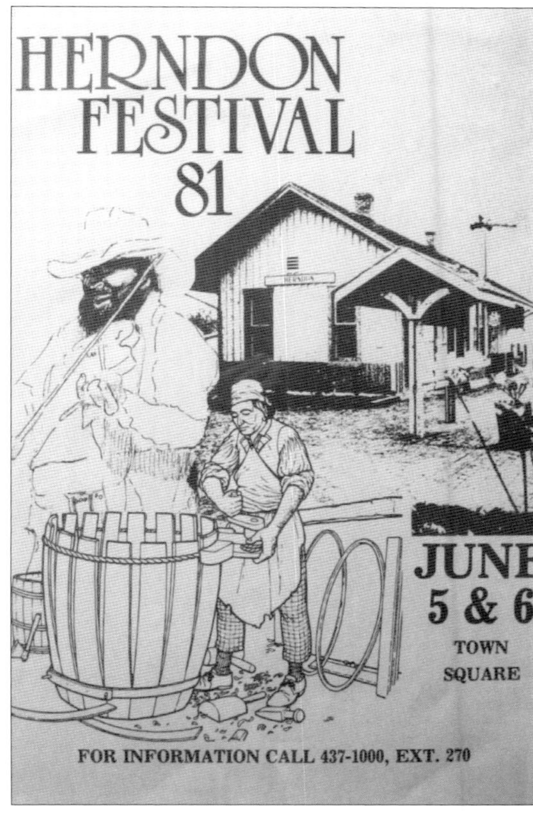

Left: Promotional poster for the first Herndon Festival in 1981. *Town of Herndon Department of Parks and Recreation.*

Below: Town Square, 1970s. The Herndon Festival was held here for many years. *Herndon Historical Society.*

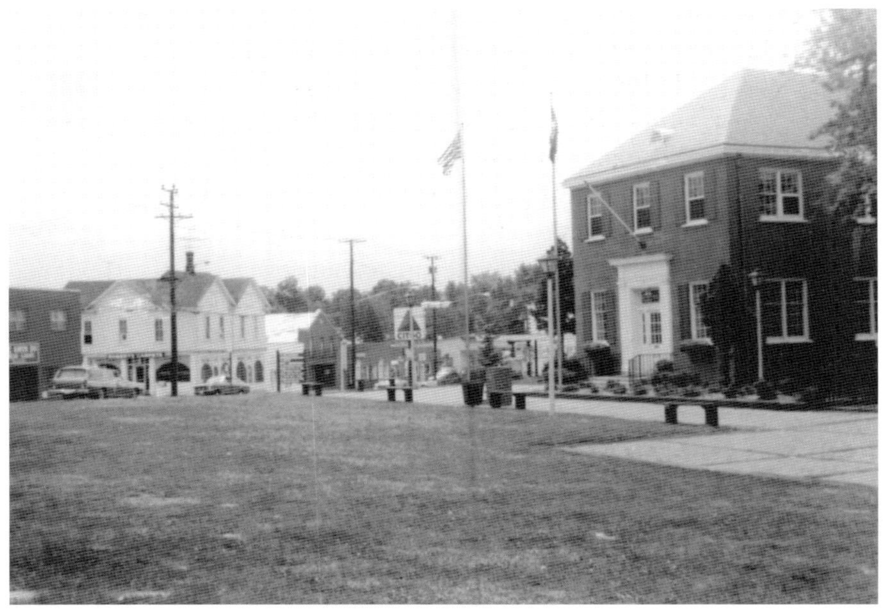

that they might need about $3,000 to fund the festival. However, as planning went on it became apparent that $8,000 to $12,000 would be needed. The planners arranged for advertising in the local newspaper, the *Herndon Observer*, but upfront money was needed to help get the first festival off the ground.

Randall approached Mayor Rust about the festival idea, asking him if the town would be willing to sponsor it, with the understanding that the festival would break even and not leave the town in the red. Randall told Rust, "Do you know what this town needs? This town needs a good party!" Rust agreed, and the town became the sponsor.

The first festival was held in 1981 in the town square by the Town Hall. It included a concert, arts and crafts, food and entertainment. The headline act was a famous bluegrass band called the Country Gentlemen. About two hundred volunteers, many from the Jaycees, staffed the festival.

That first festival was conducted on a Friday and Saturday and drew about 3,500 people. Within a couple of years, it was expanded to include Sunday. Several years later, Thursday evening and a carnival were added.

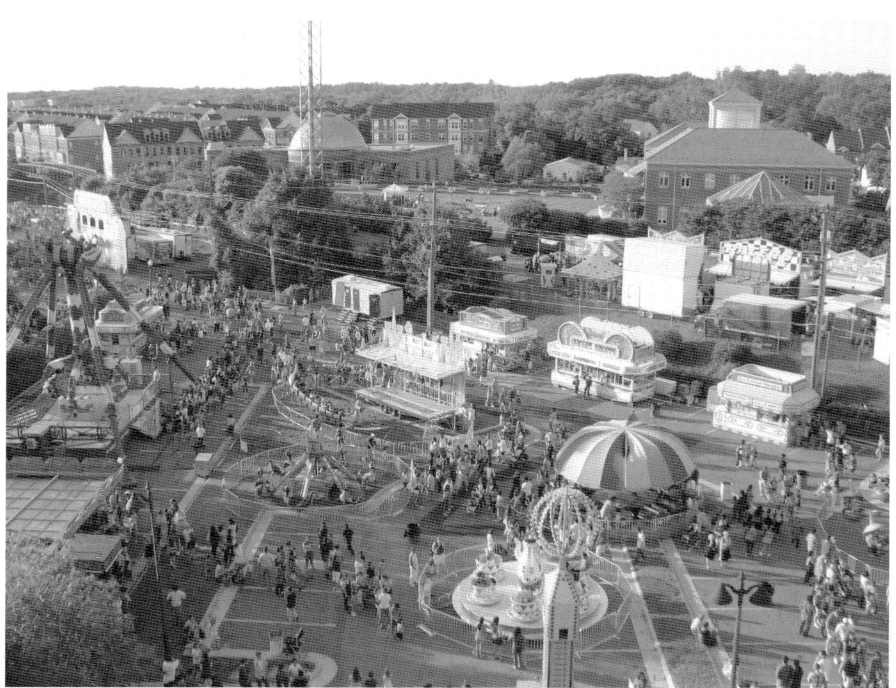

The Herndon Festival, 2014. *Town of Herndon.*

Over the course of the last many years, the Herndon Festival has come a long way. By the year 2000, it was estimated that approximately eighty-five thousand to ninety-five thousand people were attending the festival. The festival that once took place on Lynn Street and the grass around the Town Hall expanded to include all the streets and open spaces in Herndon's downtown core. A committee continues to plan the event each year, and approximately eight hundred volunteers help make it a success. Randall, who later moved to Maryland, continued to serve on the executive steering committee. Arno got his party.

For one hundred years, Herndon has had a long-standing tradition of outdoor, town-wide public events. These events make Herndon unique, bring the townspeople together, are fun for all and help raise money for worthy causes.

18

The Caboose Comes to Herndon!

The Story of How Herndon's Red Caboose Became a Town Landmark

One popular point of interest in downtown Herndon is the red caboose that sits on Lynn Street, adjacent to Herndon's railroad depot and the Washington and Old Dominion hike and bike trail—formerly the W&OD Railroad line.

The idea to procure a caboose for Herndon was originally raised by Herndon Historical Society member and train buff George Moore in January 1989. At the time, the Norfolk Southern Corporation started selling and donating its caboose fleet as they were being replaced by modern electronic "End of Train Devices." Moore, claiming "every town needs a caboose," thought it was a perfect opportunity. The Herndon Historical Society membership voted to acquire a caboose for Herndon, and a Caboose Committee was formed.

Through the efforts of the historical society's Caboose Committee, which Moore chaired, the society was able to successfully persuade the rail company to donate a 1949 Class 8 center-style cupola caboose, a design used on many U.S. railroads after World War II. The all-steel caboose was built by the Wheeling & Lake Erie Railway in its shops at Ironville, Ohio. It weighed 45,300 pounds and measured about thirty-seven feet long, ten feet wide and almost fourteen feet high. Had this forty-year-old caboose not been acquired by the historical society, it would have surely been taken to the scrapyard.

After a series of railroad company mergers, the caboose became NW 557748 when the Norfolk & Western Railroad acquired the New York, Chicago & St. Louis Railroad Company (or Nickel Plate Road) in 1964.

After another merger in the 1980s, Norfolk & Western later became the Norfolk Southern Railway.

Interestingly, the original caboose that Norfolk Southern was going to donate to Herndon was NW 557547, a different style caboose that did not have a cupola. However, Moore insisted that "a real caboose has a cupola on top!" As a result, he was able to effect a change and got a caboose with a cupola instead.

Cabooses are manned railroad cars coupled at the end of a freight train. The purpose of a caboose is to act as an operating headquarters and office for the train personnel. A conductor would spend time sitting at his desk in the caboose, filling out waybills and wheel reports having to do with the ownership, content, mileage and weight of each car of his train. Brakemen would also ride in the caboose, keeping look out to spot any trouble that might appear on the rail ahead. The brakemen would also take care of routine tasks such as switching, flagging and signaling. The caboose had bunks, as well as lockers for the trainmen to store their food. Using the caboose stove, they would cook their meals or make a hot cup of coffee.

The Caboose Committee of the Herndon Historical Society worked to plan the many logistics associated with the procurement and arrival of the caboose. In addition to the committee's many communications with the rail company, it discussed possible locations for the caboose to be displayed, coordinated with town officials, obtained approval from the town's Heritage Preservation Review Board, obtained permission from the Virginia Power Company to place the caboose on its transmission right-of-way, coordinated the transportation arrangements for the caboose and did research on what color the caboose should be painted. The plan was to place the caboose near the Herndon Depot Museum and have it be a focal point of town, a static display that would be open on select days.

Many entities assisted with the move and placement of the donated caboose. Gordon and Associates, along with the town engineer, prepared a site plan for the caboose. The caboose was delivered from Norfolk to Manassas at no charge by the railroad company. Once the caboose arrived in Manassas, the Herndon Public Works Department and the McGee Crane Rental Company loaded the caboose onto a flatbed truck for transport to its new home. The Manassas, Prince William and Herndon Police Departments assisted with the move. The efforts of the McGee Crane Rental Company were donated to the caboose effort. The Manassas fire marshal and chief inspector also assisted. The Herndon Public Works Department prepared a small section of track bed with iron rails that would serve as the resting place for the newly arriving caboose. Chantilly Crushed Stone Company donated the stone used on the track bed. Once in Herndon, the caboose was unloaded onto its new track bed.

The caboose arrived in Herndon on a cold November day with snow on the ground. The flatbed truck on which it was carried traveled on a route from the Manassas rail yard, north along Route 28 and into Herndon via Sterling Road. Some motorists honked their horns to welcome the caboose. Historical society members helped warm up both observers and workers alike, serving free coffee and donuts in the depot. Soon after, restoration work began.

Although the Town of Herndon would own the caboose and pay for its insurance, the Herndon Historical Society was responsible for its restoration, inside and out. Once in Herndon, the caboose exterior was power washed, primed, patched and painted. The paint job cost $1,600. Some windows were replaced, locks were installed and it was fitted with ladder guards. Later, interior painting was completed, and a caboose stove was installed. The W&OD lettering was painted on the exterior, even though the caboose never served on the Washington & Old Dominion Railroad. The caboose was renumbered 504 by the Herndon Historical

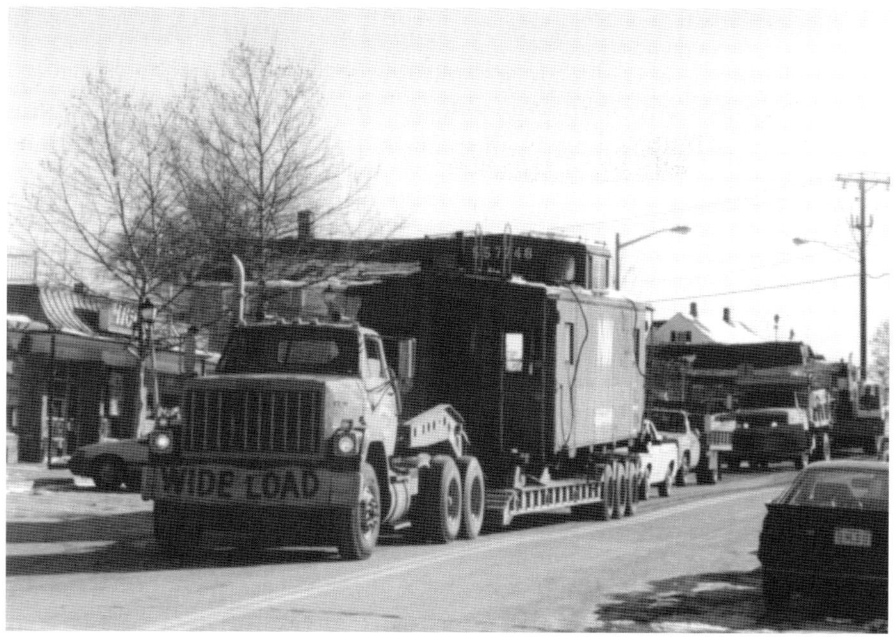

The caboose is transported down Lynn Street, 1989. *Herndon Historical Society.*

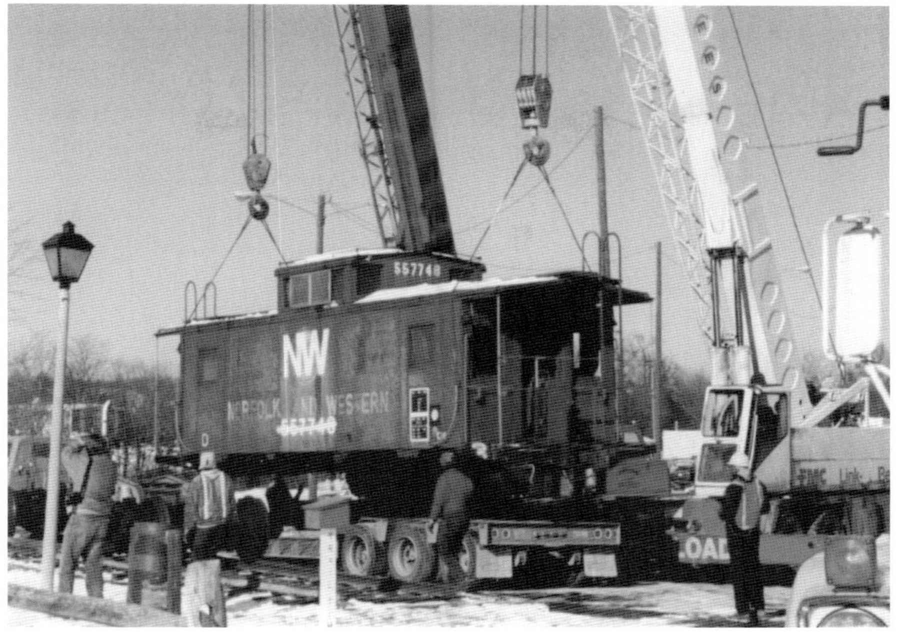

A crane sets the caboose on its new track bed in Herndon, 1989. *Herndon Historical Society.*

Society to honor the 500 Series cabooses that formerly served Herndon on the Washington & Old Dominion Railroad. In 2008, with a generous grant to the Herndon Historical Society by the Nelson and Katherine Post Foundation, the interior was further restored and the windows were improved to make them watertight.

On April 21, 1990, the historical society organized a dedication ceremony for the Herndon caboose. The society went on to organize various fundraising events, with proceeds going toward the restoration of the caboose. Fundraisers included yard sales and a benefit concert at the Industrial Strength Theatre. Many town residents and nonprofit organizations also made contributions toward the restoration of the caboose.

Following the death of George Moore in 2003, the caboose was dedicated in his memory. A memorial plaque was placed next to the caboose in his honor.

Today, the Herndon Historical Society continues to monitor the caboose's condition and to fund its interior maintenance. The caboose is open for special events, such as the historical society's annual train show. The caboose and the adjacent railroad depot are reminders of the town's rail history. The

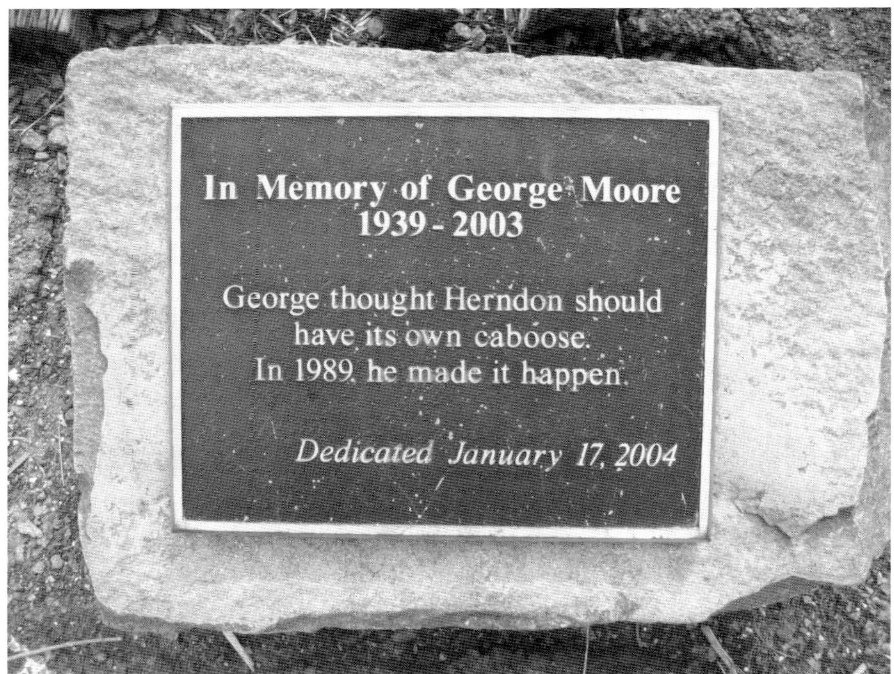

A plaque honoring George Moore is located next to the Herndon caboose. *Barbara Glakas.*

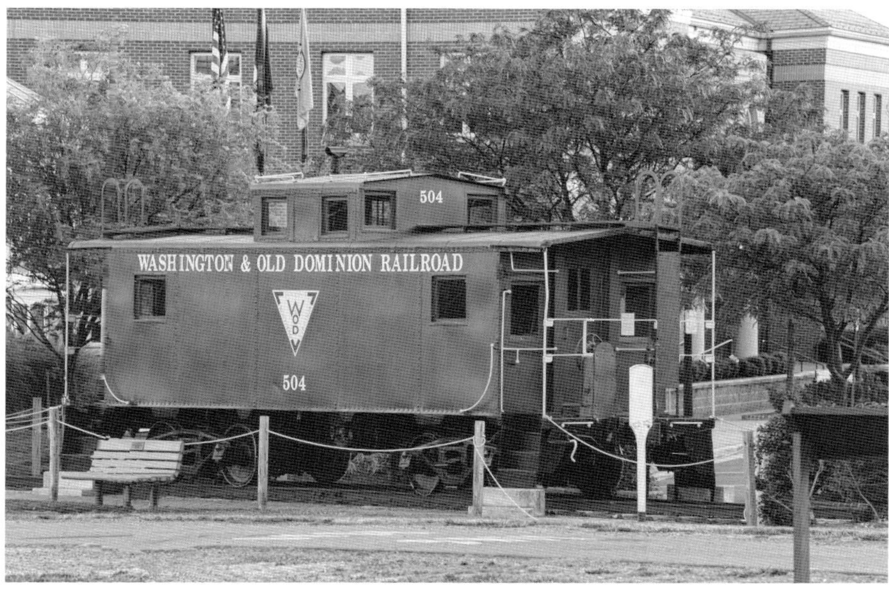

The caboose sits next to the Herndon Municipal Center. *Floyd Wellershaus.*

Herndon Depot Museum includes a room with rail artifacts, many original to the Washington & Old Dominion Railroad. The caboose is a popular stop for locals and tourists alike. On any given day, one can see wedding parties taking pictures next to the caboose or children peering into its windows.

Bibliography

Books

Bowers, Robert G., and James F. Brewer. *Cabooses of the Norfolk and Western.* Roanoke, VA: Norfolk & Western Historical Society, 1994.

Buckland, Eric W. *Mosby Men III.* Centreville, VA: That Fateful Night Press, 2012.

Buell, Thomas R. *Buell, Genealogic Notes on Buell Family.* Effingham, IL: E.W. Petty Company, 1971.

Castleman, Virginia Carter. *Reminiscences of an Oldest Inhabitant (A Nineteenth Century Chronicle).* Herndon, VA: Herndon Historical Society, 1976.

Conrad, Judy, ed. *The Herndon Observer's Neighbor to Neighbor Cookbook.* Herndon, VA: Herndon Publishing Company, Inc., 1982.

———. *Story of an American Tragedy: Survivors' Accounts of the Sinking of the Steamship Central America.* Columbus, OH: Columbus-America Discovery Group, Inc., 1988.

Cross, David. *A Tale of Two Statues: The William Wells Statues at Gettysburg and Burlington, Vermont.* Barre: Vermont Historical Society, 2005.

Fairfax County Stories, 1607–2007. County of Fairfax, VA: Fairfax County 2007 Community Citizen Planning Committee, 2007.

Finney, Jack. *Forgotten News: The Crime of the Century and Other Lost Stories.* New York: Simon & Schuster, 1986.

The Fortnightly Club and Library Association of Herndon, The First Hundred Years, 1889–1989. Herndon: Fortnightly Club and Library Association of Herndon, Virginia, 1989.

Geddes, Jean. *Fairfax County Historical Highlights from 1607*. Fairfax County, VA: Dellinger's Publishers, 1967.

Greear, Virginia. *Service Record, World War I and II, Herndon, Virginia.* Herndon, VA: Herndon Post 91, American Legion and Herndon Unit 91, American Legion Auxiliary, 1949.

Guillaudeu, David A. *Washington & Old Dominion Railroad.* Charleston, SC: Arcadia Publishing, 2013.

Hakenson, Donald C., and Charles V. Mauro. *A Tour Guide and History of Col. John S. Mosby's Combat Operations in Fairfax County, Virginia*. Alexandria, VA: HMS Productions, 2013.

Harsh, Joseph L., ed. *Yearbook: The Historical Society of Fairfax County, Virginia.* Vol. 20, *1984–1985.* Fairfax County, VA: Historical Society of Fairfax County, 1985.

Harwood, Herbert H., Jr. *Rails to the Blue Ridge: The Washington and Old Dominion, 1847–1968.* Fairfax Station: Northern Virginia Regional Park Authority, 2000.

Henriques, Peter R., ed. *Northern Virginia Heritage, A Journal of Local History*. Vol. 2, no. 2. Vienna, VA: Better Impressions, Inc., 1980.

Jones, Laura Reasoner. *Herndon.* Charleston, SC: Arcadia Publishing, 2011.

Kilmer, Kenton, and Donald Sweig. *The Fairfax Family in Fairfax County: A Brief History.* Fairfax, VA: Fairfax County Office of Comprehensive Planning in Cooperation with the Fairfax County History Commission, 1992.

Kinder, Gary. *Ship of Gold in the Deep Blue Sea.* New York: Atlantic Monthly Press, 1998.

Klare, Normand E. *The Final Voyage of the Central America, 1857*. Spokane, WA: Arthur Clark Company, 1992.

LeVine, Donald. *Herndon, The Land: 1649–1900.* Herndon, VA: self-published, 1982.

Mauro, Charles V. *Herndon: A History in Images.* Charleston, SC: The History Press, 2005.

———. *Herndon: A Town and Its History.* Charleston, SC: The History Press, 2004.

———. *A Southern Spy in Northern Virginia: The Civil War Album of Laura Ratcliffe.* Charleston, SC: The History Press, 2009.

Mosby, John S. *The Memoirs of Colonel John S. Mosby.* Boston, MA: Little, Brown, and Company, 1917.

Netherton, Nan, Donald Sweig, Janice Artmel, Patricia Hichin and Patrick Reed. *Fairfax County, Virginia, A History.* Fairfax County, VA: Fairfax County Board of Supervisors, 1992.

Payne, Brooke. *The Paynes of Virginia*. 2nd ed. Richmond, VA: W. Byrd Press, 1937.

Peck, Margaret C. *Around Herndon*. Charleston, SC: Arcadia Publishing, 2004.

———. *Stories from Floris of a Time Gone By*. Floris, VA: Floris Friends, 2000.

Poland, Charles Preston, Jr. *Dumbarton, Dranesville, Virginia*. Fairfax, VA: Fairfax County Office of Comprehensive Planning Publications Staff, 1974.

Pritchard, Jeanne Robb. *The Mouse's Tail Is Gone*. N.p.: Haiti Fund Publications, 2010.

Pryor, Elizabeth Brown. *Frying Pan Farm*. Fairfax County: Office of Comprehensive Planning Fairfax County, Virginia, and Fairfax County Board of Supervisors, 1979.

Rado, Lisa, and Karin de Weille. *Herndon: Growing Gracefully, A Case Study of the Successful Transition of a Small Virginian Community into the Modern World*. McLean, VA: Langley High School, 1983.

Ramage, James A. *Grey Ghost: The Life of Col. John Singleton Mosby*. Lexington: University Press of Kentucky, 1999.

Rose Hill Civic Association. *The Rambler, Journal of the Rose Hill Civic Association*. Alexandria, VA: private printer, June 1984.

Schneider, Lottie Dyer. *A Chronicle of the Dyer-Johnson Family*. Radford, VA: Commonwealth Press, Inc., 1963.

———. *Memories of Herndon, Virginia*. Radford, VA: Commonwealth Press, Inc., 1962.

Scott, Major John. *Partisan Life with Col. John S Mosby*. New York: Harper & Brothers, Publishers, 1867.

Thomas, Emory M. *Bold Dragoon: The Life of J.E.B. Stuart*. Norman: University of Oklahoma Press, 1986.

Wert, Jeffry D. *Mosby's Rangers*. New York: Simon & Schuster Paperbacks, 1990.

Williams, Ames W. *The Washington and Old Dominion Railroad*. Alexandria, VA: Meridian Sun Press, 1977.

——— *The Washington and Old Dominion Railroad, 1847–1968*. Springfield, VA: Capital Traction Quarterly, 1970.

Williamson, James J. *Mosby's Rangers: A Record of the Operations of the Forty-Third Battalion Virginia Cavalry, from Its Organization to the Surrender*. New York: Ralph B. Kenyon, 1896.

Young, N. Peyton. *Yearbook: The Historical Society of Fairfax County, Virginia*. Vol. 4, *1955: History of the Dividing Line Between Fairfax and Loudoun Counties*. Fairfax County, VA: Historical Society of Fairfax County, 1955.

Newspapers and Periodicals

Alexandria Gazette
Burlington Free Press
Evening Star
Fairfax Herald
Fairfax Independent
Herndon Connection
Herndon News-Observer
Herndon Observer
Herndon Times
Herndon Tribune
Local News (of Alexandria)
New York Times
Reston Times
Virginia News
Washington Post
Weekly Comet

Other Sources

African American Landowners, Churches, Schools and Businesses in Fairfax County (1860–1900). Virginia: Black Women United for Actions, 2009.

Ancestry.com.

Bicksler, Edna A. *The Beginning and the End of a Railroad.* Paper, May 1, 1979.

Celebrating One Hundred and Forty Years Methodism in Herndon, Virginia, 1857–1997. Herndon United Methodist Church.

The Congressional Medal of Honor Society.

Crocker, Anne Ward. *Mary Morrison (Lee) Castleman: Our Woman of History.* Self-published, 2000.

———. "St. Timothy's Protestant Episcopal Church, A History of the Original Church Building, 1881 to 1969." Herndon, VA: unpublished paper, 1997, 2009 (updated).

Encyclopediavirginia.org.

The Fairfax County Preservation Association.

Fairfax County Public Schools: http://www.fcps.edu/PulleyCtr/about/whowasearl.html.

FairfaxUnderground.com.

Find-A-Grave.com.
Fold3.com.
Friends of Runnymede Park.
goldstarmoms.com.
The Grand Lodge of Virginia Ancient, Free and Accepted Masons.
The Great Falls Historical Society. gfhs.org.
The Herndon Historical Society.
Herndon Holiday Homes Tour programs.
Herndon Masonic Lodge No. 264, Herndon, VA.
Historicaerials.com.
History.com.
Home Interest Garden Club. "Home Interest Garden Club of Herndon, May 28, 1935–May 28, 1985." Herndon, VA: unpublished paper, 1985.
Hopkins, G.M. *Atlas of Fifteen Miles Around Washington Including Fairfax and Alexandria Counties*. Fairfax, VA: Fairfax County History Commission, Office of Comprehensive Planning, 1986.
Insect Life. USDA bulletin, 1889.
jimmystavern.com.
Kneebone, John T. "Ku Klux Klan in Virginia." Article contributed to the *Encyclopedia Virginia*. Virginia Foundation for the Humanities, 2012.
Mauro, Charles V. *The Town of Herndon Oral History Project, 1999–2001*. 2006.
Newkirk, Pamela. *Washington Post* book review, *The Second Coming of the KKK* by Linda Gordon.
O'Connor, Kate. *Life Is a Small Town: Herndon's Past as Seen by Ten Residents*. BIS Project Report, 1993.
www.ogbc-sterling.org.
Reed, Patrick. *Fairfax County, Virginia, 1870–1900*.
Ridgely-Nevitt, Cedric. "The United States Mail Steamer George Law." *American Neptune* 4, no. 4 (October 1944.)
Schneider, Robert J. *Hills and Valleys of Experience: Memoirs of Robert Julius Schneider, a German Immigrant, from 1852–1937*. 2001.
Schug, Rita F. "The Town of Herndon." Fairfax, VA: unpublished term paper at George Mason University, 1973.
TeachingHistory.org.
Town of Herndon, Town Council Minute Books 1879–2014.
USNA.org.
The Virginia Room, Fairfax County Public Library, Fairfax, VA.
Wayne M. Kidwell American Legion Post No. 184; Herndon, VA.
Wikipedia.org.

Williams, Ruth O. *Lest We Forget: The Childhood of Ruth O. Dyer*. Unknown date.

Wood, Rebekah K. *History of the Town Square, Herndon, Virginia*. November 19, 2001.

Wynkoop, Virgie. "Herndon–Etcetera." Unpublished manuscript, 1979.

Index

I

J

K

L

M

About the Author

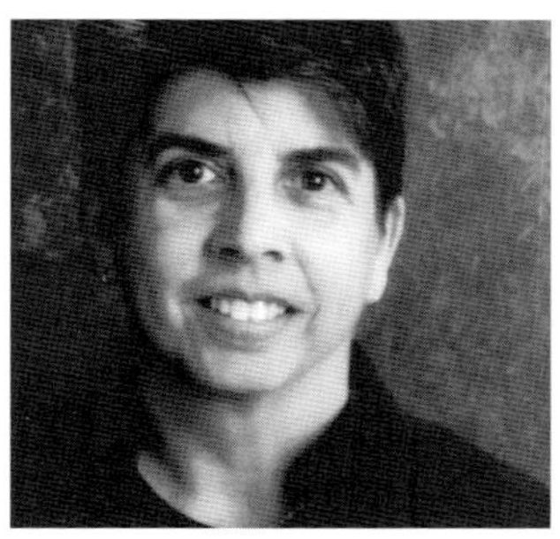

Barbara Glakas currently serves as the historian of the Herndon Historical Society. She has spent several years researching, writing stories and making videos about the history of the town of Herndon, Virginia. Barbara is a native of Fairfax County, Virginia. She is a graduate of James Madison University and is a retired teacher from Fairfax County Public Schools. Barbara currently lives in the town of Herndon.